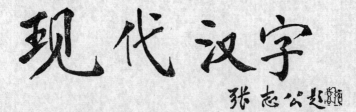

现代汉字

MODERN CHINESE CHARACTERS

Yin Binyong（尹斌庸）
John S. Rohsenow（罗圣豪）

SINOLINGUA BEIJING

First Edition 1994

ISBN 7-80052-167-2
ISBN 0-8351-2474-6

Copyright 1994 by Sinolingua, Beijing

Published by Sinolingua
24 Baiwanzhuang Road, Beijing 100037, China

Printed by Beijing Foreign Languages Printing House
Distributed by China International
Book Trading Corporation
35 Chegongzhuang Xilu, P.O. Box 399
Beijing 100044, China

FOREWORD

Chinese characters are a kind of living fossil among the writing systems of the world. They are both an ancient writing system and a contemporary writing system. In more than 3,000 years from the time of the oracle bone inscriptions to the present, the total number of characters in existence has reached about 60,000. Presently there are approximately 7,000 characters used to write contemporary Chinese. While some of the characters used today were not used in the past, nevertheless many characters used in ancient times are still in use today. If one wants to understand Chinese characters, or to do research on them, modern Chinese characters are a good place to start. Moving from the familiar to the unfamiliar, and from the simple to the more difficult are both sound principles for studying.

The study of Chinese characters in ancient times was called "xiaoxue" 小学, that is, the teaching of characters to children. In the late Qing Dynasty, this study was referred to as "wenzixue" 文字学, "scriptology", and in the 1950s as "Hanzixue" 汉字学, "Chinese characterology". In the last decade, a new sub-field has emerged, called "xiandai Hanzixue" 现代汉字学 or "modern Chinese characterology". Traditional Chinese characterology focused on the origins of Chinese characters and the evolution

i

of their forms, pronunciations, and meanings, and thus is also known as "historical Chinese characterology". Modern Chinese characterology, on the other hand, concentrates on the uses of Chinese characters in modern Chinese, including the systemization of Chinese characters as well as their use for information processing in computers. Modern Chinese characterology is a multifaceted science which, in addition to such traditional methods of analysis as the "Six Scripts" approach, also employs contemporary linguistics, statistics, information science, and computer technology. In Shanghai, two universities have already introduced courses in this subject.

Chinese is quite different from the various languages of the Indo-European family to which English belongs. Chinese is also quite different from most of the languages in the world which use alphabetic writing systems. For speakers of these languages studying Chinese and Chinese characters is quite difficult, but difficulty can incite curiosity, and even promote one's interest in studying. The Himalayas are difficult to climb, but the number of athletes wanting to scale them keeps growing. Similarly, there are many foreigners who have pressed on despite the difficulties and bravely accepted the intellectual challenge of learning Chinese and Chinese characters. Cultural exchange between East and West continues to develop daily.

Someone has referred to China as "the Land of the Great Wall, the Terra-Cotta Soldiers, and Chinese Characters". This is an interesting image. Most tourists who come to China come to see our ancient treasures. The Great Wall, the terra-cotta statues of soldiers and horses of the Emperor Qin Shi Huang and Chinese characters in fact all do represent China's ancient culture. But while the Great Wall and the terra-cotta soldiers no longer have any practical uses in modern times, Chinese characters still play a role in contemporary Chinese life. They are the official script of China. After so many years of literacy training and compulsory education, the position of Chinese characters in China has not weakened but has rather been strengthened. Sixty years ago many people thought of Chinese characters as a venerable old gentleman unsuited for modern life; now this old gentleman is learning to use a computer!

When the Western missionaries came to China at the end of the last century, they quickly realized that the majority of Chinese were illiterate, and that using Chinese characters to evangelize would be very difficult, so they devised romanized alphabets for many of the Chinese dialects, used them to translate the Bible, and then taught their converts to use these romanizations to learn their doctrine directly. In their view, using Chinese characters in the twentieth century was simply a great mistake in history. In the 1930s, under the influence of the idea from the Soviet Union that language could have a "class nature", many people felt that Chinese characters should be abandoned as a relic of China's feudal past. The truth is that Chinese characters are both China's burden and her treasure. But whether one likes them or not, abandoning the writing system used by one billion people is simply impossible. In 1958, when the Scheme for the Chinese Phonetic Alphabet (Hanyu Pinyin Fang'an) was promulgated, it was declared that Hanyu Pinyin was a system of phonetic symbols for expressing the pronunciation of Chinese characters, not an orthography to replace the Chinese characters. Today, China is slowly moving toward a situation of "digraphia", in which the characters and Hanyu Pinyin are beginning to operate as two separate writing systems for the same spoken language.

In the Jet Age, the world is growing smaller, but China still remains a great land of mystery which is just beginning to open up to the outside world. Professor Yin Binyong's book *Modern Chinese Characters* gives a complete and systematic explanation of modern Chinese characters in a lively and easy-to-read style. I hope that this work will become a "bridge" for English readers into the treasure house of Chinese culture, and will also help to change the China of the "Far East" into the China of the world.

Zhou Youguang
May 4, 1989
Beijing

PREFACE

Chinese characters have one of the longest histories of any writing system on earth. If we reckon from the earliest carved symbols recently discovered which possess the nature of a writing system, we can say that the characters have a history of about 6,000 years. If we only count from the time of the fully developed Shang Dynasty oracle bone inscriptions, we can say that they have a history of more than 3,000 years. From those ancient Chinese characters up to modern Chinese characters, although there have been many changes in their forms, from the point of view of the writing system as a whole, there has been no basic qualitative change. That one writing system should continue on for thousands of years since its creation in this way really is a unique wonder in the history of the world's writing systems. If we take into consideration the long history of Chinese characters, their wide geographical spread, and the number of people who have used them, then we may truly describe the amount of literature which has been recorded using this writing system as enormous. If one wishes to study Chinese culture, or in fact even Far Eastern culture, Chinese characters are the most important key to unlocking that treasure trove of knowledge.

But Chinese characters are also one of the most difficult writing systems in the world to master, and this appears to be even more true for those who only know an alphabetic writing system. When people first come in contact with this system of writing with its several thousand differing square shapes, on the one hand they find them rather novel, but on the other hand they are usually somewhat overwhelmed. In fact, Chinese characters are not such an unconquerable phenomenon. Any complex phenomenon on earth has its own internal regularities. If one is willing to study conscientiously to grasp their fundemental principles, then learning the basics is not hard, and advanced mastery is also possible. One of the aims of this little book is to help foreign students who have just begun to study Chinese characters, or who already have some knowledge of Chinese characters (especially those students whose native language employs an alphabetic writing system) to grasp the principles and methods of studying Chinese characters, and to gain some basic knowledge about them.

In order to provide the basis for a more complete understanding of modern Chinese characters, the first chapter of this book briefly introduces the origin, evolution, and character-formation principles of Chinese characters. The subsequent chapters then concentrate on modern Chinese characters, discussing such topics as their numbers, their forms, their pronunciations, their meanings, their ordering, and their calligraphy. The discussion of all of these topics is directed at the difficulties and needs of foreign students of Chinese, using plain, non-technical language to explain the principles of the forms, pro-

vi

nunciations, and meanings of Chinese characters in order to provide realistic, practical assistance in mastering them. In addition, appended to relevant chapters for reference are lists of characters most often written, pronounced, or used wrongly. For those who wish to pursue advanced studies, the final chapter contains an introduction to certain selected reference works of Chinese characters.

Please note, however, that this book is not simply a textbook for learning Chinese characters. Since the founding of the People's Republic, both China's government and her scholars have carried out a long series of research projects to improve and standardize modern Chinese characters, and have achieved considerable results. These include a reduction in the number of characters, simplification of many of the character forms, as well as standardization of the forms, pronunciations, and ordering of the characters. The aim of all of this work has been to make Chinese characters into a social tool which is easier to study and easier to use, and thus better suited to the task of our national reconstruction and modernization. This book also contains a comparatively detailed introduction to the results of this research in order to give foreign students of Chinese a broader and deeper understanding of this recent work on modern Chinese characters.

I wish to express my thanks to Professor Zhou Youguang for going over the original manuscript of this work and for his foreword. This work was translated from the author's original manuscript by Professor John S. Rohsenow of the University of Illinois at Chicago, U.S.A. and Ms. Mary Felley of Stanford

University, U.S.A., with assistance from Professor Victor Mair of the University of Pennsylvania, Dennis Mair, Guo Jianzhong, Peter Y. Qiu, and the author. Professor Rohsenow served as the overall English editor. Lastly, the author also wishes to thank Mr. Chen Xiaoming, senior editor of Sinolingua Press for his encouragement and advice, without which this book would not be before you now.

Y.B.Y.
Beijing
May 4, 1989

CONTENTS

1. THE CREATION AND EVOLUTION OF CHINESE CHARACTERS

In studying a subject, one should first understand its history. Thus in studying Chinese characters, it is best to begin by understanding their origin and the various ways in which they were constructed, as well as something of their later evolution. This chapter will introduce these topics.

1.1 HOW WERE CHINESE CHARACTERS CREATED?

In the past, there have been many legends pertaining to the birth of Chinese characters. Among these stories, the most popular is that characters were created by a man named Cāng Jié 仓颉. Cāng Jié was described as an extraordinary, mythical figure in order to play up the greatness of his achievement. He is said to have had four eyes and was born with the knowledge of writing. After studying the principles and affairs of the world, he developed his wondrous writing system. When he invented writing, it is said that grain fell from the sky and ghosts and demons howled through the night.

Although this story is doubtless apocryphal, it is probable that such a person as Cāng Jié really did exist. According to Chinese historical records, Cāng Jié was an official under the reign of Huáng Dì, approximately five thousand years ago. A primitive form of writing already existed long before Cāng Jié was born. His contribution, it seems, was to collect and organize this already extant system of writing and present it as a formal system. Though Cāng Jié was not as remarkable as the legends describe him to be, his collection and organization of the writing system was nonetheless an important accomplishment.

A more dependable theory as to the origin of Chinese characters is based on results obtained from archaeological finds. Scratch-mark symbols 刻划符号 found on the Yǎngsháo Culture pottery of Xī'ān's Bànpō Village in 1972 (see Fig. 01) are the earliest form of writing found to date. According to results obtained

Fig. 01: Scratch-marks found on Yǎngsháo Culture pottery of Bàn pō Village near Xi'an.

2

by the Archaeological Research Institute of the Chinese Academy of Science through carbon-14 dating, these character-symbols are approximately six thousand years old. The period of Yăngsháo Culture corresponds approximately to the latter period of China's primitive matriarchal-society culture. These scratch-marks are all symbols. They all have simple structures similar to stroke compositions and contain in embryonic form elements of Chinese characters. In addition, some of these marks are very similar to the bone and bronze inscriptions of Chinese characters made three thousand years ago. From these similarities we may conclude that these scratch-marks are not merely arbitrary decorative impressions, but meaningful symbols of a writing system. In his treatise "The Dialectical Evolution of Ancient Chinese Characters" 古代文字之辩证的发展, the prominent Chinese historian Guō Mòruò said, "We can definitely conclude that these scratch-marks are the source of Chinese characters, or at least the derivatives of primitive Chinese characters." From the evidence of these primitive characters on the Bànpō artifacts, we may say that Chinese characters already have a history of at least six thousand years, placing them among the most ancient of the world's writing systems.

Although the Yăngsháo symbols are exceedingly simple in form, they still could not have been developed by one person in a short period of time. The birth of Chinese characters was obviously the product of a long period of trial and error over many generations. It is common knowledge that human speech is as old as mankind, that is, thirty to forty thousand years old; writing is a much more recent development.

Although spoken language is mankind's one indispensable tool of communication, it has two great limitations in the area of transmitting information. The first restriction is that of space. A spoken message can reach only a small number of people and cannot carry long distances to reach greater numbers. The second limitation is that of time. Because sound dissipates immediately, there is no way to preserve important messages and pass them on to later generations.

In the initial period of primitive society, the small number of people in a tribe and limited extent of their activities meant that oral transmission of messages was sufficient for their needs. The limitations of the spoken word were not yet obvious. As society continued to progress, however, and communal clans and tribes evolved and grew, the life of a society gradually became more complex, and the limitations of the spoken word became increasingly apparent. Sole reliance on oral transmission and memory could no longer meet the needs of society's production requirements. People needed to find a means to record important matters so that they could be transmitted long distances and passed down to later times. Thus the need to develop writing appeared.

Primitive man recorded matters in two main ways: through concrete objects and through pictures. In ancient China, the most prevalent method of recording through objects was knot-tying 结绳. Knots were tied on a piece of rope as an aid to memory. This method of recording events developed quite naturally: if there were some matter that one feared one would forget and wished to record, one would tie a knot on a rope.

If it were an important affair, one would tie a large knot; if a less important matter, then a small knot. Once matters piled up, there would be many knots, large and small, on the rope (see Fig. 02). Some cultures also used ropes of different colours to

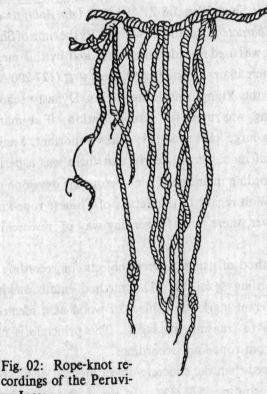

Fig. 02: Rope-knot re-
cordings of the Peruvi-
an Inca.

record different types of events, as red for war, white for peace, black for disaster or death, etc. Many cultures throughout the world have employed this knot-tying method in the past, and some continue to do so today.

Rope-knot recording 结绳记事 is mentioned briefly in ancient Chinese historical records. In the Yìjīng 易经 (*Book of Changes*) it is written, "In ancient times, knot-tying was used in administration. Later generations substituted inscribed characters for this." In the preface to Xǔ Shèn's 许慎 (ca. 58-147 AD) work Shuō Wén Jiě Zì 说文解字 (*An Analysis and Explanation of Characters*) the author writes, "By the time of Shén-nóng, knot-tying was used for administration, and by this means they governed their affairs." In Zhèng Xuán's 郑玄 (127-200 AD) commentary on the Yìjīng, this Eastern Hàn Dynasty scholar said, "Knot-tying was used for administration; if a matter was important, a large knot was tied; if less important, a small knot." These references show clearly that there was a period of rope-knot recording in ancient China before the development of characters. With regard to the details of Chinese rope-knot recording, however, there is no longer any way of researching the matter.

Another method of using concrete objects for recording is wood-notch recording 刻木记事. This method entails making a number of different marks on a piece of wood as a memory aid and in order to transmit messages. The principle is not much different from rope-knot recording.

More advanced than the concrete-object method of recording is pictorial recording 图画记事. In using objects such as rope or wood to record things, one can only record that something happened, but cannot indicate clearly what the nature of the thing was. The object method places too much pressure on one's memory. In this respect, pictorial recording is far

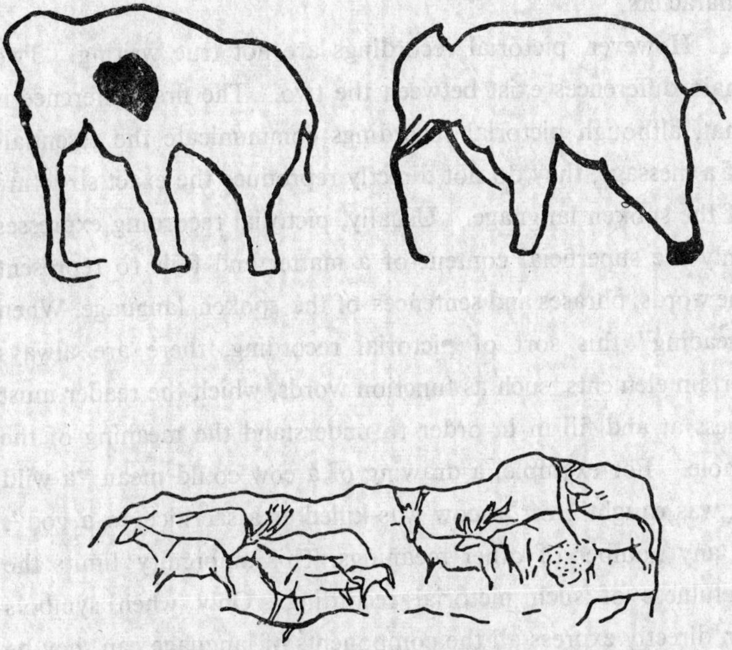

Fig. 03: Pictorial recordings in prehistoric China.

superior to object recording. A drawing of a cow, for instance, can directly convey "a wild ox was caught" or other such meanings. This method indicates the nature of the matter recorded and is thus a great improvement on rope knots or notches on a piece of wood.

Although the pictures used to record such matters do contain images representing animals and people, they are completely different in nature from pictures made for aesthetic enjoyment. Pictures used in recording are for the transmission and preservation of messages. They embody some of the essential qualities of writing, and may be considered the prototype of true characters.

However, pictorial recordings are not true writing. Two main differences exist between the two. The first difference is that, although pictorial recordings communicate the essentials of a message, they do not directly reproduce the exact structure of the spoken language. Usually, pictorial recording expresses only the superficial content of a matter and fails to represent the words, phrases and sentences of the spoken language. When "reading" this sort of pictorial recording, there are always certain elements, such as function words, which the reader must guess at and fill in in order to understand the meaning of the whole. For example, a drawing of a cow could mean "a wild ox was caught", or "a cow was killed as a sacrifice to a god", or any number of other meanings. This ambiguity limits the usefulness of such pictorial recording. Only when symbols can directly express all the components of language can they be considered true writing.

The second difference between pictorial recordings and true writing is that the former, being a form of drawing, must be as lifelike as possible to achieve their purpose. In drawing a cow, one must include the head, horns, feet, tail, and even hair in order to fully represent the animal. Moreover, not everyone's drawing of a cow will be the same; in fact, they may be quite different. The symbols of a writing system, on the other hand, should be easy to write and should have standardized, generally recognized forms. Considering these points, it becomes clear that pictorial recordings and true writing are fundamentally different in nature.

Methods of recording through concrete objects and through pictures, while not in themselves writing, nonetheless had a direct impact on the development of writing, and both may be considered the predecessors of true writing. Long and repeated use of pictorial recording resulted in the picture-forms gradually becoming simplified and schematized; in this manner, they developed into generally recognizable pictograms 图画文字.

Materials pertaining to Chinese pictograms are still scarce. By examining the pictographic symbols found on bone and bronze inscriptions (see 1.3), however, we may conclude that Chinese characters did pass through a phase of pictographic writing. The most typical of the pictograms unearthed so far are the totemic symbols 族徽符号 found on bronze inscriptions (see Fig. 04). These pictograms, cast on bronze utensils, represent a clan surname or a personal name, and indicate the maker or owner of the vessel. The next step in the development of pictograms were the bone and bronze characters (see 1.3). The Chinese characters of this period already constituted a well-developed formal writing system.

1.2 METHODS OF CHINESE CHARACTER CONSTRUCTION

The previous section discussed briefly the genesis of Chinese characters. In this section, we will go on to discuss the construction of Chinese characters. To anyone accustomed to an alphabetical writing system, it is very important to understand

Fig. 04: Comparison of pictograms, bone-inscrption characters, and modern characters.

this aspect of Chinese characters. This is because the methods of constructing Chinese characters are drastically different from anything found in the writing systems of English, Russian, or any other alphabetical system. Understanding the construction of Chinese characters can help us understand the origin of each character, and at the same time help us grasp each character in its entirety.

There are many methods of character construction. Traditional analyses are usually based on the six categories mentioned in Xǔ Shèn's philological treatise Shuō Wén Jiě Zì of the Eastern Hàn period. These six categories 六书 are based on six methods of character construction: pictographic 象形, indicative 指事, associative 会意, picto-phonetic 形声, notative 转注 and borrowing 假借. These six methods were not devised by Xǔ Shèn, but are merely his induction and summary of ancient ways of creating characters. These six methods did not all develop at the same time; some were earlier, and some later. Strictly speaking, only the first four of these categories (pictographic, indicative, associative, and picto-phonetic) are true methods of character construction; the last two categories, notative and borrowing, are really just methods of expanding the range of use of an existing character. In the following section, we will primarily discuss the first four categories, and discuss the last two only briefly.

1) Pictographic Characters 象形字

The pictographic method of character construction is based upon the depiction of an object's shape — drawing a picture of it. To express the concept "sun", one draws a sun; to ex-

11

press "moon", one draws a moon, and so on. This was the earliest method of character construction, which is obviously the culmination of the evolution of pictorial recording and pictograms.

Pictographs, however, are different from pictograms, and even more different from pictorial recordings. Pictographic characters are able to express directly the individual words of a language. Moreover, pictographic characters are simple in form, far simpler than pictures of pictograms.

Pictographic characters have the great advantage over other types of characters of having a direct visual appeal: it is often easy to remember what object a character represents just by looking at it. Below are given a few examples of pictographic characters in Chinese.

Ancient Character	Modern Character	Definition
⊙	日 RI 日	sun: a depiction of the sun
☽	月 YUE 月	moon: a depiction of the moon
〲	水 SHUI 水	water: water flowing in a curve
⅏	山 SHAN 山	mountain: mountain peaks
⻖	雨 雨	rain: rain falling from the sky
囲	田 TIAN 田	field: rice fields and their irrigation ditches

半	牛 NIU 牛		cow: a cow's head with horns
仐	羊 YANG 羊		sheep: a sheep's head with horns
馬	马 MA 马		horse: side view of a horse, showing legs, tail, and mane
尾	鸟 NIAO 鸟		bird: side view of a bird, showing its beak, claws, and wings
魚	魚 YU 鱼		fish: side view of a fish, showing its fins, scales, and tail
入	人 REN 人		person: side view of a person, showing head, hands, and legs
日	目 MU 目		eye: a person's eye, with the eyeball
口	口 KUO 口		mouth: an open mouth
凵	齿 齿		tooth: an open mouth with a row of teeth
月	舟 舟		boat: a small boat floating downstream
丽	门 MEN 门		door: a door with two swinging panels under a crossbeam
戈	戈 戈		dagger-axe: an ancient Chinese weapon
米	木 MU 木		tree: a tree, showing branches and roots
面	瓜 GUA 瓜		melon: a melon hanging on the vine

13

Pictographic characters have the merit of conveying meaning directly, but this method of character construction has severe limitations. Among the millions of objects in the world, there are many which cannot be depicted according to any shape, and there is no way to depict abstract concepts directly. For these reasons, the pictographic method was only employed during the early stages of character evolution, and was later gradually phased out of use. In the two thousand years from the Qín Dynasty to the present, only a handful of new pictographic characters have been devised — 伞 (umbrella), 凸 (convex), 凹 (concave), and a few others. Nonetheless, pictographic characters remain the foundation of the whole edifice of Chinese characters; they are all simple single-element characters 独体字 which cannot be analyzed into smaller meaningful components. They can be used as building blocks in creating new characters. They are, however, few in number: among the 9,353 Chinese characters found in the Shuō Wén Jiě Zì, only three hundred or so (4 percent of the total) are pictographic characters.

2) Indicative Character 指事字

The indicative method of character construction uses symbols to indicate abstract meanings. Indicative characters may be divided into two sub-categories as follows.

The first type uses pure symbols to express a given meaning. Very few indicative characters fall into this category:

Ancient Character	Modern Character	Definition
⌣	上 SHANG 上	above: the long curve indicates a border, above which sits a dot
⌢	下 XIA 下	below: the long curve indicates a border, below which sits a dot
—	— YI —	one: one stroke
=	二 ER 二	two: two strokes
☰	三 SAN 三	three: three strokes

The second type involves the addition of a pure symbol onto a pictographic character to express a given meaning. For example: 丿 (刀, knife) is a pictographic character. A dot added onto the side to indicate the knife's edge gives us the indicative character 刁 (刃, knife edge). The number of characters belonging to this type is somewhat larger than that belonging to the first type. A few examples of this second type:

Ancient Form	Modern Form	Explanation
木	本 BEN 本	木 is a pictographic character meaning "tree". The horizontal line across its lower half indicates "root", the meaning of the character as a whole.

15

末　末　末　木 is the tree again; the horizontal line across its top indicates the treetop, and the meaning of the whole is "branch end".

亦　亦　亦　大 is a pictographic representation of the human body. Two dots underneath the arms indicate "armpit", the meaning of the whole.

甘　甘ᵀᴵᴬᴺ 甘　甘 is a pictographic representation of a mouth; a dot in the middle shows the place where sweetness is tasted. The meaning of the whole is "sweet".

Indicative characters, like pictographic characters, belong to the category of single-element characters. The indicative method of creating characters, however, is far more limited in productivity than the pictographic method. Indicative characters make up the smallest proportion of Chinese characters. Of the 9,353 characters listed in the Shuō Wén Jiě Zì, only about one hundred, or one percent, are indicative characters.

3) Associative Characters 会意字

The associative method of creating characters combines two or more ideographic symbols to form a new character. The relationship between the several component symbols produces the new meaning. Consider for example the character 采 (采), composed of a hand above a tree. The juxtaposition of the two implies the meaning, "to pick fruit". Another example is the character 伐 (伐), composed of a lance to the right of a person. The blade of the lance is cutting off the person's head, indicating the meaning — "to cut off".

There are two main types of associative characters. The first type is called "associative characters of identical parts". These consist of the same symbol repeated to express a new meaning. A few examples:

Ancient Form	Modern Form		Explanation
〵〵	从	从	Two people, one in front of the other, means "to follow".
ᠲ	步	步	Two feet, one in front of the other, means "to walk".
炎	炎	炎	Fire on top of fire means "to blaze; hot".
磊	磊	磊	Three stones together means "a pile of stones".
林	森	森	Three trees together means "many trees; forest".
晶	晶	晶	Three suns together means "glittering".

The second type of associative characters is called "associative characters of different parts". These consist of different symbols joined to express a new meaning. This type accounts for the majority of associative characters. A few examples:

17

Ancient Form	Modern Form		Explanation
⊙	旦	旦	A sun just over the horizon means "dawn".
𣎍	莫	莫	The sun setting amid thick grass means "dusk" (the original meaning of this character).
𥁕	益	益	Water above a dish implies water overflowing; "overflowing" is the original meaning of 益.
牧	牧	牧	A hand holding a stick, with a cow on the left, means "to herd".
休	休	休	A person to the left of a tree implies someone leaning against a tree; the meaning of the character is "to rest".
及	及	及	A hand, on the right, has a grip on a person; the character means "to reach, catch up with".
集	集	集	A bird on top of a tree means "to gather", as birds gather in a tree.
鳴	鳴	鳴	A mouth to the left of a bird means "to sing, call, cry out".
寇	寇	寇	A person (left) and a hand holding a club (right) inside a house. Beating and killing people inside a house implies the meaning, "bandit".

寒 寒 Grass is spread out for insulation inside a house, while ice can be seen underneath. The person in the center is cold, and "cold" is the meaning of the character.

聲 聲(声) Beneath a stone chime (left) and a hand holding a small mallet is an ear. When the stone chime is struck, sound is heard; "sound" is the meaning.

Associative characters created later in the evolution of the writing system include: 尖 (small 小 on top and big 大 on the bottom: "tapering"), 劣 (less 少 strength 力: "weak" or "inferior"), 卡 (not above 上 and not below 下: "to wedge, get stuck"), 掰 (two hands 手 dividing 分: "to pull apart with the hands"), and 冇 (the character 有 "to have" minus two strokes: "not to have").

The associative method of creating characters is a great step forward from the pictographic and indicative methods. While both pictographic and indicative characters are single-element characters, associative characters are compound characters. The associative method combines a few simple symbols with definite meanings to create characters with new meanings. This method is clearly much more flexible and adaptive. The characters created by the pictographic and indicative methods for the most part represent concrete nouns; the associative method, however, can be used to create characters for verbs and adjectives with abstract meanings. Because associative characters are originally somewhat abstract, their meanings and usages can often be expanded. The character 鸣, for example, was originally used only to mean "to call" with respect to birds, but over time its meaning has been expanded to apply to any animal (e.g. 马鸣, "a horse whinnies") and even to inanimate objects (e.g. 雷鸣, "the thunder crashes"). Because of this flexibility, associative characters are more numerous than either pictographic or indicative characters. Of the 9,353 characters in Shuō Wén Jiě Zì, about 1,200, or 13 percent, are associative characters.

Although it is far more productive than the pictographic or indicative method, the associative method of creating characters is unable to leap outside the system of pure ideographs, or meaning symbols. This fact imposes many limitations on its productivity. Concrete objects which can be represented by a picture are of thousands of forms, and most of them are highly complicated. Merely using meaning symbols when creating characters inevitably presents difficulties. For example, the character 寒 analyzed above combines the symbols for "house", "grass", "person" and "ice" to express the simple meaning "cold". If "cold" is so difficult to represent, how can more abstract and complex concepts be represented? As a society's economy and culture progress and develop, material objects increase in number and complexity, and the language used to talk about these things must develop accordingly. In writing, purely ideographic symbols soon become unequal to the task of representing all these objects. At this point, a society is compelled to turn to the sounds of its language to develop its written

20

language further.   A new and more scientific method of creating characters then appears, known as the picto-phonetic method.

4) Picto-phonetic Characters   形声字

The picto-phonetic method of creating characters uses the combination of a phonetic component and a semantic radical to construct a character.   The phonetic indicates the pronunciation of the character, and the so-called "radical" indicates the meaning.   The combination of the two parts together thus provides both the pronunciation and meaning of the character. In the character 蝗 (locust), for example, the phonetic 皇 (huáng) tells us that the character is pronounced huáng; the radical 虫 (insect) tells us that 蝗 is a type of insect.   The radical and phonetic together give us an insect whose name is pronounced huáng — a locust.   Another example: the phonetic of the character 吐 (to spit) is 土 (tǔ), indicating that the character is pronounced tǔ, while the semantic radical is 口 (mouth), indicating that the meaning of 吐 has something to do with the mouth.

The picto-phonetic method of creating characters breaks through the restrictions binding the purely meaning-dependent pictographic, indicative and associative methods.   This method was historically a great step forward in the development of Chinese characters.   The picto-phonetic method makes it easier to create large numbers of new characters to express all kinds of concepts.   For example, by adding various radicals to the phonetic component 胡 (hú), one can create many new characters with the same pronunciation (hú) yet with different meanings:

胡 + 氵   (water) = 湖   (hú, lake)

胡 + 艹   (grass) = 葫   (hú, calabash)

21

胡 + 犭 (dog or other animal) = 猢 (hú, monkey)

胡 + 米 (rice) = 糊 (hú, paste)

胡 + 虫 (insect) = 蝴 part of 蝴蝶, (húdié, butterfly)

胡 + 王 (jade) = 瑚 part of 珊瑚, (shānhú, coral)

胡 + 鸟 (bird) = 鹕 part of 鹈鹕, (tíhú, pelican)

Similarly, by adding various different phonetic components to the radical 木 (wood, tree), one can create many different characters semantically linked to wood or trees:

木 + 干 (gān) = 杆 (gān, flagpole)

木 + 丈 (zhàng) = 杖 (zhàng, walking stick)

木 + 才 (cái) = 材 (cái, lumber)

木 + 支 (zhī) = 枝 (zhī, branch)

木 + 风 (fēng) = 枫 (fēng, maple)

木 + 乔 (qiáo) = 桥 (qiáo, bridge)

木 + 娄 (lóu) = 楼 (lóu, building of several stories)

木 + 曹 (cáo) = 槽 (cáo, trough)

The invention of this picto-phonetic method opened up a limitless horizon for the development of Chinese characters. It gradually became the dominant method for creating characters, while the other three methods gradually ceased being used. This process may be observed statistically. Of the characters used in oracle bone inscriptions current before 1000 BC, only about 20 percent were picto-phonetic. In Xǔ Shèn's Shuō Wén Jiě Zì (ca. 100 AD), more than 80 percent of the Characters listed are picto-phonetic.

Two points on the topic of picto-phonetic characters deserve our further attention.

a) Relative positions of radical and phonetic components.

Being able to recognize the relative position of radical and phonetic within a picto-phonetic character is essential to efficient study of this type of character. There are general rules governing the position of radical and phonetic, though not without some exceptions. The basic rules are as follows:

Rule 1: Radical on the left, phonetic on the right: 伙，请，
城，描，吐，油，峰，狮，饭，弦，奶，骑，绣，
珠，桐，轮，牦，曝，肝，烤，砖，睁，钟，秧，
蝗，鲤，踩，靶.

Exception: Radical on the right, phonetic on the left:
和，政，期，邱，鹦，顶，锦，剩，欣。

Rule2: Radical on the top, phonetic on the bottom.:
花，芳，岗，宇，宾，爸，竿，筷，窈，窖，罟，
露，零.

Exception: Radical on the bottom, phonetic on the top:
盒，装，驾，忍，堡，烫，背，熬.

Rule 3: Radical on the outside, phonetic on the inside:
固，围，阁，阀，匪，匾，历，厦，屏，氧，赶，
魍，衙，衷.

Exception: Radical on the inside, phonetic on the outside:
闷，勉，辩.

In the majority of picto-phonetic characters, the radical and the phonetic are easy to distinguish. In some picto-phonetic characters, however, it is very difficult to identify which is which. In the latter case, one may consult a reference book which deals with the origin of individual characters (see 8.4).

b) The function of radical and phonetic.

When each picto-phonetic character was originally created, the phonetic component was an accurate indicator of the character's pronunciation, and the radical was an accurate guide to meaning. However, owing to the changes that have occurred over long periods of development in language and writing, phonetics and radicals have both to a great extent lost their ability to represent pronunciation and meaning exactly. It is very important to be aware of this when studying picto-phonetic characters.

Because of the changes in the pronunciation of the language that have occurred between ancient and modern times, most phonetics have lost their ability to indicate pronunciation precisely. The degree of accuracy to which the phonetic indicates the pronunciation in modern picto-phonetic characters may be divided roughly into four levels:

Completely accurate: 湖, 拌, 鲤, 蝗, 伙, 城, 珠.

Fairly accurate: 妈, 背, 笨, 饭, 花, 宇, 装.

Bearing certain relations to the present pronunciation: 宾, 灯, 渡, 狼, 奸, 精, 酒, 洞, 摆, 矿, 炉.

Absolutely unrelated to the present pronunciation: 江, 海, 怀, 槐, 挥, 凉, 猎, 路, 埋, 迈.

The semantic radicals originally bore only a general relation to the meanings of individual characters; they were not equivalent to the meanings of the characters of which they formed a part. Over time, moreover, the meanings of the characters have changed, expanding and shrinking continually. The result is that the radicals of modern picto-phonetic characters

24

have only a weak and very limited ability to convey character meaning.   The degree of accuracy with which a radical expresses the meaning of its character may be divided roughly into four levels:

Represent a meaning category into which their character fits: 鲤，蝗，柏，铜，氧.

Have a direct relationship with the character's meaning: 浸，淀，扔，扶，杖，饭.

Have an indirect relationship with the character's meaning: 冷，城，助，满，粒，字.

Have no relationship with the meaning of the character: 演，给，笑，答，错，范，独，较，理，落.

The above evaluations of the meaning- and pronunciation-conveying abilities of radicals and phonetics apply only to modern Chinese characters.   Readers who are interested in knowing the original functions of radicals and phonetics should consult a reference book dealing with the derivation of Chinese characters (see 8.4.).

In addition to the four methods of creating characters discussed here, there are two other methods for expanding the range of use of characters also included in the six categories proposed by Xǔ Shèn: "notative characters" 转注字 and "borrowed characters" 假借字. Xǔ Shèn unfortunately did not give a clear definition for notative characters in his work Shuō Wén Jiě Zì. Scholars of later periods have suggested many possible definitions, trying to clear up Xǔ Shèn's ambiguity. From the examples of notative characters cited by Xǔ Shèn, we can reason as follows: if two characters belong to the same radical category, and if their pronunciation and meaning are the same or similar, then the two characters can be used to define one another. This is the probable meaning of "notative characters". For example, the two characters 顶 (dǐng, peak) and 颠 (diān, top) share the radical 页, and are close in both meaning and pronunciation. Thus they may be considered notative characters.

The "borrowed" character method makes use of homophones to attach extant characters to words lacking a written form. It works as follows: if two words have the same pronunciation, then a character representing one word may be "borrowed" and used to represent the other as well. The meaning of the character here is irrelevant; it is only borrowed for its sound. The character-borrowing method was an early development in the history of Chinese characters. Usually, a character expressing a fairly concrete meaning would be used to represent a homophonous word with a more abstract meaning. A few examples of this method are:

㠱 (其) originally was a pictographic character meaning "dustpan". It was later borrowed to write the homophonous pronoun 其 (he, it). A bamboo radical ⺮ was later added to the original character 其 to express the original meaning, "dustpan", as dustpans are usually made of bamboo in China.

夾 (亦), an indicative character, originally meant "armpit". It was borrowed to signify the homophonous adverb 亦 (also). Later, the picto-phonetic character 腋 "armpit" was created to represent the original meaning of 亦.

The character-borrowing method does not require the

26

creation of new characters, and it gives us an easy way to express abstract concepts in writing. The borrowing method uses characters as pure phonetic symbols to expand their range of use. All in all, it was an extremely convenient way of finding characters to represent words which had none. However, the borrowing method was severely limited by the ideographic nature of the Chinese character system, and was unable to develop into the main method of creating characters — a position long held by the picto-phonetic method.

1.3 THE EVOLUTION OF THE FORMS OF CHARACTERS

The discussion of the six categories of character construction and use in the previous section dealt mainly with the earliest stages of their creation and use. Most modern characters cannot be explained using the six categories. Taking pictographic characters as an example, only seldom do they resemble the object they represent. The modern character 日 (sun) has become rectangular; 月 (moon) now has a large hole at the bottom; 牛 (cow) now has only one horn; and 鱼 (fish) seems to have four legs. The pictographic essence of these characters has been altogether lost. This phenomenon is the result of over 3,000 years of continuous evolution in the forms of Chinese characters. Thus we need to understand the process of development that Chinese characters have gone through over time.

Most scholars feel that the oracle bone inscriptions of more than 3,000 years ago constitute the earliest systematic array of Chinese characters. The structural evolution that led from oracle bone inscriptions to the Chinese characters used today may be divided into three stages: (1) "Ancient writing", including oracle bone inscriptions, bronze inscriptions, and seal characters. These represent the formative stage of Chinese characters. Character structure was not yet finalized during this stage; it was not until the latter period of seal characters, small seal characters, that written forms were basically fixed. (2) The "official script". This was a transitional stage between ancient writing and modern characters, and represents the finalizing of form and the establishment of the structural foundation of modern characters. (3) Regular script. This represents the standard of modern written Chinese. Below follows a brief introduction to these three stages of development, and the forms that characterize each.

1) Oracle Bone Inscription 甲骨文

Oracle bone inscriptions represent a style of Chinese characters which appeared over 3,000 years ago, during the late Shāng Dynasty (1711-1066 BC). The examples of this writing which survive today were carved with a bronze knife on tortoise shells and ox bones, and for this reason are called 甲骨文 (jiǎgǔwén), or "shell-bone writing", in Chinese. The history of their discovery is an interesting one. Beginning in the mid-19th century, ancient inscriptions on tortoise shells and ox boneswere unearthed repeatedly. Local residents sold these "dragon bones" to pharmacies to be ground up as medicine. It was not until 1899 that someone recognized the carved symbols as writing. The oracle bones were unearthed in the village of Xiǎotún in

28

northwest Ānyáng County, Hénán Province, the site of the capital of the late Shāng Dynasty. The Shāng court had practised divination, and the oracle bone inscriptions, it was discovered, were inscriptions used for divination. Continued excavation, gathering and sorting has gone on in recent decades. Altogether more than 150,000 examples of oracle bone writing have been unearthed, and about 4,500 individual characters have been distinguished, of which about 900 are believed to have been accurately interpreted.

Since oracle bone inscriptions were carved on hard surfaces with knives, the individual strokes of the script are firm and thin.

Fig. 05: Oracle bone inscriptions.

and mostly angular. Judging by the characters interpreted so far, Chinese characters at the time of the oracle bone inscriptions made use of all the methods of creating characters discussed in the preceding section. The inscriptions show us a well-organized and relatively mature writing system, which had long since advanced beyond conveying whole messages in individual pictures, the distinctive feature of pictographic writing. In the oracle bone script, each symbol represents an individual word. In terms of form, the script had already broken away from primitive pictographic patterns and moved toward linear and contour forms. It is clear, however, that Chinese characters had advanced beyond the pictographic stage only a relatively short time before the period of the oracle bone inscriptions, and these characters still retained some of the "variable" features typical of the more primitive writing, as follows:

a) Character complexity could vary. The same character sometimes was written with many strokes, at other times with few; sometimes in one fashion, sometimes in another. Thus, one character could have several or even dozens of different forms. The character 羊 (sheep), for example, had at least four different forms: 𐅣 𐅣 𐅣 𐅣 𐅣 𐅣 YÁNG

b) Character positioning could vary. The same character might equally well be written upright, upside-down, reversed, or obliquely. The character 豕 (猪, pig), for example, had several possible positions: 𐅣 𐅣 𐅣 𐅣 ZHŪ

c) Character size could vary. The size of an oracle bone character was often determined by its complexity; a more complex character would be larger than a simple one. A large character could be up to several times the size of a small one; there was no standard size.

d) Textual format could vary. Oracle bone inscriptions were written in a vertical line, from top to bottom; but the order of the lines could be either from right to left or from left to right. Again, there was no fixed rule.

Oracle bone writing was in use for approximately three hundred years, and in that time went through considerable changes, which will not be elaborated upon here.

2) Bronze Inscription 金 文 JĪN WÉN

Bronze inscriptions are a style of Chinese characters which were current during the late Shāng Dynasty and throughout the Zhōu Dynasty (1066-256 BC). Most of the examples which survive today are from the Zhōu period, cast on bronzeware. They were most commonly cast on bells and cauldrons, and

Fig. 06: Bronze inscriptions.

31

bronze inscriptions are for this reason also called "bell-bronze writing" 钟鼎文 in Chinese. Bronze inscriptions have been discovered continuously since 500 or 600 AD, but long remained unresearched. Not until after 1000 AD did the number of scholars and scholarly works devoted to bronze-inscription research begin to grow.

In terms of their content, bronze inscriptions differ from oracle bone inscriptions, being concerned mainly with naming the makers and owners of the implements on which they are cast. Auspicious and congratulatory phrases are usually included as well. The number of characters on a single bronze piece was greater than that on a typical oracle bone; some bronzes bear several hundred characters. There are extant between five and six thousand pieces of cast and engraved bronze, from which about 3,000 individual characters have been collated. Of these, nearly 2,000 can be accurately interpreted.

Most bronze inscriptions were first written with a calligraphy brush, carved into a mold and then cast, but some were carved directly onto the bronze. In terms of form, the bronze characters are thicker and more curving than oracle bone characters; they are also more regular in size.

The structure and composition of the characters in these bronze inscriptions are quite similar to those of the oracle bone inscriptions. This is not surprising, as they were the continuation and development of oracle bone writing. Bronze inscription character structure, like its predecessor, has the trait of variability of form — 虫 (insect) could be written),), or)

— and variable positioning — 射 (to shoot) could be written ⟨glyph⟩, ⟨glyph⟩ or ⟨glyph⟩ But bronze inscription characters are more symmetrical and regular in size, their format is more fixed, and their strokes are simpler in form than those of oracle bone characters. All these features indicate the relative advancement of the bronze script. (Another feature of bronze inscriptions, "totemic" characters, constitutes a remnant of pictographic writing. See Fig. 04.)

3) Seal Script 篆 书 ZHUÀN SHŪ

The seal script was a style of Chinese characters used by the Qín State of the late Zhōu Dynasty and the Spring-Autumn and Warring States Periods (722-221 BC). The first Qín emperor, after uniting China and establishing the Qín Dynasty (221-206 BC), decreed seal script the standard of writing for the entire country. 篆 (zhuàn), the Chinese name for the seal script, means "to pull or stretch out long", and seal characters are characterized by elongated strokes. Seal characters are regular in form, with even, gently-curving strokes, and are roughly square in shape — as are almost all forms of Chinese characters that postdate them (see Fig. 07).

Seal characters may be divided chronologically into great seal script 大篆 and small seal script 小篆. Great seal script was used during the early years of the Qín State. It is similar in appearance to bronze script, but its character structure is more regular and symmetrical. A typical example of great seal script may be seen in the stone drum inscriptions discovered in the early Táng Dynasty in what is now Sānzhìyuán, Bǎojǐ,

33

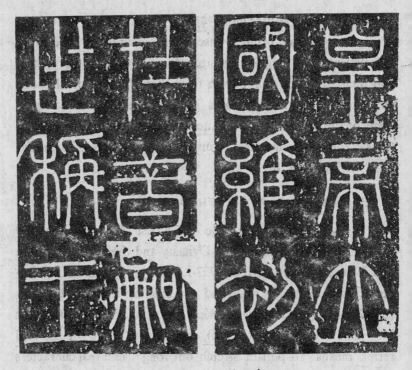

Fig. 07: Small seal script.

in Shaanxi Province. The "stone drums" are ten bun-shaped pieces of stone, each several feet across. On each is carved in great seal script a set of ten quatrains describing the hunting expeditions of the Qín ruler.

Small seal characters were a simplification of great seal script. They are neater in appearance than great seal script, and are more unified in terms of written form. Small seal characters already existed before the first Qín emperor united China; when the emperor unified the writing system, he abolished all scripts of other states and made small seal characters the standard.

The development of small seal characters was an important stage in the evolution of Chinese character structure. Small seal characters differ from ancient writing in the following ways:

a) They break away from pictographic forms, moving more towards linear and symbolic forms;

b) They leave behind the "variations" of oracle bone and bronze scripts, finalizing structure and establishing the square shape characteristic of later characters;

c) They contain many more picto-phonetic characters.

Xǔ Shèn's work Shuō Wén Jiě Zì provides a look at typical small seal characters. This work, China's first complete dictionary, lists 9,353 small seal character forms (see 8.4).

4) Official Script 隶 书 Lì Shū

Official script was a style of Chinese characters used during the Qín and Hàn (206 BC-220 AD) dynasties. After the first Qín emperor unified the character system, small seal characters were used for official and governmental documents; at the same time, however, a different form of script, called "clerks' script" or "plain script" was current among the people. Clerks' script became widespread because, although small seal characters were simpler in structure than their predecessors, their curving strokes were difficult and time-consuming to write. Lesser officials in local levels of the government, attending to relatively unimportant documents, adopted the common script in use among the people to keep afloat of the sea of documents. This script later acquired official approval, whence its Chinese name,

35

隶书 (official script).　Official script is of two types:　Qín official
and Hàn official.　Qín official script is the cursive form of small
seal characters, and in many respects retains the overall form of
seal characters.　Hàn official script makes a full break with seal
script form, developing its own independent form (see Fig. 08).

The change from small seal characters to official script was

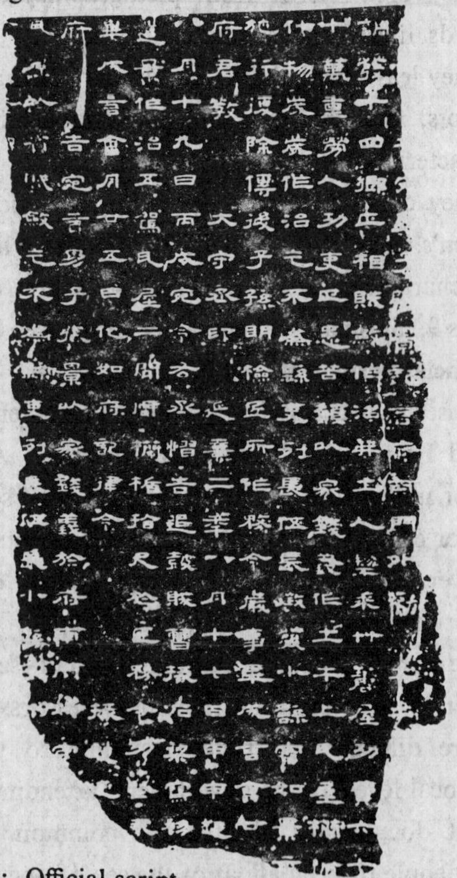

Fig. 08:　Official script.

36

the most thoroughgoing and large-scale transformation ever of Chinese character structure. This transformation is called the "official change" 隶变 in works on the history of Chinese character development. After this official change, pictographic forms vanished entirely from the script, and Chinese characters turned into a purely symbolic writing system. The official script was thus an extremely important transitional phase between ancient and modern writing.

Official script differs from seal characters and more ancient scripts in the following ways:

a) Strokes are level and straight. Ancient scripts used curving, naturalistic strokes to better approximate the objects portrayed. But official script placed a premium on convenience and speed, and to this end curving lines were made straight. This fundamentally altered the pictographic nature of the writing system.

b) Character structure is simplified. For convenience, official script simplified and neatened character structure. The overall number of strokes was reduced, and both radical and phonetic components were simplified. Some different character components were simply merged into one, as when the components 彳 亻 彳 艸 屮 and 几 all came to be written 大 when they appeared at the bottom of a character.

c) Composition is adjusted. In order to make character forms square and neat, official script made large changes in character composition. For example, certain single-element characters were assigned a modified and simplified new form when they appeared as parts of larger characters. Thus 水

(water) in certain situations becomes 氵, 手 (hand) becomes 扌, 犬 (dog, animal) becomes 犭, 心 (heart) becomes 忄, 衣 (clothing) becomes 衤, and 示 (to show) becomes 礻.

The official change established the structural foundation of modern Chinese characters, but in the process it wrought havoc with the original character structure. Many characters originally created using the six methods of character constructions were so altered in form that they could no longer be analyzed or interpreted. Despite this loss, however, we must regard the official change as a quantum leap forward in the evolution of Chinese character structure.

5) Regular Script 楷 书 KǍI SHŪ

Regular script is a style of Chinese characters that has been in continuous use for 1,800 years, from the later years of the Hàn Dynasty to the present day. Regular script was a direct development of official script. The official script had already reformed the Chinese characters that had been in use for over two thousand years; regular script went a step farther in standardizing and regularizing them.

Regular script and official script are structurally not very different. Nevertheless, they differ in two other aspects: a) individual strokes in official script undulate, while those of regular script are smooth and straight; and b) the official script still retains some of the form of seal characters, while regular script departs wholly from seal form (see Fig. 09). The square structure, straight and level lines, and clear strokes of regular script make it easy to read and write; for this reason, it received widespread welcome among the people. It is now respected as the

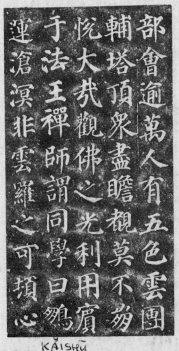

Fig. 09: Regular script.

KAISHŪ

standard of Chinese character structure, whence its Chinese name, 楷书 (model script; other names include true script 真书, ZHĒN SHŪ correct script 正书, and correct model 正楷). After the invention ZHÈNG SHŪ, of printing, regular script was circulated even more widely as ZHĒNG KĂI the standard. With the support lent it by such famous calligraphers as Wáng Xīzhī, Ōuyáng Xún, Yán Zhēnqīng, Liǔ Gōngquán, Sū Shì, Huáng Tíngjiān, Mǐ Fú and Zhào Mèngfǔ, regular script increasingly became the form for students of characters and calligraphy to master.

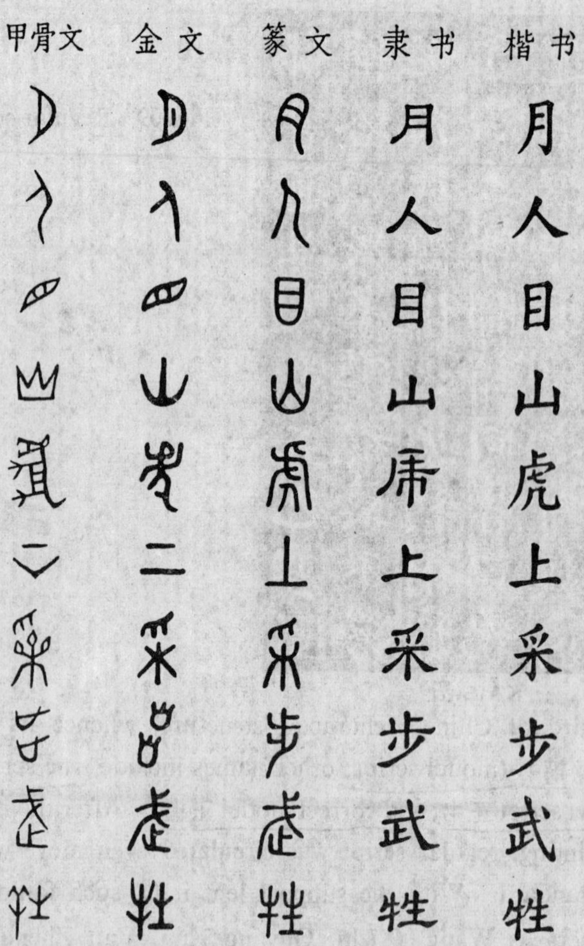

甲骨文	金文	篆文	隶书	楷书
				月
				人
				目
				山
				虎
				上
				采
				步
				武
				牲

Fig. 10: Comparison of oracle bone, bronze, seal, official and regular scripts.

40

Regular script is the representative form of modern Chinese character structure. Figure 10 compares the five most important Chinese character styles and structures: oracle bone, bronze, seal, official, and regular scripts.

Besides the five styles of characters introduced above, there are two other important forms: "grass" characters and "running" characters.

Grass characters script 草书 is an offshoot of official script, being the "shorthand" form of that script. The word "grass" in the name is actually part of several Chinese words meaning "careless, illegible". The purpose of using grass characters is to increase the speed of writing as much as possible. To that end, grass characters retain only the basic outline of the character; strokes are often omitted, and different character components written all the same . Grass script also tends to link separate strokes into one wherever possible. This linking produces vigorous calligraphic flourishes. When grass script first developed, it still retained some of the form of official script, and was more or less legible. Later on, however, the script became more and more cursive and more and more illegible, to the point where sometimes characters could not be read by anyone except the person who wrote them. At this point grass script ceased to be useful as a means of transmitting information, and entered the realm of calligraphic art, written purely for esthetic enjoyment.

Running script 行书 was a development of regular script; specifically, it is the handwritten form of regular script. Although regular script is the model for Chinese script and is easy

41

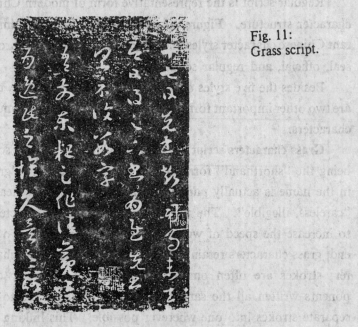

to read and write, to write it out stroke by stroke actually takes a lot of time and trouble. To remedy this shortcoming, a more convenient style of script — running script — developed on the foundation of regular script. Regular characters may be likened to a person standing straight and still, while running characters are more like a person strolling along in a leisurely manner. This is the origin of the script's Chinese name, 行书 ("walking" or "running" script). Running script stands somewhere between regular script and grass script in form, and although some strokes are connected, the whole is still very legible and retains the basic form of regular script (see Fig. 12). Since this script is easy to read and write, it has come into widespread use. Running script has a high practical value, and is commonly used in writing letters, taking notes, and so on.

Fig. 12: Running script.

1.4 THE PRINCIPAL LAWS OF CHINESE CHARACTER DEVELOPMENT

Through the introduction to the evolution of the form of characters provided in this chapter, we can observe the principal trends of Chinese character development over the past several thousand years:

1) Abstraction

Characters have evolved from concrete visual symbols depicting material objects into the abstract symbols of a pure writing system.

2) Simplification

Characters have evolved from complicated pictographic symbols into simple, easy-to-write linear symbols.

3) Phoneticization

Characters have evolved from ideographs directly expressing concepts into phonetic symbols directly expressing sounds.

These three principal trends reflect the laws of Chinese character evolution, which accord with the historical principles of the evolution of writing worldwide.

2. THE NUMBER OF CHINESE CHARACTERS

Almost everyone who studies and uses Chinese characters will ask one question: How many characters are there altogether in Chinese? It is natural that people are concerned with this question. Basically, Chinese characters are independent isolated units. Each symbol has to be memorized by rote one by one. For those who are more familiar with alphabetic writing systems, this is indeed not an easy task. Thus the number of Chinese characters has turned out to be a significant factor for the degree of difficulty in the study of Chinese characters. Is it necessary to completely learn this huge quantity of Chinese characters? If not, then how many is it necessary to learn? Which should be learned first and which can be postponed? In this chapter we are going to discuss these questions.

2.1 HOW MANY CHINESE CHARACTERS ARE THERE?

This is a question which no one can answer clearly and accurately. It is said that an emperor of ancient China once asked one of his very erudite ministers how many characters he knew. The minister answered, "There are as many Chinese characters as there are hairs on the body of an ox. I only know enough to cover one leg."

Chinese characters are widely used throughout the Far East. Besides the Han Chinese themselves, some minority nationalities in China, plus people in Japan, Vietnam, Korea, and some other regions have also used them. It is nearly impossible to collect and count all the characters in their different forms which have ever appeared from ancient times to the present. While it is true that the number of Chinese characters is not infinite, accurate statistics would be very difficult to compile.

A relatively practical approach is to investigate the number of characters collected in dictionaries from each Chinese dynasty. Of course, no such dictionaries were compiled at the time of the oracle bone and bronze inscriptions. The Jiǎ Gǔ Wén Biān 甲骨文编 (*Compilation of Oracle Bone Inscriptions*), a comparatively comprehensive modern day collection of oracle bone inscriptions, contains 4,672 characters. The Jīn Wén Biān 金文编 (*Compilation of Bronze Inscriptions*) similarly contains 3,093 characters. We may say that these figures are incomplete, because from these two periods of history characters are still continuously being discovered, and of course after three thousand years, many of these older characters are probably lost forever.

Ever since Xǔ Shèn compiled the Shuō Wén Jiě Zì in the Eastern Hàn Dynasty, we have had formal dictionaries. The following is a list of comprehensive Chinese character dictionaries with their years of publication and the number of characters contained:

46

Name of Dictionary	Year of Publication	Number of Characters
Shuō Wén Jiě Zì 说文解字	(ca.) 100 A.D.	9,353
Zì Lín 字林	4th C, A.D.	12,824
Yù Piān 玉篇	543 A.D.	16,917
Guǎng Yùn 广韵	1008 A.D.	26,000
Lèi Piān 类篇	1039 A.D.	31,000
Jí Yùn 集韵	1067 A.D.	53,525
Zì Huì 字汇	1615 A.D.	33,179
Zhèng Zì Tōng 正字通	1670 A.D.	33,000
Kāngxī Zìdiǎn 康熙字典	1716 A.D.	47,035
Zhōnghuá Dà Zìdiǎn 中华大字典	1915 A.D.	48,000
Dà Hàn-Hé Cídiǎn 大汉和辞典	1959 A.D.	49,965
Zhōngwén Dà Cídiǎn 中文大辞典	1968 A.D.	49,905
Hànyǔ Dà Zìdiǎn 汉语大字典	1986 A.D.	56,000

From the above list, we may see that the quantity of Chinese characters collected in dictionaries has increased over time. It had reached nearly 50,000 by the time of the Kāngxī Zìdiǎn, and is now close to 60,000 with the recently published Hànyǔ Dà Zìdiǎn. Even so, we still from time to time come across some characters used for colloquial expressions, dialects, or in the names of places or people which are rarely used characters and are not found in dictionaries. Taking this into account, we may make an approximate guess that the total number of ancient and present-day characters altogether is around 60,000 or so.

But *why* are there so many Chinese characters? The primary reasons are discussed below:

1) The large number of Chinese characters is determined by the nature of the language they represent. Characters are written signs for recording language. The type of elements which the characters record influences their number. For instance,

子 曰：学而时习之，不亦说（悦）乎？

Zǐ yuē: xué ér shí xí zhī, bù yì yuè hū?

Confucius said: Isn't studying and reviewing from time to time a pleasure?

This sentence consists of eleven characters in ancient Chinese. These eleven characters actually represent eleven words. We may say, then, that ancient Chinese characters are word-characters 词文字. But things have changed a great deal in the case of modern Chinese. Nowadays the Chinese characters mostly represent the morphemes of the language. For example, in modern Chinese we usually say 学习 (xuéxí, study), 复习 (fùxí, review), 练习 (liànxí, practice), etc., instead of using the single form xí 习 to express all of those concepts. Thus modern Chinese characters may be called morpheme characters 词素文字. Some people combine the two concepts and refer to them as

48

word-morpheme characters 词-词素文字. But whatever you call them, because the characters represent all the morphemes and words in the language, their number is inevitably going to be extremely large. Alphabetic writing systems, on the other hand, have as their basic elements symbols which (more or less) represent the basic sound units, or phonemes, of the morphemes and words of language, so that only a few dozen phonetic symbols, often in the form of "letters", are sufficient.

(2) The large number of characters is also a result of the method of coinage of the Chinese writing system. The character-making method 造字法 in Chinese is not mono-principled, but rather multi-principled. The same word is often represented by different characters formulated on the basis of different character-making principles. Even the same character-making principle has given rise to differing character variants for the same word. For example, the character 牢 in Mandarin, which means "jail", historically has three variant forms, all formed on the basis of the associative principle of character formation: 㸚 an ox in a cowshed; 㸙 a sheep in a sheep pen, and 㺊 a horse in a stable. The word sǎn 伞 (umbrella) is generally represented picto-phonetically by the character 傘, but it can also be represented picto-phonetically by the character 繖. It is difficult to argue that one basis is inherently better than another. When the picto-phonetic principle began to be applied, the phenomenon of characters for the same word having variant forms became quite common.

It is true that it can make just as much sense to represent the same word by one method of coinage or component as another. For example, the word for "cat" has been represented both by the character 猫 with the semantic "animal" radical, and by the character 貓 with another "animal" radical; "gun" both with a "wood" radical 槍, and a "metal" radical 鎗; "cannon" both with a "fire" radical 炮 and a "stone" radical 砲. "Lips" are just as much related to the "mouth" radical 唇, as they are to the "flesh" radical 脣. Similarly, for a given word, one phonetic part may represent the pronunciation of the word just as well as another; thus the word gū meaning "mushroom" may have its pronunciation equally well represented by the character 菇, or the character 菰, and the word chuí meaning "hammer" has been represented both by 錘 and 鎚. As noted above, the number of Chinese characters is already quite large due to the fact that they represent both words and morphemes. They become even more numerous when we have such cases of the same word being represented by different character forms. In ancient days this was referred to as chóng-wén 重文 (alternate forms). The 9,353 characters given above in the famous Shuō Wén Jiě Zì dictionary excludes an additional 1,163 such alternate forms also contained in the dictionary. In the case of the great Kāngxī Zìdiǎn, which contains 47,035 characters, there are more than 20,000 such alternate character forms. For the same word 丘 (qiū, hill), there are eight variant characters used to write it: 丘, 𠀉, 岖, 𡵓, 𡉥, 坴, 坵, 𡊵。

3) The vast numbers of Chinese characters also stem from their continuous accumulation over the ages. The increasingly large number of characters given for the various dictionaries and wordbooks listed above stems from the fact that each suc-

cessive generation of dictionary compilers continued to accumulate any and all characters from the vast sea of ancient writings (including previous wordbooks and virtually any sort of writings of their predecessors) regardless of whether or not a character was ever used more than the one time it was coined. In fact, a great number of these characters became "dead characters" 死字 long ago simply by virtue of the great changes in the language over the centuries. Yet many of these characters have continued to remain in these wordbooks forever. Some people have humorously referred to them as "dead characters without cemetaries".

For instance, the Kāngxī Zìdiǎn contains 481 characters composed with the "horse" radical, among which the majority are "dead characters":

犸:	a one year old horse	馴:	an eight year old horse
駣:	a three or four year old horse	駓:	a stout horse
騋:	a horse over seven hands tall	馼:	a horse over eight hands tall
騵:	a horse with a white belly	驔:	a horse with a white forehead
驕:	a horse with white legs	騱:	a horse with completely white forefeeet
駧:	a horse with one white eye	駋:	a white horse with dark lips
騩:	a horse with a white tail	騚:	a horse with four white hoofs

骃：a horse with mixed black and white hair

駹：a horse with black hair and a white forehead

騢：a horse with mixed red and white hair

駓：a horse with mixed yellow and white hair

騧：an indigo horse

驖：a blood black horse

騂：a red and yellow horse

騟：a violet horse

駂：a light black horse

騧：a yellow horse with dark lips

驎：a horse with dark lips

騚：a horse with a yellow mane

騜：an indigo horse with black spots

騤：a red horse with a black mane

In contrast, we can see that there are only 143 characters employing the "horse" radical in the twentieth century dictionary Cí Hǎi 辞海 (Sea of Words), and fewer than 80 such in the contemporary Xiàndài Hànyǔ Cídiǎn 现代汉语词典 (*Dictionary of Modern Chinese Words*) and the Xīnhuá Zìdiǎn 新华字典 (Xīnhuá *Dictionary*), from which we may conclude that the majority of the 47,035 characters in Kāngxī Zìdiǎn are now dead ones.

4) As noted above, special characters for words in dialects, colloquialisms, proper names of people and places, as well as many special words used for scientific and technological terminology all add to the number of Chinese characters. Many examples can be given. Wǔ Zétiān 武则天, a well-known empress of the Táng Dynasty, herself coined nineteen Chinese characters, including the character 曌, indicating that the sun and moon are shining in the heavens, which she used as her own

name. Later this character was mistakenly written as 塁, and thus two more new characters were added to the language. Modern chemists have also coined quite a few new characters for the newly discovered chemical elements, such as 锕 for actinium, 镅 for americium, 镧 for lanthanum, etc.

Thus we can see the principal causes for the large number of Chinese characters. Obviously, the approximate figure of 60,000 characters mentioned earlier is simply the aggregate of all the characters which have ever appeared from past to present. Such a figure is not very meaningful in terms of its practical value. First, the alternate forms described in point (2) above should be excluded from calculation, as they are merely variant ways of writing the same characters. Second, the large number of "dead" characters described in point (3) should also be excluded as those characters have become useless in modern times. If these two types of characters are excluded, then the remainder of Chinese characters totals only between ten and twenty thousand. For example, the contemporary dictionary Cí Hǎi contains 14,872 characters, which still includes a number of variant forms and dead characters. Thus we may say that the number of Chinese characters of practical value today is between ten and twenty thousand.

2.2 THE SYSTEMATIZATION OF CHINESE CHARACTERS

That the number of Chinese characters should be as high as 20,000 is still quite amazing. Such a large quantity of characters means that learning and using them can be quite burdensome, as well as causing great difficulties in technical applications such as typing, printing, and computer entry of characters. To systematize Chinese characters means to make a comprehensive investigation to determine which characters are absolutely necessary, and which ones are less frequently used or not used at all. Obviously the first step is to thoroughly eliminate those characters that are entirely obsolete in order to reduce the difficulties of study and technical application. Since the founding of the People's Republic of China, the Committee for the Reform of the Chinese Language has done a lot of work in this area, which we shall now examine in some detail under two headings.

1) Eliminate Alternative Forms of Characters

This refers to those alternative character forms 异体字 discussed in the previous section. The definition of such characters is two or more characters whose pronunciation and meaning are entirely the same, which differ only in written form. Examples can be seen in the variant characters for "cat" 猫/貓; "lip" 唇/脣; "mushroom" 菇/菰; and "hammer" 锤/鎚 mentioned above. Obviously it is completely unnecessary to have such alternative written forms in the language, as it only makes learning to read and write more difficult. In his famous short story Kǒng Yǐjǐ 孔乙己, Lu Xun satirized the old scholar Kǒng's pride in showing off his ability to write the four alternative forms of the character 回 (huí, to return) 囘囬囶.

The alternative character forms originate from the methods of coining Chinese characters. As noted above, these methods are multi-principled rather than mono-principled. Even employing one particular method of character formation, such as the picto-phonetic principle, there are many cases where one morpheme was represented by a number of different picto-phonetic characters arbitrarily. Thus it is a fact that a character may have more than one form representing the same meaning and pronunciation.

We should also remember that Chinese characters were produced by the Chinese people over the centuries. Referring to the legendary official in charge of historical records in the court of the Yellow Emperor, the famous Chinese writer Lu Xun remarked in *A Layman's Remarks on Writing* 门外文谈: "There was more than one 仓颉 Cāng Jié. Some people carved little diagrams on knife handles and some drew pictures on windows and doors. Thus by mutual agreement and word of mouth, the number of characters increased." For instance in ancient times the character 果 (fruit) was created. This was a pictographic character, the lower half of which 木 represents "wood" and the upper half of which 田 represents the actual fruit. Later the "grass" or "vegetable" radical ⺿ was added to the top of the character, making it a picto-phonetic character. Thus the characters 果 and 菓 came to overlap. For another example, someone in one place created a character 岩 by the associative character\formation principle: mountains and stones together designate a mountain "crag", pronounced yán. In another place the character 巖 was created picto-phonetically by combining the "mountain" radical with the phonetic component 嚴, also pronounced yán. But somewhere else it was felt that writing the character that way with the "mountain"

55

radical on the top made the character too elongated, so the radical was moved to the left, giving a third variant 巗. Thus the one word pronounced yán came to have three alternative character forms. It was also through this type of process that the character forms became differentiated into the different so-called "styles" of characters, such as the zhèng tǐ 正体 or formal style, the sú tǐ 俗体 or popular style, the bié tǐ 别体 or alternate form, the biàn tǐ 变体 or changed form, etc. There are a lot of these different forms, and all of them have been collected into dictionaries and used in publications. Their increasing social currency of course created chaos in the system of Chinese characters as a whole as well as creating great inefficiency for people learning to read and write.

Such variant character forms may generally be grouped into the following six classes. (For the purpose of contrast, some old style complex character forms are used here.)

a) Different methods were used in coining the same character:

伞	umbrella (pictograph) *SĂN*	=	繖 (picto-phonetic)
岳	hill (pictograph) *QIÚ*	=	嶽 (picto-phonetic)
泪	tears (associative) *LÈI*	=	淚 (picto-phonetic)
岩	crag (associative) *YÁN*	=	巖 (picto-phonetic)
鬥	fight (associative) *DÒU*	=	鬧 (picto-phonetic)
奸	liason (picto-phonetic)	=	姦 (associative)
羴	smell of mutton (picto-phonetic)	=	羴 (associative)
渺	vast and vague (picto-phonetic)	=	淼 (associative)

b) Different radical components were used for the same character coined picto-phonetically:

猫 = 貓 cat MĀO   狸 = 貍 racoon   貛 = 貛 badger

猪 = 豬 pig   鷄 = 雞 chicken jī   雕 = 鵰 vulture

堤 = 隄 dike   阶 = 堦 flight of   址 = 阯 address
                          steps

秕 = 粃 blasted   糯 = 稬 glutinous   糠 = 穅 chaff

籼 = 秈 long-grained rice   粘 = 黏 sticky

糖 = 餹 sugar   哗 = 譁 noise   咬 = 齩 bite

咏 = 詠 chant   唇 = 脣 lip   悖 = 誖 contrary

遍 = 徧 times   膀 = 髈 shoulder   炮 = 砲 cannon

焊 = 銲 weld   煉 = 鍊 smelt   辉 = 煇 splendor

迹 = 跡 trace   枪 = 鎗 gun   棱 = 稜 edge

橹 = 艣 scull   礦 = 鑛 ore/mine   捆 = 綑 bind

暖 = 煖 warm   鋪 = 舖 shop/store   館 = 舘 shop/

                                                    house

耽 = 眈 delay   懒 = 孄 lazy   球 = 毬 ball

婿 = 壻 son-in-law   侄 = 姪 nephew   弦 = 絃 string

鳖 = 鼈 turtle   凉 = 涼 cool   蓑 = 簑 straw rain

                                                    cape

c) Different phonetic components were used in making the same picto-phonetic characters:

柏 = 栢 cypress   绷 = 繃 tighten   馒 = 饅 steamed

                                                    bun

眯 = 瞇 squint   泛 = 汎 overflow   蝶 = 蜨 butterfly

璃 = 琍 glass   鐮 = 鎌 sickle   杆 = 桿 pole

菇 = 菰 mushroom   糠 = 粇 chaff   秸 = 稭 stalks

綫 = 線 line   勋 = 勳 merit   汹 = 洶 turbulent

57

吃 = 喫 eat	錘 = 鎚 hammer	笋 = 筍 shoots
鰐 = 鱷 crocodile	臉 = 瞼 cheek	烟 = 煙 smoke
胭 = 臙 rouge	咽 = 嚥 swallow (v)	韵 = 韻 rhyme
涌 = 湧 gush		

d) The phonetic and radical parts were not consistantly arranged in the same picto-phonetic character. The various parts of the characters were arranged in various configurations, thus creating more character variants. For example:

綿 = 緜 silk floss	隣 = 鄰 felt	够 = 夠 revive
秋 = 秌 autumn	氈 = 氊 felt	蘇 = 蘓 take
飄 = 飃 blown about	峰 = 峯 peak	拿 = 舍 take
概 = 槩 general	期 = 朞 time period	啟 = 启 reveal
耕 = 畊 plough	棋 = 棊 chess	胸 = 曾 bosom
略 = 畧 omit	紙 = 帋 paper	峨 = 峩 high
鵝 = 鵞 goose	岸 = 屵 bank	裏 = 裡 inside
龕 = 匚 women's toilet case	闊 = 濶 vast/wealthy	匯 = 滙 converge

脅 = 脇 side of body 慚 = 慙 ashamed/shameful

Some character variants involve both changes in the radical or phonetic component, and in their relative positioning as well. For instance:

翻 = 繙 overturn	蜂 = 蠭 bee	荡 = 盪 swing
睹 = 覩 witness	嘆 = 歎 sigh	歌 = 謌 song
肛 = 疘 anus	歡 = 讙 cheer	救 = 捄 rescue
溪 = 谿 creek	膻 = 羶 smell of mutton	腮 = 顋 cheek
焰 = 燄 flames	吻 = 脗 kiss	蚊 = 螡 mosquito

58

e) Some variant forms of characters were created by the later addition of a superfluous radical to the original character. This phenomenon is aptly described by the four-character idiom "huà shé tiān zú" 画蛇添足 (drawing a snake and adding legs to it). For example:

麻 = 蔴 hemp   豆 = 荳 bean   果 = 菓 fruit

梁 = 樑 beam   動 = 働 move   丘 = 坵 hill

席 = 蓆 mat   帚 = 箒 broom   嘗 = 嚐 taste

升 = 昇 rise   殷 = 慇 fervent   欲 = 慾 desire

愈 = 癒 cure   沾 = 霑 stain   匆 = 忽 hasty

f) Some characters have variant ways of writing a component part. For example:

留 = 畱 stay   畝 = 畞 ≈0.15 acre   朵 = 朶 stem

亘 = 亙 continuous   回 = 囘 return   捷 = 捿 triumph

晋 = 晉 raise   插 = 挿 insert   撑 = 撐 prop

册 = 冊 book volume

In December 1955, the Committee for the Reform of the Chinese Language and the Ministry of Culture jointly published a "List of the First Group of Standardized Forms of Variant Characters" 第一批异体字整理表. Included in this list were 810 sets of variant characters ranging from at least two, to six per set. Of a total of 1,865 characters, 1,055 were eliminated by standardization. With the publication of this list, these 1,053 abrogated character variants were entirely eliminated from use in all national level newspapers, periodicals, and books. Exceptions are made in the case of reprinting ancient books using their original characters or in names and surnames that require special character forms. (A minority of characters in the list were modified when the Scheme for Simplifying Chinese Characters was published in 1956. Now the Complete List of Simplified Characters, finalized in 1964, is taken as the uniform standard. See Appendix 2 to this book).

Certain principles were observed in deciding which of the alternative forms to keep and which to eliminate. Basically, there are two principles:

i) Follow custom: that is, the forms chosen to be the standard forms were those forms in wide currency, while those of rare or limited currency were abandoned.

ii) Choose the simpler form: character variants with comparatively fewer strokes and structurally simpler configurations were preferred over those with more strokes and more complex structures.

A combination of these two principles was used to determine which forms were to be kept and which were to be abandoned. For example:

Characters Chosen:			Characters Eliminated
嘆	sigh	TÀN	歎
凉	cool	LIÁNG	涼
泪	tears	LÈI	淚
烟	smoke	YĀN	煙菸
岩	crag	YÁN	巖巗嵒
暖	warm	NUǍN	烧晅煗
拿	take	NÁ	舒拏挐
携	bring		擕攜攜攜

咱　　we/I　　　　　　　　　　 喒偺喒偺
窗　　window CHUĀNG　　　　 窓窻窻牎牎

In fact the task of systematizing characters with alternate forms is not yet finished. There are still quite a few presently in use which need to be systematized. Besides such individual characters, there are also cases of so-called "compound words with alternate forms" 异体词. These are usually disyllablic words which carry the same meaning and prounuciation, but with different written forms. For example: 疙瘩 (knob/knot) is also written as: 疙疸，纥縼，咯哒，咯嗒，圪垯，圪塔，屹嵖，all pronounced gēda, with the same meaning. Other examples are 耿直 (frank and upright), pronounced gěngzhí, also written as 梗直 or 鲠直; and 委靡 (listless), pronounced wěimǐ, also written as 萎靡. These kinds of "alternate compound forms" also need to be normalized.

2) Change Rarely Used Characters in the Names of Places

Many place names in China employ rarely seen characters handed down from ancient times. Research shows that there are over five hundred such specialized characters used in place names above the county level throughout China. These specialized characters are only used in these place names and nowhere else in current usage. Some are so rarely encountered that they are difficult to learn to recognize, memorize, and write, for instance 盩厔 (Zhōuzhì) County in Shaanxi Province, 鳛水 (Xíshuǐ) County in Guizhou Province, 亹源 (Ményuán) Hui Nationality Autonomous County in Qinghai Province, to give but a few typical examples. If such rare, special purpose characters used in place names are replaced by homonymous, more

61

common characters, then not only will the difficulty of learning and writing them be reduced, but the total number of characters will also be reduced as well. Between 1956 and 1964, with the approval of the State Council, thirty-five such place names of counties and prefectures were changed. Some examples:

Original Forms:	Revised Forms:
铁骊县（黑龙江）	铁力县
瑷珲县（黑龙江）	爱辉县
亹源回族自治县（青海）	门源回族自治县
和阗专区（新疆）	和田专区
和阗县（新疆）	和田县
于阗县（新疆）	于田县
婼羌县（新疆）	若羌县
雩都县（江西）	于都县
大庾县（江西）	大余县
虔南县（江西）	全南县
新淦县（江西）	新干县
新喻县（江西）	新余县
鄱阳县（江西）	波阳县
寻邬县（江西）	寻乌县
鬱林县（广西）	玉林县
酆都县（四川）	丰都县
石砫县（四川）	石柱县
越嶲县（四川）	越西县
呷洛县（四川）	甘洛县
婺川县（贵州）	务川县

鰼水县（贵州）	习水县
商雒专区（陕西）	商洛专区
盩厔县（陕西）	周至县
郿县（陕西）	眉县
醴泉县（陕西）	礼泉县
郃阳县（陕西）	合阳县
鄠县（陕西）	户县
雒南县（陕西）	洛南县
邠县（陕西）	彬县
鄜县（陕西）	富县
葭县（陕西）	佳县
沔县（陕西）	勉县
栒邑县（陕西）	旬邑县
洵阳县（陕西）	旬阳县
汧阳县（陕西）	千阳县

The work of systematizing such rarely used characters in place names is continuing.

2.3 THE FREQUENCY OF OCCURRENCE, RATE OF CURRENCY, AND WORD FORMATION CAPABILITY OF CHINESE CHARACTERS

As noted in the first section of this chapter, the total aggregate of both ancient and present-day Chinese characters is about sixty thousand. However, if we eliminate those alternate and "dead" characters, the number of practical use is by now between ten and twenty thousand. But even this large figure is not truly representative of the number of characters that must be learned. From the point of view of reading and writing, the number should be much smaller.

One needs to recognize more characters than one needs to write. But how many characters are enough to enable one to read general books and periodicals? According to the experience of several large scale printing houses over many years, type-pieces for approximately seven to nine thousand different characters are sufficient to print all kinds of books and magazines, including a variety of publications on specialized subjects. As far as general publications for the public at large, seven thousand characters are quite sufficient for general reading.

The number of characters required for writing is much fewer than that required for reading. A statistical study of Sun Yat-sen's book Sān Mín Zhǔyì 三民主义 (*The Three Principles of the People*) shows that the book employs only 2,134 different characters. The famous novel Luòtuo Xiángzi 骆驼祥子 (*Rickshaw Boy*) by Lǎo Shè 老舍 is over one hundred thousand characters in length, yet it employs only 2,413 different characters. All five volumes of the Máo Zédōng Xuǎnjí 毛泽东选集 (*Selected Works of Mao Zedong*) altogether contain more than 900,000 characters, yet only 3,136 different characters are used. From these statistics we can see that a little over three thousand characters is adequate for writing books.

Based on these facts, we may conclude that, excluding professionals in such specialized fields as archaeology, history, philology, etc., generally speaking, if one can recognize seven thousand characters and correctly write three thousand of these, then one has already obtained a fairly high standard. And in fact, such a standard is beyond the reach of much of the Chinese population.

The next problem which presents itself is which of these seven thousand characters should be learned first, and which later? In other words, which characters are most frequently used, and which ones are less often or even rarely used? Of course we cannot decide the rates of currency and frequency on the basis of individual judgement, because different people have different experiences, specializations, and educational backgrounds, which would naturally give rise to differences of opinion on the frequency and currency of different characters, and thus there is no uniform standard. Obviously such decisions should only be made after detailed research and statistical investigation on the number and frequency of characters in current use so that our judgments can be made on the basis of scientifically objective data. In the following three sections, we shall investigate the bases for calculating the frequency of occurrence, the rates of currency, and the word-formation capability of Chinese characters.

1) The Frequency of Occurrence of Chinese Characters
In order to make a statistical investigation of the frequency of Chinese characters, we should select a number of different articles on various subjects from newspapers, magazines, and such publications, all of about the same length. This data is taken as the sample 抽样 base. The total aggregate number of characters in these samples is called the total sample aggregate

总字数. The number of times of occurrence of any one character in this total aggregate we may call the "degree of occurrence" 出现次数 of that character. For example, if the total sample aggregate contains 21,600,000 characters, and the character 我 (wǒ, I) occurs 89,091 times, while the character 你 (nǐ, you) occurs 20,053 times, then the degree of occurrence of the character 我 is 89,091 and that of the character 你 is 20,053. The frequency of occurrence 出现频率 of any one character is the ratio of the degree of occurrence of that particular character in relation to the total aggregate number of characters in the overall sample. Thus in the two examples just cited:

The frequency of occurrence of 我 =
$$89,091/21,600,000 = 0.0041246$$

The frequency of occurrence of 你 =
$$20,053/21,600,000 = 0.0009284$$

According to the principles of statistics, the larger the total aggregate sample, the more representative (and therefore accurate) are both the number of times of occurrence and the frequency of occurrence. Therefore, in doing this type of statistical sampling work, one's total sample aggregate should not be too small.

Obviously a character with a higher frequency of occurrence is used more often than one with a lower frequency. So in the example just above, 我 is more frequently used than 你. To give another example, if we look at the frequency of characters used to represent the names of common animals based on the same sample, their rates of occurrence are 马 (mǎ, horse) 26,866, 猪 (zhū, pig) 3,654, 牛 (niú, ox/cow) 3,478, 羊 (yáng, sheep) 2,575, 狗 (gǒu, dog) 1,197, and 猫 (māo, cat) 257. Thus the frequency of occurrence of a character is an important index in measuring its degree of use in the total system of Chinese characters.

We can therefore make a table of frequency of Chinese characters containing several thousand of them listed in order of their relative degrees and frequency of occurrence based on a large sampling. The following shows the first 28 characters listed at the beginning of such a frequency table, based on a total aggregate sample of 21,629,376 characters*:

No.	Character	Pron.	Degree of Frequency of Occurrence	Frequency of Occurrence	Accumulative Frequency
1	的	de	830302	0.0383877	0.0383877
2	一	yī	270949	0.0125269	0.0509146
3	是	shì	211842	0.0097942	0.0607088
4	在	zài	204459	0.0094528	0.0701616
5	了	le/liǎo	177299	0.0081971	0.0783587
6	不	bù	174234	0.0080554	0.0864141
7	和	hé	161754	0.0074784	0.0938925
8	有	yǒu	150015	0.0069357	0.1008282
9	大	dà	148500	0.0068657	0.1076939
10	这	zhè	138426	0.0063999	0.1140938
11	主	zhǔ	131991	0.0061024	0.1201962
12	中	zhōng	129005	0.0059643	0.1261605
13	人	rén	126375	0.0058427	0.1320032

*See Zheng Linxi, Gao Jingcheng, *A Frequency Table of Chinese Characters* 汉字频度表 published by the Committee for the Reform of the Chinese Language, Aug. 1980.

14	上	shàng	119011	0.0055023	0.1375055
15	为	wéi	113913	0.0052666	0.1427721
16	们	men	113101	0.0052290	0.1480011
17	地	dì	108618	0.0050218	0.1530229
18	个	gè	107623	0.0049758	0.1579987
19	用	yòng	102435	0.0047359	0.1627346
20	工	gōng	98549	0.0045563	0.1672909
21	时	shí	97539	0.0045096	0.1718005
22	要	yào	97436	0.0045048	0.1763053
23	动	dòng	96432	0.0044584	0.1807637
24	国	guó	96337	0.0044540	0.1852177
25	产	chǎn	93541	0.0043247	0.1895424
26	以	yǐ	91031	0.0042087	0.1937511
27	我	wǒ	89191	0.0041236	0.1978747
28	到	dào	88008	0.0040689	0.2019436

Accumulative frequency累积频率, the right-most column in the above table, is the cumulative sum of the continuous addition of the percentages of frequency, obtained by adding the percentage of frequency of occurrence of the character listed to the sum total of the percentages of frequncy of all of the characters preceding it. Thus, for example, the accumulative frquency of 0.0783587 given in the righthand column for character number 5, 了 le/liao, is the sum obtained by adding together all of the frequency percentages for characters 1 through 5. This is an important concept because it tells us, for example, that the total accumulative frequency of the 28 characters listed above is a little over 0.20. In other words, if you know these 28 characters, then you will on average recognize 20 percent of the Chinese characters that you encounter in reading most general articles.

Thus if we examine the frequency table given below we can see that if you know the first 163 characters on the above-mentioned frequency list, you should recognize 50 percent of the characters you meet in most newspapers and magazines; and if you know the first 2,400 characters, you should recognize 99 percent of such characters. Thus we may say that it is enough for the average person to know 4,000 characters, and thus recognize 99.9 percent of the characters he or she encounters. The final entry in this table (6,359 characters) is a total based on such a statistical investigation of a large sample, and approximates the figure of 7,000 characters mentioned above as the maximum number of characters necessary for most reading purposes.

This list may also be used to make an approximate estimate of the size of your own Chinese character vocabulary. While reading a newspaper, note the total number of characters in the articles you read. Then determine the number of characters you recognize by subtracting the number of all instances of characters which you do not recognize. For example, if the total number of characters in the newspaper article(s) you read was 125,000, and there are 1,140 instances of characters you do not recognize or do not know, then by subtraction, the number of characters that you do recognize is 123,860 or 99.1 percent of the total of 125,000. Based on the assumption that the distribution of characters in the article(s) you chose approximates the general sample, then you may use the frequency table "in reverse" to estimate that you know approximately the first 2,500 characters on the list.

Character No. In Freq. List	Accumulative Frequency
28	20%
163	50%
243	60%
363	70%
560	80%
950	90%
2,400	99%
3,804	99.9%
5,265	99.99%
6,359	100%

2) The Rate of Currency of Chinese Characters

Although the degree of occurrence of a Chinese character is a significant figure in calculating its overall frequency of occurrence, nevertheless in the case of individual characters, some deviation may occur, especially in the case of characters with relatively low frequencies of occurrence. Let's look at some concrete examples. If we take as our sample five différent articles or pamphlets of similar lengths on different subjects, the number of times of occurrence of the five characters 篆 (zhuàn, seal), 弊 (bì, fraud), 焚 (fén, to burn), 怜 (lián, pity), and 趁 (chèn, take adventage of) might happen to be 30 instances of each of these five characters. May we then conclude that the frequencies of occurrence of these five characters are basically similar? Not necessarily. This will become clear if we look at the distribution 分布 of these five characters in each of the five different source materials:

Char.	Pron.	I	II	III	IV	V	Total
篆	zhuàn	0	30	0	0	0	30
弊	bì	0	0	2	0	28	30
焚	fén	2	0	26	2	0	30
怜	lián	16	1	2	6	5	30
趁	chèn	4	3	7	8	8	30

The most striking datum is the character 篆 (zhuàn) which occurs thirty times in sample article II and not at all in any of the other sample articles. Obviously there is a problem in our selection of the basis of our overall sample. Probably article II is an essay on the history of ancient Chinese characters in which such terms as 大篆 (dàzhuàn, great seal script), 小篆 (xiǎozhuàn, small seal script) and 篆书 (zhuàn shū, seal script) are repeatedly used, so that its degree of occurrence is greatly increased. Similarly, we can see that the other characters also have more or less this same kind of skewed distribution within our sample. Obviously it would be a mistake to conclude from each of the overall totals of 30 instances that these characters are similar in frequency of occurrence when their distribution even within such a limited sample is so uneven.

One lesson we may draw from this is to make our samples as representative as possible by increasing the size of the sample, both in terms of the number of different articles in it as well as the total volume of characters. Avoiding small samples and specialized articles will eliminate problems such as those mentioned in the example above. Another point is to pay attention not simply to a character's frequency of occurrence, but also to its distribution 分布 of occurrences, and, even more importantly, to its rate of currency 通用率. The index of the rate of currency of a character may be expressed in terms of its degree or ratio of currency. Let us calculate the degrees of currency 通用度 for each of the five characters mentioned in the example above.*

篆　zhuàn　$=(\sqrt{0}+\sqrt{30}+\sqrt{0}+\sqrt{0}+\sqrt{0})^2/5=6$

弊　bì　$=(\sqrt{0}+\sqrt{0}+\sqrt{2}+\sqrt{0}+\sqrt{28})^2/5\approx9$

焚　fén　$=(\sqrt{2}+\sqrt{0}+\sqrt{26}+\sqrt{2}+\sqrt{0})^2/5\approx13$

怜　lián　$=(\sqrt{16}+\sqrt{1}+\sqrt{2}+\sqrt{6}+\sqrt{5})^2/5\approx25$

趁　chèn　$=(\sqrt{4}+\sqrt{3}+\sqrt{7}+\sqrt{8}+\sqrt{8})^2/5\approx29$

The rates of frequency for each of these five characters become much clearer when considered together with their degrees of currency. If we examine the formula used for computing the degree of currency*, we can see that the degree of currency of a character is smallest when the distribution of the numbers of times of its occurrence is the most uneven throughout the sample, as in the case of the first character 篆 (zhuàn). On the other hand, when the distribution of a character is close to being equal, as in the case of 趁 (chèn), then the degree of currency is closer

---

*Yin Binyong, *A Method for Estimating the Degree of Currency of Words and Phrases* 词语通用度的一种估计方法. Paper presented to the Fifth Meeting of the Chinese Linguistics Society, Guangzhou, December 1987.

to the number of times of occurrence. Of course, the maximum degree of currency occurs when the distribution is exactly even and the two figures are equal.

Adding up the degrees of currency of all of the characters in the frequency list will give us the total aggregate of degrees of currency. The ratio of the degree of currency of any one character and this total aggregate is called the rate of currency of that character. This rate of currency is the index for measuring the degree of currency of Chinese characters.

3) The Word Formation Capability of Chinese Characters

One point to remember, of course, is that Chinese characters mostly do not occur in isolation, but rather combine with other characters to make polymorphemic/polysyllabic words. From the point of view of word-building, most Chinese characters may be put into one of two categories. One category contains characters such as 人 (rén, person), 学 (xué, study), and 好 (hǎo, good), which can be used both as independent monosyllabic words (e.g. 他在学中国话 Tā zài xué Zhōngguóhuà, He's studying Chinese), and also as constitutent elements of longer polysyllabic words such as 学习 (xuéxí, study), 大学 (dàxué, university), 中学生 (zhōngxuéshēng, middle school student), 生物学 shēngwùxué, biology), etc. The other category consists of characters such as 殖 (zhí, breed), 辉 (huī, brightness), and 慰 (wèi, console), which cannot be used alone as monosyllabic words, but only occur as components in polysyllabic words such as 殖民地 (zhímíndì, colony), 生殖 (shēngzhí, reproduction), 光辉 (guānghuī, brilliance), 辉煌 (huīhuáng, magnificence),

慰问 (wèiwèn, entertain, sympathize), 安慰 (ānwèi, console), etc.

The number of different words (both monosyllabic and polysyllabic) which a character may enter into is called the word formation capability 构词力 of that character. For example, the character 蚯 (qiū) can enter into only one word, 蚯蚓 (qiūyǐn, earthworm), so its word formation capability is 1. However, 学 (xué, study) can constitute one hundred and twenty-one such words, such as 学 (xué, study), 学习 (xuéxí, study), 中学 (zhōngxué, middle school), 大学生 (dàxuéshēng, university student), 植物学 (zhíwùxué, botany) etc., so its word formation capability is 121. When we learn the character 蚯 (qiū) we only have access to part of the one compound word 蚯蚓 (qiūyǐn, earthworm), while we gain potential access to one hundred and twenty-one compound words by mastering the character 学 (xué). Obviously the character 学 is much more widely used than 蚯, so we can say that the word-building capability of a character is also an reflection of both its degrees of frequency and currency.

Below is a table of the top ten Chinese characters in terms of their word formation capacities. In the column headed "Word Formation Capability as a Monosyllable", the number given indicates the number of different parts of speech that character may represent when it occurs alone as a monosyllabic word. Thus, for example, the character 大 (dà, big) listed in third position in the table below can function either as an adjective or an adverb when it occurs alone as a monosyllabic word. Under the heading "Word Formation Capability in Polysyl-

74

lables", the columns sub-headings "Head", "Mid" and "End"
represent the number of instances when the character occurs
in the initial, middle, or final position in a polysyllabic word;
for example, Head: 大学 (dàxué, university), Mid: 放大镜
(fàngdàjìng, magnifying glass), End: 广大 (guǎngdà, wide-
ranging).

The word formation capacity of Chinese characters only
reflects one aspect of the degrees of frequency and currency of
Chinese characters, but is not equivalent to the rates of occur-

No.	Char.	Pron.	Word Formation Capability as Monosyllable	Word Formation Capability in Polysyllables			Total
				Head	Mid	End	
1	子	zǐ	1	11	32	624	668
2	不	bù	1	227	266	6	500
3	大	dà	2	202	53	39	296
4	心	xīn	1	88	55	143	287
5	人	rén	1	68	51	158	278
6	一	yī	2	192	65	16	275
7	头	tóu	4	31	41	187	263
8	气	qì	3	58	25	151	237
9	无	wú	1	133	79	3	216
10	水	shuǐ	1	121	20	67	209

rence or currency. To give some concrete examples, some characters such as 的 (de, of), 了 (le, perfective aspect marker), 是 (shì, to be), 我 (wǒ, I), 又 (yòu, again), 吧 (ba, OK?), 很 (hěn, quite), 但 (dàn, but), etc. have very limited word formation capabilities, yet are among the most frequently used characters. Therefore, word formation capability can be used only as a reference index for measuring the degrees of frequency and currency of Chinese characters.

2.4 FREQUENTLY USED CHARACTERS, GENERALLY USED CHARACTERS, AND CHARACTERS FOR SPECIALIZED USE

1) Frequently Used Characters 常用字

Everyone seems to know what this term means, and yet it is difficult to give it a clear definition. It is also hard to give it a definite scope. Generally speaking, characters which have a very high frequency of occurrence and are indispensible for reading and writing for most people of average education can be considered to be frequently used characters.

The first educator to make a systematic study of frequently used characters in China was Chén Hèqín 陈鹤琴. His "Glossary of Characters Used in Written Language" 语体文应用字汇, published in June 1928, listed 4,261 frequently used characters. The "List of Frequently Used Characters" 常用字表 published by the Sichuan Academy of Educational Sciences in August 1946, contains 2,000 characters. After the founding of the People's Republic, to meet the needs of illiteracy elimination work the Central Ministry of Education issued a "List of Frequently Used Characters", also containing 2,000 characters, which was published in June 1952. This list was compiled after consulting all previous such lists and after seeking opinions from all quarters.

In 1987, the State Language Commission and the State Education Commission jointly conducted a research project on frequently used characters. In addition to the previously mentioned works, more than a dozen other materials were consulted, including the "List of 3,500 Characters for Learning with Correct Pronunciation" 识字正音3,500字表 published in January 1954 by the editors of the China Dictionary Editorial Board, the *Collection of Symbols for Encoding Information Exchange: Basic Volume* 信息交换用汉字编码字符集·基本集, compiled by the National Bureau of Standards (May 1981), in which the first level of characters is 3,755, and the 3,190 characters contained in the "List of Character Vocabulary for the National Chinese Language Textbook Series for the Six-Grade Primary School", published by the People's Educational Publishing House. After repeated discussion, comparisons, and consultations with all levels of society, the "List of Frequently Used Characters in Modern Chinese" 现代汉语常用字表 was finally published in 1988, based on frequency of use, distribution in various subjects, word formation capability, and practical conditions of daily use, as well as the above-mentioned earlier works. This 1988 list contains the 3,500 most frequently used characters, among which the first 2,500 are to be taught in the primary schools, and the remaining 1,000 at the middle school level. These 3,500 characters are listed at the end of this chapter for reference.

2) Generally Used Characters　通用字

Generally used characters are those commonly needed for all types of published materials in modern Chinese, common to a wide variety of subjects.　These stand in contradistinction to characters for specialized use (see next section), which are only used in certain specialized fields.

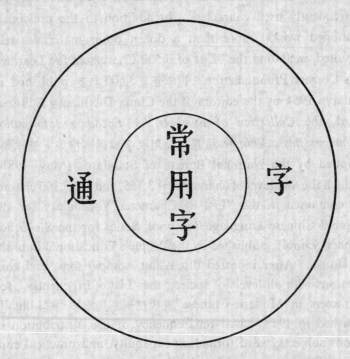

The range of generally used characters is greater than that of frequently used ones.　All frequently used characters are also generally used characters, but not vice versa. This relationship is similar to that of a small circle enclosed by a larger one, as indicated by the figure on the right.

In 1987, while researching the frequently used characters, the State Language Commission also studied these generally used characters as well. This research was based on the following various representative lists and dictionaries of characters in general use:

"List of Chinese Character Forms for General Printing" 印刷通用汉字字形表, containing 6,196 characters, published in January 1965 by the Ministry of Culture and the Committee for the Reform of the Chinese Language.

"Frequency List of Chinese Characters" 汉字频度表, containing 6,374 characters, compiled in December 1976, by the Frequency Investigation Group of Project No. 748.

Dictionary of Modern Chinese 现代汉语词典, containing 8,373 characters, compiled in December 1978, by the Institute of Linguistics of the Chinese Academy of Social Sciences.

Xinhua Dictionary 新华字典, containing 7,668 characters, published by the Commercial Press in 1979.

The first and second levels of characters defined in *Collection of Symbols for Encoding Information Exchange: Basic Volume* 信息交换用汉字编码字符集·基本集, containing 6,763 characters, published in May 1981, by the National Bureau of Standards.

Standard Telegraph Code Book 标准电码本, containing 7,292 characters, produced in 1983 by the Ministry of Post and Telecommunications.

"Comprehensive Frequency List of Characters in the Social and Natural Sciences" 社会科学、自然科学综合汉字频度表, contiaining 7,754 characters, compiled by the Beijing Institute of Aviation and the Committee for the Reform of the Chinese Language in March 1985.

"News and Information Currency Frequencies" 新闻信息流通频度, containing 6,001 characters, was produced in January 1987 by the Xinhua News Agency Technology Research Institute.

Thus the "List of Generally Used Characters in Modern Chinese" 现代汉语通用字表, was finally produced in March 1988, at the same time as the publication of the list of frequently used characters, based on an investigation of the earlier works just given, plus consideration of the factors of frequency of use, distribution, word formation capability, and applicability to daily life mentioned earlier. This list of characters in general use contains 7,000 characters, exactly twice the number in the "List of Frequently Used Characters".

3) Characters for Specialized Use 专用字

As noted above, these are characters which are only used within certain limited and specialized subjects or fields, such as the following:

a) Characters used in scientific and technological fields 科技专用字, such as the names of chemical elements, plants, and animals, etc. These are numerous, but fall outside the list of characters for generalized use.

b) Characters used in people's names, 人名专用字 both surnames and personal names. Many of these fall outside the general list.

c) Characters used in place names 地名专用字, some of

which are fairly rare and cannot be found either in the general list, or even in most ordinary dictionaries.

d) Characters pertaining to ethnic minorities (nationalities) and religions 民族和宗教专用字, such as the names of some of China's ethnic minorities, special terms for religious practices, etc. There are only a few such characters of this type which fall outside the general list.

e) Characters relating to occupations 行业专用字. Certain trades or occupations have a small number of characters for terms used only within their own specializations, which are rarely used in general publications, even though they may have a high frequency within that profession.

f) Special characters used especially for transliterating the sounds of foreign words and names 译音专用字. These are few in number and not many fall outside the general list.

g) Special characters for dialects 方言专用字, used to write certain words with special pronunciations found in China's many regional dialects, but not in standard Mandarin. Almost all of these many characters fall outside the general list.

h) Characters from ancient Chinese 文言专用字或古汉语专用字, no longer used in modern Chinese, but encountered in reading classical works from ancient times, especially those characters representing the names of ancient things. These are numerous, and beyond the scope of the general list.

i) Special characters used for spoken language 口语专用字。To represent colloquial words rarely used in written style, some special characters are used. Such characters often are used to represent dialect words, and have a strong local color.

Because these characters have no fixed standard forms, they are not usually found in dictionaries.

j) Special characters used in non-Hàn languages 非汉语专用字。These are characters created by ethnic minorities or other nations imitating Chinese characters. Some have been used in Chinese publications. For example, the Japanese *kanji* 辻 (tsuji), usually used as a name, the Vietnamese character 枞, used as a place name, and the square-shaped characters developed by some of China's ethnic minorities.

There is no clear line that can be drawn between the generally used characters and these characters for specialized use. Some characters which were originally used only in specialized areas have become generally used, and even frequently used, characters, because of their increasingly wider usage.

APPENDIX: LIST OF FREQUENTLY USED CHARACTERS IN MODERN CHINESE

现代汉语常用字表

This list contains the 3,500 most frequently used characters. Before the mark "●" are from the first 2,500 characters, and after the "●" are from the remaining 1,000 characters.

1	**stroke**	一乙
2	**strokes**	二十丁厂七卜人入八九几儿了力乃刀又●匕刁
3	**strokes**	三于干亏士工土才寸下大丈与万上小口巾山千乞川亿个勺久凡及夕丸么广亡门义之尸弓己已巳子卫也女飞刃习叉马乡
4	**strokes**	丰王井开夫天无元专云扎艺木五支厅不太犬区历尤友匹车巨牙屯比互切瓦止少日中冈贝内水见午牛手毛气升长仁什片仆化仇币仍仅斤爪反介父从今凶分乏公仓月氏勿欠风丹匀乌凤勾文六方火为斗忆订计户认心尺引丑巴孔队办以允予劝双书幻●丐歹戈夭仑讥冗邓
5	**strokes**	玉刊示末未击打巧正扑扒功扔去甘世古节本术可丙左厉右石布龙平灭轧东卡北占业旧帅归且旦目叶甲申叮电号田由史只央兄叼叫另叨叹四生失禾丘付仗

83

代仙们仪白仔他斥瓜乎丛令用甩印乐句匆册犯外处
冬鸟务包饥主市立闪兰半汁汇头汉宁穴它讨写让礼
训必议讯记永司尼民出辽奶奴加召皮边发孕圣对台
矛纠母幼丝●艾夯凸卢叭叽皿凹囚矢乍尔冯玄

6　strokes
式刑动扛寺吉扣考托老执巩圾扩扫地扬场耳共芒亚
芝朽朴机权过臣再协西压厌在有百存而页匠夸夺灰
达列死成夹轨邪划迈毕至此贞师尘尖劣光当早吐吓
虫曲团同吊吃因吸吗屿帆岁回岂刚则肉网年朱先丢
舌竹迁乔伟传乒乓休伍伏优伐延件任伤价份华仰仿
伙伪自血向似后行舟全会杀合兆企众爷伞创肌朵杂
危旬旨负各名多争色壮冲冰庄庆亦刘齐交次衣产决
充妄闭问闯羊并关米灯汗污江池汤忙兴宇守宅字安
讲军许论农讽设访寻那迅尽导异孙阵阳收阶阴防奸
如妇好她妈戏羽观欢买红纤级约纪驰巡●邦迂邢芋
芍吏夷吁吕吆屹延迄臼仲伦伊肋旭匈凫妆亥汛讳讶
讹讼阱弛阴驮驯纫

7　strokes
寿弄麦形进戒吞远违运扶抚坛技坏扰拒找批扯址走
抄坝贡攻赤折抓扮抢坞孝均抛投坟抗坑坊抖护壳志扭
块声把报却劫芽花芹芬苍芳严芦劳克苏杆杠杜材村
杏极李杨求更束豆两丽医辰励否还歼来连步坚旱盯
呈时吴助县里呆园旷围呀吨足邮男困吵串员听吩吹
呜吧吼别岗帐财针钉告岂乱利秃秀私每兵估体何但
伸作伯伶佣低你住位伴身皂佛近彻役返余希坐谷妥
含邻岔肝肚肠龟免狂犹角删条卵岛迎饭饮系言冻状
亩况床库疗应冷这序辛弃冶忘闲间闷判灶灿弟汪沙
汽沃泛沟没沈沉怀忧快完宋宏牢究穷灾良证启评补
初社识诉诊词译君灵即层尿尾迟局改张忌际陆阿陈
阻附妙妖妨努忍劲鸡驱纯纱纳钢驳纵纷纸纹纺驴纽

84

●玖玛韧抠扼汞扳抢坎坞抑拟抒芙芜苇芥芯芭杖杉
巫权甫匣轩卤肖吱吠呕呐吟呛吻吭邑囷吮岖牡佑佃
伺囵肛肘甸狈鸠彤灸刨庇吝庐闰兑灼沐沛汰沥沦汹
沧沪忧诅诈罕屁坠妓姊妒纬

奉玩环武青责现表规抹拢拔拣担垣押抽拐拖拍者顶
拆拥抵拘势抱垃拉拦拌幸招坡披拨择抬其取苦若茂
苹苗英范直茄茎茅林枝杯柜析板松枪构杰述枕丧或
画卧事刺枣雨卖矿码厕奔奇奋态欧垄妻轰顷转斩轮
软到非叔肯齿些虎肤肾贤尚旺具果味昆国昌畅明易
昂典固忠咐呼鸣咏呢岸岩帖罗帜岭凯败贩购图钓制
知垂牧物乖刮秆和季委佳侍供使例版侄侦侧凭侨佩
货依的迫质欣征往爬彼径所舍金革斧爸采受乳贪念
贫肤肺肢肿胀朋股肥服胁周昏鱼兔孤忽狗备饰饱饲
变京享店夜庙府底剂郊废净盲放刻育闸闹郑券卷单
炒炊炕炎炉沫浅法泄河沾泪油泊沿泡注泻泳泥沸波
泼泽治怖性怕怜怪学宝宗定宜审宙官空帘实试郎诗
肩房诚衬衫视话诞询该详建肃录隶居届刷弦承孟孤
陕降限妹姑姐姓始驾参艰线练组细驶织终驻驼绍经
贯●玫卦坷坏拓坪坤拄拧拂拙拇拗茉昔苛苦苟苞苗
苔枉枢枚枫杭郁矾奈奄殴歧卓县哎咕呵咙呻咒咆咖
帕账贬贮氛秉岳侠侥侣侈卑剑刹肴觅忿瓮肮肪狞庞
疟疙疚卒氓炬沽沮泣泞泌沼怔怯宠宛衩祈诡帚屉弧
弥陌陌函姆虱叁绅驹绊绎

奏春帮珍玻毒型挂封持项垮挎城挠政赴赵挡挺括拴
拾挑指垫挣挤拼挖按挥挪某甚革荐巷带草茧茶荒茫
荡荣故胡南药标枯柄栋相查柏柳柱柿栏树要咸威歪
研砖厘厚砌砍面耐耍牵残殃轻鸦皆背战点临览竖省
削尝是盼眨哄显哑冒映星昨畏趴胃贵界虹虾蚁思蚂

虽品咽骂哗咱响哈咬咳哪炭峡罚贱贴骨秒钟钢钥钩
卸缸拜看矩怎牲选适秒香种秋料重复竿段便俩贷顺
修保促侮俭俗俘信皇泉鬼侵追俊盾待律很须叙剑逃
食盆胆胜胞胖脉勉狭狮独狡狱狠贸怨急饶蚀饺饼弯
将奖哀亭亮度迹庭疮疯疫疤姿亲音帝施闻阀阁差养
美姜叛送类迷前首逆总炼炸炮烂剃洁洪洒浇浊洞测
洗活派洽济洋洲浑浓津恒恢恰恼恨举觉宣室宫宪
突穿窃客冠语扁袄祖神祝误诱说诵垦退既屋昼费陡
眉孩除院娃姥姨姻娇怒架贺盈勇怠柔垒绑绒结绕
骄绘给络骆绝绞统●契贰砧玲珊拭拷拱挟垢垛拯荆
茸荐荚茵茴荞荠荤荧荔栈柑栅柠枷勃柬砂泵砚鸥轴
韭虐昧盹咧呢昭蛊勋哆咪哟幽钙钝钠钦钧钮毡氢秕
俏俄俐侯徊衍胚脆胎狰饵峦奕咨飒闺闽籽娄烁炫洼
柒涎洛恃恬恤宦诚诬祠海屏屎逊陨姚娜蚤骇

10 strokes 耕耗艳泰珠班素蚕顽盏匪捞栽捕振载赶起盐捎捏埋
捉捆捐损都哲逝捡换挽热恐壶挨耻耽恭莲莫荷获晋
恶真框桂档桐株桥桃格校核样根索哥速逗栗配翅辱
唇夏础破原套逐烈殊顾轿较顿毙致柴桌虑监紧党晒
眠晓鸭晃响晕蚊哨哭恩唤啊唉罢峰圆贼贿钱钳钻铁
铃铅缺氧特牺造乘敌秤租积秧秩称秘透笔笑笋党债
借值倚倾倒倘俱候俯倍倦健臭射躬息徒徐舰舱般航
途拿爹爱颂翁脆脂胸胳脏胶脑狸狼逢留皱饿恋桨浆
衰高席准座脊症病疾疼疲效离唐资凉站剖竞部旁旅
畜阅羞瓶拳粉料益兼烤烘烦烧烛烟递涛浙涝酒涉消
浩海涂浴浮流润浪浸涨烫涌悟悄悔悦害宽家宵宴宾
窄容宰案请朗诸读扇袜袖袍被祥课谁调冤谅谈谊剥
恳展剧屑弱陵陶陷陪娱娘通能难预桑绢绣验继●耘
耙清匿埂捂捍袁捌挫挚捣捅埃耿聂荸莽莱莉莹莺梆

栖桦栓桅桩贾酌砸砰砾殉逞哮唠哺剔蚌蚜畔蚣蚪蚓
哩圃莺唁哼唉哨唧峻赂赃钾铆氨秫笆俺赁倔殷耸舀
豺豹颁胯胰脐脓逛卿舵鸯馁凌凄衷郭斋疹紊瓷羔烙
浦涡涣涤涧涕涩悍悯窍诺诽祖谆崇恕娩骏

11 strokes 球理捧堵描域掩捷排掉堆推掀授教掏掠培接控探据
掘职基著勒黄萌萝菌菜萄菊萍菠营械梦梢梅检梳梯
桶救副票戚爽聋袭盛雪辅辆虚雀堂常匙晨睁眯眼悬
野啦啊晚啄距跃略蛇累唱患唯崖崭崇圈铜铲银甜梨
犁移笨笼笛符第敏做袋悠偿偶偷您售停偏假得衔盘
船斜盒鸽悉欲彩领脚脖脸脱象够猜猪猎猫猛馅馆凑
减毫麻痒痕廊康庸鹿盗章竟商族旋望率着盖粘粗粒
断剪兽清添淋淹渠渐混渔淘液淡深婆梁渗情惜惭悼
惧惊惨惯寇寄宿窑密谋谎祸谜逮敢屠弹随蛋隆隐婚
婶颈绩绪续骑绳维绵绸绿●琐麸琉琅措捺捶赦埠捻
掐掂掀掷掸掺勘聊娶菱菲萎葡萤乾萧萨菇彬梗梧梭
曹酝酗厢硅硕奢盔匾颅彪眶晤曼晦冕啡畦趾啃蛆蚯
蛉蛀唬喽唾啤啥啸崎逻崔崩婴赊铸铛铝铡铣铭矫秸
秽笙笤偎傀躯兜衅徘徙舶舷舵敛翎脯逸凰猖祭烹庶
庵痊阎阐眷焊焕鸿涯淑淌淮淆渊淫淳淤淀涮涵惦悴
惋寂窒谍谐裆袱祷谒谓谚尉堕隅婉颇绰绷综绽缀巢

12 strokes 琴斑替款堪搭塔越趁趋超提堤博揭喜插揪搜煮援裁
搁搂搅握揉斯期欺联散惹葬葛董葡敬葱落朝辜葵棒
棋植森椅椒棵棍棉棚棕惠惑逼厨厦硬确雁殖裂雄暂
雅辈悲紫辉敞赏拿晴署最量喷晶喇遇喊景践跌跑遗
蛙蛛蜒蛾喝喂喘喉幅帽赌赔黑铸铺链销锁锄锅锈锋
锐短智毯鹅剩稍程稀税筐等筑策筛筒答筋筝傲傅牌
堡集焦傍储奥街惩御循艇舒番释禽腊脾腔猾猴然馋
装蛮就痛童阔善羡普粪尊道曾焰港湖渣湿温渴湾渡

87

游滋溉愤慌惰愧愉慨割寒富窜窝窗遍裕裤裙谢谣谦
属屡强粥疏隔隙絮嫂登缎缓编骗缘●琳琢琼揍堰揩
揽揖彭揣搀搓壹搔葫募蒋蒂韩棱椰焚椎棺椰椭粟棘
酣酥硝硫颊雳翘凿棠晰鼎喳遏晾畴跋跛蛔蜓蛤鹃喻
啼喧嵌赋赎赐铧锌甥掰氮氯黍筏胼粤逾腌腋腕猩猬
愈敦痘痢痪竣翔奠遂焙滞湘渤渺溃溅湃愕惶寓窘窨
雇谤犀隘媒媚婿缅缆缔缕骚
13   strokes   瑞魂肆摄摸填搏塌鼓摆携搬摇搞塘摊蒜勤鹊蓝墓幕
蓬菁蒙蒸献禁楚想槐榆楼概赖酬感碍碑碎碰碗碌雷
零雾雹输督龄鉴睛睡眯鄙愚暖盟歇暗照跨跳跪路跟
遣蛾蜂嗓置罪罩错锡锣锤锦键锯矮辞稠愁享签简毁
舅鼠催傻像躲微愈遥腰腥腹腾腿触解酱痰廉新韵意
粮数煎塑慈煤煌满漠源滤滥滔溪溜滚滨梁滩慎誊塞
谨福群殿辟障嫌嫁叠缝缠●瑟鹉瑰搪聘斟靴靶蓖蒿
蒲蓉楔椿楷榄楞棚酪碘硼碉辐辑频睦睦瞄嗜嗦暇畸
跷踩蜈蜗蜕蛹嗅嗡嗤署蜀幌锚锥锨锭锰稚颓筷魁衙
腻腮腺鹏肆猿颖煞雏馍溜禀痹廓痴靖誊漓溢溯溶滓
溺寰窥窟寝裥裸谬媳嫉缚缤剿
14   strokes   静碧璃墙撇嘉摧截誓境摘摔聚蔽慕暮蓑模榴榜榨歌
遭酷酿磁愿需弊裳颗嗽蜻蜡蝇蜘赚锹锻舞稳算箩管
僚鼻魄貌膜膊察鲜疑馒裹敲豪膏遮腐瘦辣竭端旗精
歉熄熔漆漂漫滴演漏慢寨赛察蜜谱嫩翠熊凳骡缩●
赘熬赫蔫蔷蔗蔼熙蔚兢榛榕酵碟碴碱碳辕辖雌墅
喊踊蝉嘀幔镀舔熏箍箕箫舆僧孵瘩瘟彰粹漱漾慷寡
寥谭褐褪隧嫡缨
15   strokes   慧撕撒趣趟撑播撞撤增聪鞋蕉蔬横槽樱橡飘醋醉震
霉瞒题暴瞎影踢踏踩踪蝶蝴嘱墨镇靠靠稻黎稿稼箱箭
篇僵躺僻德艘膝膛熟摩颜毅糊遵潜潮懂额慰劈●撵

撩撮撬擒墩撰鞍蕊蕴樊樟橄敷豌醇磕磅碾憋嘶嘲嘹
蝠蝎蝌蝗蝙嘿幢镊镐稽篓膘鲤卿褒瘪瘤瘫凛澎潭潦
澳潘澈澜澄憔懊憎翩褥谴鹤憋履嬉豫缭

16	strokes	操燕薯薪薄颠橘整融醒餐嘴蹄器赠默镜赞篮邀衡膨
		雕磨凝辨辩糖糕燃澡激懒壁避缴●撼擂擅蕾薛薇擎
		翰噩橱橙瓢磺霍霎撤冀踱踩螟螗螟噪鹦黔穆篡篷篱
		篙儒膳鲸瘾瘸糙燎濒憾懈窿缰

17	strokes	戴擦鞠藏霜霞瞰蹈螺穗繁辫赢槽檬燥臂翼聚●壕貌
		檬橹檩檀礁磷瞭瞬瞳瞪曙踢蟋嚎赡镣魏簇偏徽爵朦
		臊鳄糜癌懦豁臀

| 18 | strokes | 鞭覆蹦镰翻鹰●藕藤瞻嚣鲭癫瀑襟璧戳 |

| 19 | strokes | 警攀蹲颤瓣爆疆●攒蘑蘑藻鳖蹭蹬簿薄蟹靡癣羹 |

| 20 | strokes | 壤耀躁嚼嚷籍魔灌●鬓攘蠕巍鳞糯譬 |

| 21 | strokes | 蠢霸露●霹躏髓 |

| 22 | strokes | 囊●蘸镶瓤 |

| 23 | strokes | 罐 |

| 24 | strokes | ●矗 |

3. THE SHAPES OF CHINESE CHARACTERS

Chinese characters are not only numerous in quantity, but also complex in structure. Thousands of Chinese characters have thousands of different shapes. Sometimes two completely different characters are differentiated only by a single dot or stroke, as for example, 折 (zhé, bend) vs. 拆 (chāi, disassemble); 弋 (yì, a semantic radical meaning a type of arrow) vs. 戈 (gē, dagger-axe, used as a surname); 亳 (bó, house) vs. 毫 (háo, a long, fine hair/milli-). Sometimes the same constituent elements can form entirely different characters simply by a rearrangement of their positioning within a character, as in 呆 (dāi, confounded) vs. 杏 (xìng, apricot); 吟 (yín, chant) vs. 含 (hán, include), etc. Given this complexity of structure of Chinese characters, what can be done to make them easier to learn? The best way is to analyze their composition, in other words to "dissect" them into their component parts just as we would disassemble a machine in order to understand its structure. This is the best way to master the various configurations of the thousands of Chinese characters efficiently.

3.1 ANALYZING THE STRUCTURE OF CHINESE CHARACTERS

Most present-day Chinese characters are more or less square in form, which is why they are often called fāngkuài zì 方块字,

meaning "square" or "block-style" characters. A small number of characters can be taken as whole units, without dissection. These we may call single-element characters 独体字. Dú Tǐ Zì The majority of characters, however, are compound-element characters 合体字 and can be decomposed into smaller component parts. We may say that Chinese characters may generally be classified into four categories on the basis of their structural form, as the chart below indicates:

Name of Structure	Shape	Percent	Examples
Single Structure 单一结构		3%	Pictographic: 日 月 水 山 牛 羊 人 口 木 Ideographic: 一 二 三 上 下 刃 本 亦 甘
Right-Left Structure 左右结构		65%	Picto-phonetic: 河 摸 请 城 吐 蜂 蝗 和 政 鹦 Assoc. Compounds: 林 牧 明 鸣 埋 休 涉 折 野 朝
Over-Under Structure 上下结构		23%	Picto-phonetic: 花 岗 宇 筷 零 装 驾 忍 烫 背 Assoc. Compounds.: 炎 旦 益 尖 家 焚 思 采 查 突
Enclosing Structure 包围结构		9%	All-round Enclosure: 回 因 国 囚 图 囵 Three-side Enclosure: 同 凤 凶 函 区 医 Two-side Enclosure: 历 居 司 氧 过 起

In addition to the above dichotomies, a very small number of Chinese characters are divided into three parts, such as:

Left-Middle-Right Structure: 树，弼，掰…

Upper-Middle-Lower Structure: 器，嚣，赢…

Triangle-shaped Structure: 品，晶，森…

Let us now examine in detail the component parts which may make up a Chinese character:

1) Side Components 偏 旁

As shown above, most Chinese characters can be decomposed into two primary parts (with a very small number which decompose into three primary parts). Because of this fact, these primary component parts of a character are called piān-páng 偏旁 (side components). In fact, the original meaning of this term was limited to right-left structures only, with the left side being called piān 偏, and the right side called páng 旁. But now the term has been extended to all two-part characters, left-right, over-under, and enclosing structures with two component parts. For example:

摸 (mō, touch): left （扌）-right （莫） structure

明 (míng, bright): left （日）-right （月） structure

花 (huā, flower): over （艹）-under （化） structure

尖 (jiān, point): over （小）-under （大） structure

国 (guó, country): （囗） enclosing （玉） structure

医 (yī, medical): （匚） enclosing （矢） structure

氧 (yǎng, oxygen): （气） enclosing （羊） structure

过 (guò, pass): （辶） enclosing （寸） structure

Some of these side components can function as independent characters in Chinese; these are referred to as 独体字 (single-element characters). Other side components cannot function as independent characters; most of these are ancient characters or latter-day transformations thereof. For example:

Side components as independent characters: 口日月山弓马石鸟舟青其皇音

Side components as non-independent elements: 匚宀辶广 亻刂彡忄讠勹县聿

According to statistics, there are altogether 1,500 such side components, including both independent and non-independent ones.

Note that, unlike strokes (see Chapter 7), these side components are not merely elements that structually form Chinese characters, but are rather more closely connected with the semantics and phonetics of the characters as a whole. From the point of view of the character composing system, 合体字 (hétǐ zì, compound-element characters) formed by two or three primary parts are almost all either picto-phonetic characters or associative compound characters. (See Chapter 1.) In the former, one part indicates the meaning and the other part(s) the pronunciation of the entire character; in the latter type, both components are related to the meaning of the character as a whole. For example:

Picto-phonetic characters: 河摸和政花岗装忍历氧

Associative compound characters: 从休明炎益尖家焚采囚

2) Component Parts 部 件

After Chinese characters have been analysed into their primary compositional components, many of these may be further dissected into even smaller and relatively independent parts, called bùjiàn 部件 (component parts). Let us take the characters 筷 (kuài, chopstick) and 鹦 (yīng, parrot) as examples:

	Side Components	Component Parts
筷 (Over-under)	⟶ ⺮ ＋ 快 ⟶	⺮ ＋ ⺈ ＋ 忄 ＋ 夬
鹦 (Left-right)	⟶ 婴 ＋ 鸟 ⟶	贝 ＋ 贝 ＋ 女 ＋ 鸟

Component parts are qualitatively different from side components. Generally speaking, side components are usually related to the entire character of which they form a part in terms of meaning and/or pronunciation, as noted above. After further decomposition, however, the resultant component parts may not necessarily bear any such relation to the entire character. For example, if we divide the character 唱 (chàng, sing) into its two side components 口 (kǒu, mouth) and 昌 (chāng, prosperous), it is obvious that they are related to the entire character in terms of meaning and pronunciation. But further analysis of the right hand side component 昌 into its component parts 日 (rì, day) and 曰 (yuē, quoth) the direct relationship to the original overall character 唱 is obviously lost. Thus we may say that such component parts are purely formal (graphological) units in the construction of the forms of Chinese characters, and do not necessarily have the direct relationship in terms of semantics and pronunciation which side components usually have in the composition of Chinese characters.

The component parts of Chinese characters are usually simpler in structure than side components, and are much smaller in number. Research on contemporary Chinese characters suggests that there are a little over four hundred component parts, of which only two or three hundred are used frequently. A knowledge of these can be helpful in analyzing, memorizing, and writing Chinese characters (as well as for understanding some of the modern computer input systems based on character components). Thus the following characters may be more easily mastered if viewed in terms of their component parts:

烧 (shāo, burn) three parts: 火 + 戈 + 兀

望 (wàng, look towards) three parts: 亡 + 月 + 王

赢 (yíng, win) five parts: 亡 + 口 + 月 + 贝 + 凡

There are many popular character analysis couplets 析字对联, used as mnemonic devices by Chinese children to help memorize how to write Chinese characters, which are based on an analysis of the characters into side components and component parts. Here are some examples:

鸿　是　江　边　鸟，　蚕　为　天　下　虫。

Hóng shì jiāng biān niǎo; cán wéi tiān xià chóng.

Hóng 鸿 (wild goose) is a bird (鸟) by a river (江),

Cán 蚕 (silkworm) is a worm (虫) under heaven (天).

冻　雨　洒　人：　东　两　点，　西　三　点；

Dòng yǔ sǎ rén: dōng liǎng diǎn, xī sān diǎn;

切　瓜　分　客：　上　七　刀，　下　八　刀。

Qiē guā fēn kè: shàng qī dāo, xià bā dāo.

冻雨 freezing rain 洒人 soaks people:

东 (east) has two dots 冫 and 西 (west) has three 氵;

切瓜 cutting melon 分客 to apportion among guests:

The upper half has seven cuts, the lower half has eight.

　　This is a play on words. The last sentence means the former character 切 (qiē, to cut) is composed of the characters 七 (qī, seven) and 刀 (dāo, knife), and the latter character 分 (fēn, apportion) is composed of the characters 八 (bā, eight) and 刀 (dāo, knife).

The use of this term "component part" 部件 is often extended beyond its strict definition for convenience. Thus, for example, 口 (kǒu, mouth) is both an independent single element character and a character component. Thus the character 吧 (ba, how about . . . ?) can be analysed either as two side components or as two component parts. Generally speaking, side components are emphasized when characters are being analyzed from the character-composing point of view, while component parts are stressed when characters are being analyzed in terms of their graphological structure. Thus in terms of side components the character 路 (lù, road) is analyzed as a combination of 足 (zú, foot) and 各 (gè, each), while graphologially it is analyzed as being composed of the component parts 口, 止, 夂, and 口.

3) Strokes 笔画

If we wish to analyze the component parts even further, we must do so in terms of their bǐ huà 笔画 or "strokes". Strokes are the smallest elements in the structure of Chinese characters. When one is writing in the "regular style" script, each individual stroke is delineated by continuous uninterrupted contact of one's pen with the paper. The simplest characters such as 一(yī, one) or 乙 (yǐ, B) have only one stroke, while the most complicated ones may have over thirty strokes, such as 齉 (nàng, snuffle). After the Chinese characters were simplified (see next section), most characters now generally have nine or ten strokes.

These so-called Chinese character "strokes" consist of

dots and lines. Because these dots and lines assume various shapes and configurations, the strokes may be categorized into six basic types: 点 (diǎn, dots), 横 (héng, horizontal strokes), 竖 (shù, downward vertical strokes), 撇 (piě, downward southwesterly strokes), 捺 (nà, downward southeasterly strokes), and 挑 (tiǎo, upward twisting strokes). Altogether more than thirty kinds of stroke types can be formed out of these six basic strokes through combination and connection. See the following list:

Stroke Name	Basic Type	Direction	Compound Types of Basic Strokes
dot 点	` ` `		𠃌 𠃌 乃
horizontal 横	— —	left to rt.	
vertical 竖	| |	up to down	𠃋 亅 𠃍
downward southwest. 撇	ノ ㇏	upper rt. to downward left	乚 𠃊
downward southeast 捺	㇏ ㇏	upper left to downward rt.	————
upward twisting 挑	㇀ ノ	downward left to upper rt.	————

Every Chinese character is composed of some of these basic strokes, and thus every character may be analyzed into its component strokes. For example:

人 (rén, person), 2 strokes: ノ ㇏
习 (xí, study), 3 strokes: 𠃌 丶 ㇀
方 (fāng, square), 4 strokes: 丶 一 ノ 𠃌
丙 (bǐng, third), 5 strokes: 一 丨 𠃌 ノ 丶

伐　(fá, attack),　　　6 strokes:　　ノ 丨 一 乚 ノ 丶

沟　(gōu, ditch),　　　7 strokes:　　丶 丶 丿 丿 フ 乙 丶

弧　(hú, arc),　　　　8 strokes:　　フ 一 ㄥ ⁻ノ 丨 丶 乚

娜　(nuó, graceful),　9 strokes:　　ㄑ ノ 一 コ 一 一 ノ ㇆ 丨

虑　(lù, consider),　10 strokes:　丨 一 一フ 一 乚 乚 乚 丶 丶

The sequence of producing the strokes in writing a Chinese character is called the stroke order 笔顺 which follows certain basic important principles. This question will be discussed in detail in Chapter 7, Section 2, "The Writing of Chinese Characters".

The last question we should examine briefly in this section is the issue of how Chinese describe Chinese characters orally, for example, over the telephone, when it is not possible to actually write or see their shapes. The most common method for orally identifying a character in such a situation is to place it in a larger familiar verbal context, e.g., in a polysyllabic word, according to a fixed formula. Thus, if one cannot tell which character pronounced zhī is being referred to, the other party might say "知道" 的 "知" ("zhīdào" de "zhī", It's the zhī in the word zhīdào [to know]). This is the most common way of identifying characters verbally when they cannot be written, but of course it does not at all help to identify the shape of the character if the hearer does not know the compound word, or does not know how to write the character in question in the first place.

In certain commonly encountered situations, e.g, describing or distinguishing the writing of Chinese surnames, certain relatively fixed formulae have evolved. For some surnames, one may identify the surname in question with that of some famous person, e.g. 她姓曹，曹操的曹 (Tā xìng Cáo, Cáo Cāo de Cáo. She is surnamed Cáo 曹, the same Cáo as in Cáo Cāo*). Alternatively, for a number of surnames, certain fixed analytic formulae exist, e.g. 木子李 (mù-zǐ Lǐ, Lǐ consists of the character 木 [mù, wood] and the character 子 [zǐ, a noun suffix]) Other such examples are 双木林 (shuāng-mù Lín, double-wood Lín) or 三横王 (sān héng Wáng, Wáng with three horizontal strokes). These formulaic expressions have now become conventionalized as idioms and must be memorized as such.

In addition to such fixed formulae, it is still sometimes necessary to describe or distinguish the shapes and organization of written Chinese characters without being able to demonstrate them graphically. In such situations, again the Chinese tend to describe Chinese characters orally in terms of the side components, component parts, strokes, and their arrangement as discussed previously in this section. Thus to avoid any possible confusion, one usually distinguishes the surname 黄 (Huáng, yellow) by describing it as 草頭黄 (cǎo-tóu Huáng, Huáng with grass on top), referring to the so-called "grass' or vegetation radical ⺾ used in Chinese dictionaries. Again there are many common formulae for such descriptions, both for the most commonly occurring components, and for their positioning within a Chinese character. Thus, if a certain character is described as having, e.g., a 山字旁 (shān zì páng, mountain side component), we know from the "X zì páng" formula that the

* A famous historical figure in the novel *Romance of the Three Kingdoms.*

"mountain" component is on the left side of the character. Similarly 草字头 (cǎo zì tóu) means that the "grass" component is at the top of the character in question, while 心字底 (xīn zì dǐ) tells us that the "heart" component is positioned at the bottom of the character. Of course in some cases, the various components of a character are simply described by way of combining components, whole characters, and strokes in the description. For example, the surname 卞 (Biàn) is described as 下字上加一点 (xià zì shàng jiā yī diǎn), "the character 下 (xià, below) with a dot stroke added on the top", etc.

For reference, here is a list of some commonly used formula names for some Chinese character radicals and components. Note that these are colloquial formulae used in speech to describe characters or in talking about consulting dictionaries, etc., rather than their historically accurate technical designations.

Component:	Name:	Pronunciation:	Meaning:
一	一横	yī héng	one horizontal stroke
丨	一竖	yī shù	one vertical stroke
丶	一点	yī diǎn	one dot stroke
丿	一撇	yī piě	one left-falling stroke
二	两横	liǎng héng	two horizontal strokes
亻	单立人	dān lì rén	single standing person
亠	文字头	wén zì tóu	top of the character wén
宀	秃宝盖儿	tū bǎo gàir	a bald "treasure cover"
冫	两点水	liǎng diǎn shuǐ	two dots of water
刂	立刀	lì dāo	upright knife
勹	包字头	bāo zì tóu	top of the character "wrap"

100

卩	单耳朵	dān ěrduo	single ear blade
匚	匚字框	jiàng zì kuāng	enclosure for the character "artisan"
厂	偏厂儿	piān chǎngr	slanted "factory" character
尢	尤字旁	yóu zì páng	side of the character yóu
土	提土	tí tǔ	slanted earth
宀	宝盖儿	bǎo gàir	treasure cover
	宝字头	bǎo zì tóu	top of the character "treasure"
彐	横山	héng shān	horizontal mountain
几	风字框	fēng zì kuāng	enclosure of the character "wind"
彡	三撇	sān piě	three left-falling strokes
忄	竖心	shù xīn	vertical heart
扌	提手	tí shǒu	rising hand
夂	反文儿	fǎn wénr	a turned wén character
夊	折文儿	zhé wénr	a bent wén character
氵	三点水	sān diǎn shuǐ	three dots of water
灬	四点火，	sì diǎn huǒ	four dots of fire
	四点水	sì diǎn shuǐ	four dots of water
饣	食字旁	shí zì páng	side of the character "edible"
犭	反犬	fǎn quǎn	turned dog
玉	侧玉	cè yù	side jade
	斜玉	xié yú	slanted jade
	王字旁	wáng zì páng	side of the character wáng

101

广	病字头	bìng zì tóu	top of the character bìng
皿	皿字底儿	mǐn zì dǐr	vessel base
礻	示字旁	shì zì páng	side of the character "show"
禾	禾字旁	hé zì páng	side of the character "grain"
⺮	竹字头	zhú zì tóu	top of the character "bamboo"
纟	绞丝旁	jiǎo sī páng	twisted silk side
罒	偏四	piān sì	a squat "four" character
艹	草字头	cǎo zì tóu	top of the character "grass"
衤	衣字旁	yī zì páng	"clothing" character side
⻊	足字旁	zú zì páng	"sufficient" or "foot" character side
辶	走之儿	zǒu zhīr	a walking zhī character
廴	建字旁	jiàn zì páng	side of the character "construct"
阝	双耳朵	shuāng ěr duo	double ear-blade
	左耳朵	zuǒ ěr duo	left ear-blade
	右耳朵	yòu ěr duo	right ear-blade
雨	雨字头	yǔ zì tóu	top of the character "rain"
癶	登字头	dēng zì tóu	top of the character "ascend"

| 虍 | 虎字头 | hǔ zì tóu | top of the character "tiger" |

3.2 THE SIMPLIFICATION OF CHINESE CHARACTERS

A considerable number of Chinese characters have numerous strokes and complex structures, which can cause difficulties in learning to write and remembering them. As a result, over the centuries there have naturally come into being character variants with fewer strokes and simpler structures to replace many of the overly complex ones. These are known as 简体字 (jiǎntǐzì) or "simplified characters", as opposed to the 繁体字 (fántǐzì) or "complex characters". These simplified character forms generally were produced by the populace and enjoyed currency among them in their everyday hand-writing, but were never officially accepted by scholars or the government, who referred to them as 俗字 (sú zì) or "vulgar characters". The term simplification of Chinese characters 汉字简化, then, refers to the change from complex to simple in the shape and number of strokes of Chinese characters.

Chinese characters have a long history of simplification, which in fact started almost from their beginning. We find simplified characters even in the oracle bone inscriptions of the Shāng Dynasty three thousand years ago. We may say that Chinese characters have undergone a ceaseless process of simplification, from complex to simple, starting from the time of the oracle bone inscriptions, down through the bronze inscriptions, seal script, official script, and standard script. Let us examine the evolution of the pictographic character now written as 车 (chē, vehicle):

Fig. 13: Changes in   from complex to simple: oracle
bone inscription, bronze inscription, and small seal script.

Some of the simplified characters now in use today (see
appendix) began to appear as early as pre-Qín Period, and more
and more came into being during subsequent dynasties.   Let
us look at some examples:

Pre-Qín period (before 246 B.C): 从尔丰个礼气弃与洒栖杀
舍网无启虫云…

Hàn Dynasty (206 B.C.-200 A.D.): 办达复盖号继夹荐据夸
来帘粮麦脉确属台万薭岩痒涌杂灾…

Wèi, Jìn, and North-South Dynasties (220-581 A.D.):   碍
笔床断离乱猫弥狭声双袜邮…

Suí-Táng Period (581-907 A.D.): 宝缠辞籴巢干（乾）挂怜
绳凶庄…

Sòng-Yuán Period (960-1368 A.D.):   埚边蚕惨称痴当灯点
独对肤刚过观画还机节旧类恋临灵刘炉屡峦论罗梦庙难齐岂迁窃
亲穷权劝伤圣实寿虽体条铁听厅务献阳养医义阴蝇犹屿渊园远韵
灶斋皱昼烛浊纵邹…

Míng-Qīng Period (1368-1911 A.D.):   罢帮摆贝宾布（佈）
触担胆挡夺坟奋凤妇赶钢岗顾归锅怀坏欢环祸讯几剂艰娇厘厉联
么门脑乔桥扫晒牵县绣爷鱼枣毡毡这郑绉…

Although these simplified characters were easier to learn,
to write, and to remember, and therefore became accepted among
the common people who could write, they were never officially

104

recognized by the governments under the dynasties, and therefore did not have a formally legitimate status. After the founding of the People's Republic of China in 1949, however, in order to promote education and reduce the difficulties involved in the study of Chinese characters by the great masses of people, those simplified characters which already were in wide currency in society began to be collected and standardized. After several years of discussion, revision, and consultation throughout the country, the "Scheme for Simplifying Chinese Characters" 汉字简化方案 was officially published in January, 1956. At the time of its publication, the State Council of China declared: "Simplified characters should be used uniformly in national publications and written documents. the original complex-style characters should cease being used, except in the case of reprinting ancient books and other such special cases." In 1964, the "Complete List of Simplified Characters" 简化字总表 was compiled and published by the Committee for the Reform of the Chinese Language. Based on the "Scheme for Simplifying Chinese Characters" mentioned above, the 1964 list contained a total of 2,236 simplified characters, eliminating 2,264 complex-style characters mainly through the principle of simplifying certain complex radicals and side components whenever they occurred in a complex-style character. After more than twenty years of experience, the Committee (now renamed the State Language Commission (Guójiā Yŭyán Wénzì Gōngzuò Wěi-yuánhuì)) in October 1986 republished the "Complete List of Simplified Characters" with a few minor revisions. (See Appendix 2.) The purpose of republishing the list was to establish definite norms for the forms of Chinese characters and to clarify any confusion over the standard forms of the characters in the society at large.*

The "Complete List of Simplified Characters" (1986 version) has three sections:

Section One: Simplified characters which are not used as simplified side components. That is, the simplified characters in this section are only used independently, and do not also occur in this simplified form as components of other characters. For example, the character 儿 is the simplifed form of the character 兒 ér, meaning "son", but it only occurs in this form as an independent character, not as a component of any other characters. Thus the surname 倪 Ní cannot be written as 伲. There are 350 such simplified characters in this section.

Section Two: Simplified side components and simplified characters which can also be used as simplified side components. This section is subdivided into two parts: (a) 132 simplified characters which can be used both as independent characters and also as side components in other characters, as for example, 东 the simplified form of the complex character 東 (dōng, east) which can occur both as an independent simplified character, and as a side component in a number of other characters such as 冻（凍），陈（陳）， 栋（棟）， 鸫（鶇） (b) Fourteen simplified side components which can occur only as side components, but not as independent characters. For example, the

*On December 29 1977 the Committee had published a "Draft Scheme for a Second Chinese Character Simplification" 第二次汉字简化方案草案 in order to solicit opinions, but because of widely divergent reactions, it was withdrawn with the approval of the State Council on June 24, 1986.

simplified side component 讠 the simplified versoin of the so-called "speech radical" formerly written as 言, can only be used as a side component, as in 计 (計), 订 (訂), 讣 (訃), 讥 (譏), 议 (議), etc., but not for the independent character 言 yán, meaning "speech".

Section Three: Altogether 1,753 simplified characters which can be derived from the simplified characters and side compo-whibh nents listed in Section Two.

Thus there are altogether 2,235 simplified characters (plus 14 simplified side components) in the three sections. Some people who have learned only complex-style characters may ask whether it is difficult to learn so many simplified characters, but the answer is "no". Actually, among these simplified characters, the basic ones are the 350 in Section One and the 132 in Section Two, together totalling only 482 which make up the core simplified characters. These are not difficult to learn, firstly, because most of them have long been in popular use anyway, so that many people already know them. Secondly, the characters have not been simplified randomly, but rather according to certain principles. In the majority of cases there is some relation between the old complex-style characters and their new simplified forms, either in terms of their shape or in terms of the principles underlying their formation. In order to help in the mastery of these simplified characters, let us analyze the methods by which characters are simplified:

1) New Side Components Replace Old Ones.

Complex, difficult side components are replaced by comparatively simple ones. For example, the phonetic component

龠 in the complex character 鑰 (yào, key) is difficult to write, so the character has been simplified to 钥. Again, the radical component 骨 in the complex character 骯 (āng, dirty) is also difficult to write, and was therefore simplified into 肮. In most cases of replacing old complex side components by new simpler ones, it is usually the phonetic part which is simplified. Let us look at some examples:

襖——袄	斃——毙	補——补	燦——灿
懺——忏	襯——衬	遲——迟	礎——础
擔——担	燈——灯	遞——递	墳——坟
溝——沟	漢——汉	積——积	極——极
價——价	艦——舰	膠——胶	僅——仅
塊——块	臘——腊	禮——礼	聯——联
憐——怜	糧——粮	療——疗	爐——炉
廟——庙	擬——拟	僕——仆	瓊——琼
權——权	確——确	擾——扰	灑——洒
勝——胜	嘆——叹	鐵——铁	襪——袜
犧——牺	蝦——虾	選——选	憶——忆
擁——拥	優——优	運——运	贓——赃
趙——赵	這——这	證——证	種——种
鑽——钻	邊——边	達——达	隊——队
進——进	遷——迁	陰——阴	猶——犹
辭——辞	觀——观	劇——剧	亂——乱
戲——戏	郵——邮	戰——战	對——对
劉——刘	難——难	獻——献	鳳——凤
蘋——苹	竊——窃	憲——宪	藥——药
筆——笔	歷——历	窮——穷	屬——属
態——态	圖——图	團——团	園——园
國——国			

2) Parts of Characters Are Used in Place of Entire Ones.

By this method, some side components or component parts of complex-style characters are eliminated, leaving their most representative parts to replace the whole original complex form. This is analogous to a sketch done by a painter who outlines the most salient features of his subject. For example, the complex character 習 (xí, study) is replaced by its component part 习, the old character 飛 (fēi, flying) by 飞, 電 (diàn, electric) by 电, and 奮 (fèn, struggle) by 奋. Here are some additional examples:

奪——夺	兒——儿	糞——粪	鞏——巩
廣——广	號——号	繭——茧	競——竞
開——开	墾——垦	誇——夸	虧——亏
纍——累	類——类	隸——隶	滅——灭
畝——亩	瘧——疟	盤——盘	傘——伞
掃——扫	澀——涩	聲——声	獸——兽
術——术	雖——虽	塗——涂	務——务
壓——压	醫——医	鑿——凿	燭——烛
築——筑	濁——浊	產——产	蟲——虫
豐——丰	滙——汇	殼——壳	離——离
麗——丽	虜——虏	鹵——卤	錄——录
慮——虑	寧——宁	氣——气	親——亲
殺——杀	質——质	孫——孙	條——条
鄉——乡	尋——寻	厭——厌	業——业

Note that some such characters, in addition to losing some side components or parts, are also changed a bit in their structure, as for example 傘——伞 (sǎn, umbrella), 獸——兽 (shòu, animal), 麗——丽 (lì, beautiful), etc.

3) "Grass Style" Characters Are Transformed into Regular Script Forms.

Character forms originating in the cursive "grass style," which has fewer strokes, have been adapted into standard regular kǎi shū style to replace some complex characters. There are only a few characters simplified in this way, for example:

報——报	貝——贝	書——书	長——长
車——车	發——发	見——见	樂——乐
侖——仑	馬——马	買——买	賣——卖
門——门	烏——鸟	農——农	齊——齐
豈——岂	師——师	爲——为	韋——韦
烏——乌	寫——写	壽——寿	專——专
堯——尧			

4) Homophonic Substitution

Under this method, the original complex character is replaced by a character for a homophone which has fewer strokes. This method in fact has ancient precedents, and is historically quite common; it is in fact exactly the same as the phonetic loan characters 假借 (jiǎjiè) mentioned previously in our discussion of character creation systems. (See 1.2 above.) In the "Complete List of Simplified Characters" there are not many characters simplified by this method. Here are some examples:

錶——表	纔——才	衝——冲	醜——丑
齣——出	鬥——斗	範——范	乾——干
穀——谷	颳——刮	後——后	鬍——胡

110

薑——姜	裏——里	麵——面	闢——辟
捨——舍	鬆——松	係——系	葉——叶
餘——余	籲——吁	鬱——郁	隻——只
準——准	雲——云	闆——板	蔔——卜

Homophonic substitution means combining two characters with the same pronunciation but different meanings into one. It is important, however, that there be no confusion of meaning. The examples of homophonic substitution given just above have long been in use in China. For example, the more complex character 後 (hòu, behind) is substituted by the character 后 (hòu, empress) because the two are so far apart in meaning that in context there is no likelihood of confusion.

5) Creating New Characters

If none of the above four methods are applicable, and it is necessary to simplify a character, a new one has to be created, usually either by the picto-phonetic or associative compound methods. Such characters may be called "new" in contrast to older complex foms they replace, but in fact many of them have already been in currency for more than a thousand years, for example, 万 (wàn, ten thousand), 双 (shuāng, pair), 体 (tǐ, body). Some other examples are:

驚——惊	護——护	響——响	叢——丛
膚——肤	憂——忧	衆——众	體——体
竈——灶	雙——双	萬——万	歲——岁
塵——尘			

If the 482 most basic simplified characters are mastered, then by applying the principle of extension by analogy of the side components 偏旁类推 given in section three in the List, the writing of more than 2,000 characters can be understood. For example, if you know that the simplified forms of the old complex characters 貝 (bèi, cowrie shell), 車 (chē, vehicle), and 門 (mén, door/gate) are 贝, 车, and 门, respectively, then by analogical extension when these characters appear as side components of other characters, their writing is also simplified.

贝——贞则负贡员财呗狈责厕贤账贩贬...　142 characters;

车——轧军轨阵库连轩诨郓轫轭匦转库...　81 characters;

门——闩闪们闭间闯闹扪闵闷闰闲间闹...　68 characters.

Thus it may be seen that mastering simplified characters is not difficult if the above principles by which they are formed are understood.

3.3 THE STANDARDIZATION OF THE FORMS OF CHINESE CHARACTERS

Many centuries of use have produced variations in the forms of many Chinese characters. Although these variations in form may be slight, they nevertheless present a hinderance to the normalization and standardization of Chinese characters. Because of this, for example, two variant forms of the same character may differ in the number of strokes composing them. Thus the character 争 (zhēng, contend) has only six strokes, while its variant form 爭 has eight strokes. This naturally creates problems in compiling and consulting dictionaries.

This lack of uniformity of Chinese characters is most clearly seen in the difference between handwritten 手写体 and printed forms 印刷体 of characters. Many characters used to take one form in books and newspapers and another form when written.

Here are some examples of pairs of characters, with the printed form given first, and the handwritten form second: 眞/真 (zhēn, true); 直/直 (zhí, straight); 靑/青 (qīng, blue-green); 黃/黄 (huáng, yellow); 絕/绝 (jué, sever); 益/益 (yì, benefit); 研/研 (yán, grind/study); 旣/既 (jì, since); 爭/争 (zhēng, strive); 巨/巨 (jù, huge); 敎/教 (jiāo, teach). Apart from such differences between printed and handwritten forms, sometimes one character even had two different printed forms. For example, the character 旣 (jì, since) just mentioned has two different printed forms: 旣 and 既.

In order to standarize the forms of the Chinese character for educational and other purposes, in May 1964 the Ministry of Culture and the Committee for the Reform of the Chinese Language jointly published the "List of Chinese Character Forms for General Printing". This list includes 6,196 Sòng style characters 宋体字 for general use in printing (excluding some characters used for printing ancient books and for other special purposes). This list fixes the standardized forms for these 6,196 characters, as well as the number of strokes and their order for writing each one. Since that time, except in special cases, all printed publications must follow this List as a standard, which is also the standard to be taught in schools.

The "List of Chinese Character Forms for General Printing" defines the standardized forms according to the subsequent three principles: (1) if the same character in the Sòng style has variations in strokes or structure, the one which is most easily identifed and easily written should be chosen; (2) if the form of a Sòng style printed character differs in strokes or structure

113

from the hand-written "regular style", then the Sòng style form ought to approximate the hand-written regular style as much as possible; (3) emphasis is to be put on the practical concerns of ease of learning rather than on adherence to the traditions of characterology, as for example in the simplification of the component 次 (with three dots) to 次 (with two dots) in such characters as 羡 (xiàn, admire, formerly written as 羨), and 盗 (dào "rob", formerly written 盜), because the component 次 (with two dots) can occur as an independent character (cì, meaning "sequence"), and is thus easier to remember.

After the publication and implementation of the "List of Chinese Character Forms for General Printing", people began to refer to the forms in the list as the "new character forms" and to call the previous ones the "old character forms". In order to see the difference between the "new" and "old" let us make a few simple comparisons. There are three primary types of differences:

1) **Changes in the Shapes of Strokes** (The older form is given first, and the new form second):

Vertical "dots" become right-slanting ones:

安——安, 之——之, 方——方, 文——文,

Horizontal "dots" become right-slanting:

言——言, 今——今, 社——社, 氏——氏,

Downward southwesterly "dots" slant to the right:

淮——淮, 兼——兼, 屏——屏, 戶——户,

Downward southeasterly strokes become "dots":

卜——卜, 朴——朴, 刃——刃, 匆——匆,

Slightly downward southwesterly strokes become horizontals:

丰——丰，　　耕——耕，　　刊——刊，　　蚕——蚕，

呈——呈；

Horizontal strokes become downward southwesterly ones:

舌——舌，　　敌——敌，　　插——插，　　板——板；

Vertical downward southwesterly strokes become vertical:

非——非，　　排——排　　临——临；

Horizontal strokes ending the left side components become upward-twisting ones:

巧——巧，　　地——地，　　理——理，　　岬——岬，

孩——孩，　　站——站，　　到——到，　　取——取，

牧——牧；

Downward southeasterly strokes ending the left side components become "dots":

斌——斌，　　炮——炮，　　种——种，　　颇——颇，

料——料，　　麸——麸，　　短——短，　　郊——郊；

The final downward southeasterly strokes of components within enclosing structures are changed into "dots":

困——困　　达——达　　闪——闪　　医——医，

菊——菊，　　枢——枢，　　迟——迟，　　返——返。

2) Changes in the Forms of Component Parts or Single characters

In order to facilitate the naming and writing of certain characters, a great number of adjustments were made in the forms of some characters, especially in the forms of certain component parts:

a) Separate strokes are connected in certain component parts:

草——草，　　卉——卉，　　奔——奔，　　研——研，

屏——屏，　　着——着，　　象——象，　　兔——兔，

鬼——鬼，　　敖——敖，　　叟——叟，　　瓦——瓦，

制——制，　　巨——巨，　　骨——骨，　　牙——牙，

㠯——以，　　印——印　　侯——候，　　片——片，

成——成，　　及——及，　　函——函。

The purpose of the change is to reduce the number of strokes for convenience in writing.

b) Connected strokes are separated in certain component parts: 骋——骋，　　聘——聘，　　污——污，　　夸——夸，

号——号，　　周——周。

The purpose of separating them in this way is to make it easier to name and remember the various component parts. For example, 粤 may now be remembered as being composed of the two components 由 and 亏, and the character 周 (zhōu, circuit), may be remembered as consisting of 冂, 土 and 口.

c) The number of strokes in characters or components is reduced:

宫——宫，　　郎——郎，　　既——既，　　兔——兔，

争——争，　　奥——奥，　　速——速，　　羡——羡，

者——者。

These changes are effected not only to facilitate the writing of characters, but also their naming and memorization. For example, the surname 吕 (lǔ) is now composed simply of two "mouth" 口 components; the internal core of the character 奥 (ào, abstruse), either as an independent character or as a component of other characters, is now simply written as 米 (mǐ, rice), as the old core component 釆 is not easily named; and — as noted previously — using 次 (cì, sequence) as the component part in such characters as 盗 and 羡, instead of the former

116

component 次, which has no name, similarly facilitates both reference and memorization.

d) The form of a component part is changed to resemble as much as possible the handwritten style. In the following characters, 入 (rù, enter) is changed to 入 (rén, person):

內——内,　　全——全,　　余——余,　　肉——肉,

八 is changed to ⸯ :

送——送,　　遂——遂,　　盆——益,　　酋——酋,
兼——兼,　　兌——兑,　　曾——曾;

八 is changed to ⸯ, or eliminated altogether:

半——半,　　滕——滕,　　平——平,　　尚——尚,
肖——肖,　　敝——敝;

儿 is changed to 八, or eliminated altogether:

罕——罕,　　空——空,　　交——交,　　陸——陆,
商——商,　　橘——橘,　　俊——俊,　　甚——甚,
詹——詹,　　焖——焖,　　迴——迥,

儿 is changed to 几 :

微——微,　　亮——亮,　　虎——虎,

刀 and 勹 are changed to ⼑ or 几, etc.:

陷——陷,　　負——负,　　兔——兔,　　危——危,
色——色,　　沒——没;

and other similar such changes:

祿——绿,　　溫——温,　　攜——携,　　敎——教,
捏——捏,　　晉——晋,　　直——直,　　眞——真,
角——角,　　拔——拔,　　冊——册,　　皐——皋,
搖——摇,　　將——将,　　吳——吴,　　兪——俞,
etc.

117

3) Changes in the Structural Relations Between Component Parts

For some characters, the forms of their component parts are basically unchanged, but the arrangement of these parts within the character has been altered, primarily to make them easier to describe, remember, and write. For example:

Old Forms of Characters: 黙 盛 惑 盇

New Forms of Characters: 默 盛 惑 盇

In order to normalize and standardize the forms of the characters, the "List of Chinese Character Forms for General Printing" also contains definite rules for the structural arrangement of the forms of the characters. For example, characters such as 毛，走，尢，是，鬼，风，爪，支，尧，尺，瓜， etc. when used as left-side components are all to be written as "enclosing structures", as for example in the characters 毡，赶，尬，题，魁，飓，爬，翅，翘，咫，飚； but characters such as 麦 and 鼠, etc., when used as left-side components, are to be proportioned in "left-right" structures as in 麸 and 鼩. Similarly, characters such as 麻，鹿，厌， etc., when used as upper-side components are to be proportioned as enclosing structures, thus: 摩，麂，餍 rather than as over-and-under structures.

For the reader's convenience, the contrastive list of 48 new and old component forms from the contemporary dictionary Xiàndài Hànyǔ Cídiǎn is given here:

Old Form	New Form	Examples
1. 艹	艹	花草
2. 辶	辶	连速

118

3.	开	开	型研
4.	丰	丰	艳沣
5.	巨	巨	苣渠
6.	屯	屯	纯顿
7.	瓦	瓦	瓶瓷
8.	反	反	板饭
9.	丑	丑	纽枢
10.	龙	龙	拔茏
11.	印	印	茚
12.	耒	耒	耕耘
13.	吕	吕	侣营
14.	攸	攸	修倏
15.	争	争	净静
16.	产	产	彦産
17.	羊	羊	差养
18.	并	并	屏拼
19.	吴	吴	蜈虞
20.	角	角	解确
21.	奂	奂	换痪
22.	俯	尚	敝弊
23.	耳	耳	敢严
24.	者	者	都著
25.	直	直	值植
26.	黾	黾	绳鼋
27.	咼	咼	過蜗
28.	垂	垂	睡郵
29.	食	食	飲飽
30.	郎	郎	廊螂

31.	彔	录	渌篆
32.	㿿	昷	温瘟
33.	骨	骨	滑骼
34.	鬼	鬼	槐嵬
35.	爲	为	偽媯
36.	旣	既	溉厩
37.	蚤	蚤	搔骚
38.	敖	敖	傲遨
39.	莽	莽	漭蟒
40.	眞	真	慎填
41.	䍃	䍃	摇遥
42.	殺	殺	摋鍛
43.	黃	黄	廣横
44.	虛	虚	墟歔
45.	異	異	冀戴
46.	象	象	像橡
47.	奧	奧	澳襖
48.	普	普	谱镨

(Note: For purposes of contrast, some complex-style characters have been included in the above list.)

3.4 CHARACTERS EASILY MISWRITTEN BECAUSE OF THEIR SIMILARITY OF FORM

A major cause of the miswriting of characters is their similarity of form. This is why a beginning student of the language should carefully analyze the structures of Chinese characters and clearly differentiate their forms. There are two possibilities of miswriting a Chinese character. One is to write it in such a way that it is not a Chinese character at all, as for example when the character 拜 (bài, do obeisance) is mistakenly written as 拝, which is not a character, or when 迎 (yíng, welcome) is miswritten as 迊. The second error is to write a character with another meaning by mistake, as for example to write 候 (hòu, await) for 侯 (hóu, marquis), 治 (zhì, control) for 冶 (yě, smelting), or 暑 (shǔ, summer) for 署 (shǔ, department), etc. The first type of error is called writing cuòzì 错字 (wrong [i.e., non-existant] characters) whereas the second type of error is referred to as writing biézì 别字 (inappropriate [i.e. wrongly used] characters). But in both cases the error comes from a failure to understand characters or parts of characters which are similar in form and therefore easily confused.

Most of the mistakes in character writing are related to one part of the characters, that is to say, that either one of the side components or one of the component parts is miswritten. Therefore we should pay particular attention to these recurrent parts, especially to those which are similar in form and thus easily confused. An effective method of avoiding this type of mistake is to analyze the characters into their component parts.

For the reader's reference, there follows a list of forty most commonly confused side components and component parts, plus some representative characters. (For the Hanyu Pinyin readings, please refer to 4.1 below.)

1) 阝 vs. 卩

阝 (on the right side) was originally written as 邑 (yì), meaning "city", so that characters with the 阝 radical on the right side usually have some semantic connection with towns or cities. 卩, on the other hand, originally meant "bone joint", so characters with this radical generally and originally had something to do with parts or joints. For example:

阝——都 (dū, capital), 郭 (guō, outer city wall), 郡 (jùn, prefecture), 邦 (bāng, nation), 部 (bù, section), 邮 (yóu, postal).

卩——节 (jié, joint), 脚 (jiǎo, foot), 叩 (kòu, kowtow), 卸 (xiè, disassemble/unhitch), 却 (què, step back), 印(yìn, seal), 即 (jí, approaching).

2) 冫 vs. 氵

Characters with the "two dots of water" radical (冫) usually are related to "cold", while those with "three dots of water" (氵) are related to water or liquid. For example:

冫——冷 (lěng, cold), 冻 (dòng, freeze), 凛 (lǐn, stern, cold), 凝 (níng, congeal), 冶 (yě, smelting), 冲 (chōng, dash, flush).

氵——河 (hé, river), 治 (zhì, control), 泽 (zé, pool), 汛 (xùn, flood), 洁 (jié, clean), 泳 (yǒng, swim).

3) 廴 vs 辶

The "walking radical" 辶 is often associated with movement or distance. It should not be confused with the radical 廴, which may have to do with buildings or structures when used as the primary radical.

廴——建(jiàn, construct), 廷 (tíng, palace), 延 (yán, extend).

辶——过(guò, surpass), 巡 (xún, patrol), 返 (fǎn, return), 还 (huán, return), 通 (tōng, pass through), 远 (yuǎn, far), 迫 (pò, approach, press).

4) 厶, 𠂇 **and** 衣

Note the following representative characters, plus those which are formed from them by extension:

𠤎——长 (cháng, long), plus: 张, 帐, 账, etc.

𠂆——畏 (wèi fear), 展 (zhǎn, unfold), 丧 (sàng, loss), 辰 (chén, dawn), plus: 偎, 碾, 振, etc.

衣——衣 (yī, clothing), 表 (biǎo, graph), 农 (nóng, agriculture), 袁 (Yuán, a surname), plus: 依, 褙, 浓, 猿, etc.

5) 又, 夂, 攵, **and** 欠

Note that 又, 攵 and 欠 are usually used as right-hand components, whereas 夂 usually is not:

又——叙 (xù, narrate), 叔 (shū, uncle), 取 (qǔ, fetch). 淑 (shū, fair), 娶 (qǔ, marry).

攵——收 (shōu, receive), 攻 (gōng, attack), 放 (fàng, release), 牧 (mù, herd), 政 (zhèng, politics), 救 (jiù, rescue), 致 (zhì, send), 敛 (liǎn, restrain).

欠——欣 (xīn, glad), 欲 (yù, desire), 欧 (Ōu, Europe), 欺 (qī, oppress), 饮 (yǐn, drink), 欢 (huān, joyous), 款 (kuǎn, funds), 嗽 (sòu, cough).

夂——处 (chù, pliace), 夏 (xià, summer), 复 (fù, repeat), 陵 (líng, tomb), 俊 (jùn, handsome), 冬 (dōng, winter), 各 (gè, each), 路 (lù, road), 条 (tiáo, strip), 蜂 (fēng, bee), 修 (xiū, mend).

6) 土 **vs.** 士

土, the "earth" radical, originally had to do with the soil, but nowadays there are some characters in which this relationship is not clear. It is important to memorize some key examples, and distinguish it from characters containing 士, the "scholar" radical.

土——坐 (zuò, sit), 尘 (chén, dust), 堵 (dǔ, plug up), 至 (zhì, arrive), 去 (qù, go), 社 (shè, society), 圣 (shèng, sage), 圭 (guī, jade tablet).

士——壮 (zhuàng, strong), 吉 (jí, lucky), 志 (zhì, will), 壳 (ké/qiào, shell), 声 (shēng, sound), 壶 (hú, pot), 壹 (yī, one).

7) 彐 vs. 互

Most characters with 彐 as a component are pronounced lù, with a few pronounced lü or bō, whereas those containing the 互 component are not pronounced this way. For example:

彐——录 (lù, record), 禄 (lù, emolument), 碌 (lù, mediocre), 绿 (lü, green), 氯 (lǜ, chlorine), 剥 (bō, exploit).

彑——缘 (yuán, reason), 椽 (yuán, timber), 篆 (zhuàn, seal), 掾 (yuàn, subordinate official), 彝 (yí, wine vessel), 喙 (huì, snout), 蠡 (lí, seashell).

8) 凡, 卂 and 丸

Characters which use 凡 as a side component generally are pronounced like fán, while those containing 卂 are pronounced like xùn.

凡——帆 (fān, sail), 矾 (fán, vitriol), 钒 (fán, vanadium), 梵 (fán, Sanskrit).

卂——迅 (xùn, fast), 讯 (xùn, question), 汛 (xùn, flood).

丸——丸 (wán, ball), 纨 (wán, fine silk), 执 (zhí, grasp), 挚 (zhì, sincere), 蛰 (zhé, hibernate), 热 (rè, hot), 垫 (diàn, cushion).

Note that the character 染 (rǎn, dye) contains the component 九 (jiǔ, nine) on top, not 丸 (wán, ball).

9) 己, 巳, 巳 **and** 巳

The character 巳 (yǐ, already), which is "half-closed", can only occur as an independent character, but not as a component of any other character, whereas the other three can so occur:

己——己 (jǐ, self), 记 (jì, remember), 忌 (jì, taboo), 纪 (jì, record), 起 (qǐ, upward), 岂 (qǐ, how can . . . ?) 配 (pèi, match), 妃 (fēi, imperial concubine).

巳——祀 (sì, sacrifice), 异 (yì, different), 导 (dǎo, direct), 包 (bāo, wrap), 巷 (xiàng, lane), 撰 (zhuàn, compose).

巳——范 (fàn, model), 犯 (fàn, transgress), 卷 (juǎn, roll up), 厄 (è, evil), 危 (wēi, danger), 仓 (cāng, storehouse), 宛 (wǎn, winding), 怨 (yuàn, enmity), 苑 (yuàn, garden).

10) 少 **vs.** 少

Note that the component 少 only appears at the bottom of characters, while 少 (shǎo, few), as an independent character never appears in this bottom position.

少——沙 (shā, sand), 抄 (chāo, copy), 秒 (miǎo, a second), 妙 (miào, wonderful), 劣 (liè, inferior), 省 (shěng, province), 雀 (què, sparrow).

少——步 (bù, step), 涉 (shè, wade), 陟 (zhì, mounting). (Note that 少 occurs as the bottom part of 步 and characters derived from it.)

11) 戈, 戈, 戋 **and** 弋

Note that 戈 only appears in the character 尧 (Yáo, the simplified form of the name of the legendary sage originally written as 堯), and characters derived from it. 戈, is the simplifed form of …. 弋 (yì, retrievable arrow) has one less stroke than 戈 (gē, dagger-axe), which usually occurs in characters relating to weapons.

戈——尧 (Yáo, a name), 浇 (jiāo, sprinkle), 烧 (shāo, burn), 绕 (rào, coil), 晓 (xiǎo, dawn/know), 挠 (náo, scratch).

戈——划 (huá, paddle), 戏 (xì, opera), 战 (zhàn, war), 戡 (kān, suppress), 戳 (chuō, stab), 戮 (lù, kill), 栽 (zāi, plant), 裁 (cái, cut[paper etc.]).

戋——钱 (qián, money), 浅 (qiǎn, shallow), 贱 (jiàn, cheap), 溅 (jiàn, splash), 饯 (jiàn, give a farewell dinner), 线 (xiàn, thread), 残 (cán, incomplete), 践 (jiàn, trample), 笺 (jiān, writing paper).

弋——式 (shì, style), 试 (shì, test), 拭 (shì, wipe), 代 (dài, replace), 武 (wǔ, military), 斌 (bīn, urbane), 赋 (fù, bestow on), 腻 (nì, greasy), 贰 (èr, two [used on cheques, banknotes, etc.]).

12) 大 vs. 犬

大 (dà, big) and 犬 (quǎn, canine) are often confused when used as components due to their differing only by one "dot".

大——庆 (qìng, celebrate), 类 (lèi, species), 奖 (jiǎng, reward) 契 (qì, contract), 驮 (tuó, carry on the back).

犬——厌 (yàn, detest), 哭 (kū, weep), 莽 (mǎng, rank grass), 臭 (chòu, stinking), 伏 (fú, submit), 器 (qì, implement).

13) ㄚ vs. 羊

Note that ㄚ occurs in the enclosed part of the character 鬲 (lì, an ancient cooking tripod) and all characters of which

126

it is a part, while 丷 occurs within the enclosed part of the character 南 (nán, south) and those characters of which it is a component.

丬——鬲 (lì, cooking tripod), 隔 (gé, separate), 融 (róng, melt), 鬻 (yù, vend).

丷——南 (nán, south), 献 (xiàn, offer), 楠 (nán, nanmu wood), 喃 (nán, murmur).

14) 𠃓, 㐅 and 易

𠃓 is the simplified form of the component 昜 and replaces it in all cases except 阳 (yáng, sun), the simplified form of 陽, and 伤 (shāng, wound), the simplified form of 傷, which must be memorized. Those characters with ... as a phonetic component all rhyme with -ang. Those with 易 (yì, easy) as a phonetic component all rhyme with -i.

𠃓——汤 (tāng, soup), 荡 (dàng, away), 烫 (tàng, scald), 场 (chǎng, field), 肠 (cháng, intestine), 畅 (chàng, unimpeded), 扬 (yáng, raise), 杨 (yáng, poplar), 疡 (yáng, sore), 殇 (shāng, die young), 觞 (shāng, wine cup).

㐅——伤 (shāng, wound), 饬 (chì, readjust).

易——錫 (xī, tin), 踢 (tī, kick), 剔 (tì, debone), 惕 (tì, careful), 蜴 (yì, lizard), 赐 (cì, bestow).

15) 天 vs. 夭

Characters containing 天 (tiān, heaven) as a phonetic component are generally pronouned to rhyme with -an (with the exception of 吞 [tūn, swallow]). Characters containing 夭 (yāo, witch) as a component, on the other hand, generally have such finals as -ao, -uo, or -üe. For example,

127

天——袄 (ǎo, short jacket), 妖 (yāo, demon), 笑 (xiào, smile laugh), 沃 (wò fertile), 跃 (yuè, leap).

天——添 (tiān, add), 舔 (tiǎn, lick), 蚕 (cán, silkworm), 吞 (tūn, swallow).

16) 攵 vs. 支

Characters which employ 支 as a side component take -i in their pronunciation, with the one exception of 鼓 (gǔ, drum). There are only a few characters which employ 攵 as a component, so those can be memorized individually.

支——技 (jì, skill), 伎 (jì, trick), 枝 (zhī, branch), 肢 (zhī, limbs), 歧 (qí, branching), 翅 (chì, wing), 豉 (chǐ, fermented soya beans), 鼓 (gǔ, drum).

攵——敲 (qiāo, knock), 寇 (kòu, bandit).

17) 仓 vs. 仑

仓 is the simplified form of 倉 (cāng, storehouse), while 仑 is the simplified form of 侖 (lún, coherence). Because both may be employed as side components in other characters and they are so similar in form, they are often confused. Please note the following examples:

仓——沧 (cāng, dark-blue [sea]), 伧 (cāng, rude), 抢 (qiǎng, rob), 枪 (qiāng, gun), 呛 (qiàng, choke), 疮 (chuāng, ulcer), 舱 (cāng, cabin), 苍 (cāng, dark green).

仑——沦 (lún, sink), 伦 (lún, logic), 抡 (lūn, brandish), 轮 (lún, wheel), 论 (lùn, discuss), 囵 (lún, whole), 纶 (lún, black silk ribbon), 瘪 (biě, shrivelled).

18) 日，曰， and 目

Characters which take 日 (rì, sun) as their radical are often related in meaning to "sun", "day", or "time", and should be distinguished from those taking 曰 (yuē, quoth), which is wider in form. Several characters written with 冃, the ancient character for 帽 (hat), are related to headgear. The component 冖 only occurs on the top of those characters or components in which it appears.

日——时 (shí, time), 映 (yìng, shine), 晴 (qíng, sunny), 旦 (dàn, dawn), 春 (chūn, spring), 早 (zǎo, morning), 普 (pǔ, universal), 旧 (jiù, old).

曰——最 (zuì, most), 量 (liáng, measure), 沓 (tà, crowded), 渴 (kě, thirsty), 曼 (màn, graceful), 旨 (zhǐ, purpose), 曹 (Cáo, a surname), 曾 (Zēng, a surname).

冃——冒 (mào emit), 帽 (mào, hat), 冕 (miǎn, crown).

19) 衤 vs. 礻

Characters with the side component 礻, which is a variation of the independent character 衣 (yī, clothing), are generally related to clothing or cloth in meaning. Characters with the side component 礻, which is a variation of the character 示 (shì, show), often have to do with luck or religion.

礻——祈 (qí, pray), 祷 (dǎo, pray), 祝 (zhù, celebrate), 礼 (lǐ, courtesy), 福 (fú, blessings), 祥 (xiáng, luck), 禄 (lù, official preferment), 祸 (huò, misfortune), 祠 (cí, ancestral temple), 社 (shè, association).

衤——补 (bǔ, mend), 衬 (chèn, lining), 衫 (shān, shirt), 袜 (wà, sock), 袄 (ǎo, jacket), 袖 (xiù, sleeve), 袍 (páo, robe), 被 (bèi, quilt), 裤 (kù, pants), 裙 (qún, skirt), 袒 (tǎn, bare-chested), 裸 (luǒ, naked), 褂 (guà, gown), 褥 (rù, mattress), 襟 (jīn, garment front).

20) 今 vs. 令

Because of their similarity of form, these two characters as side components are easily confused. Generally characters using 今 (jīn, today) as a side component have finals such as -in, -an, or -en, while a majority of those containing 令 (lìng, command) are related in pronunciation to ling, with a minority only beginning with the initial l-. Compare:

今——矜 (jīn, pity), 衿 (jīn, front of a garment), 衾 (qīn, quilt), 琴 (qín, zither), 黔 (qián, black), 贪 (tān, corrupt), 念 (niàn, think of), 含 (hán, contain), 吟 (yín, chant), 岑 (cén, high hill).

令——拎 (līng, carry), 羚 (líng, antelope), 泠 (líng, cool), 零 (líng, zero), 龄 (líng, age), 铃 (líng, bell), 伶 (líng, actor), 领 (lǐng, neck), 岭 (lǐng, mountain range). 邻 (lín, neighbor), 怜 (lián, pity), 冷 (lěng, cold).

Note that 冷 (lěng, cold) and 泠 (líng, cool and refreshing) are different characters.

21) 王 vs. 玉

There are only a few characters which use the character 玉 (yù, jade) as a side component and these mostly refer to some sort of precious stone. The remaining characters all take the character 王 (wáng, king) as a radical or a component, and most of these rhyme with -uang.

王——汪 (wāng, deep and vast water), 枉 (wǎng, crooked), 望 (wàng, expect), 旺 (wàng, prosperous), 匡 (kuāng rectify), 框 (kuāng, frame), 筐 (kuāng, basket), 眶 (kuāng, eye socket), 诓 (kuāng, deceive), 狂 (kuáng, crazy), 诳 (kuáng, lies), 逛 (guàng, stroll), 皇 (huáng, emperor), 惶 (huáng, anxiety), 煌 (huáng, brilliant), 蝗 (huáng, locust), 呈 (chéng, submit), 全 (quán, complete), 琴 (qín, zither), 班 (bān, class).

玉——碧 (bì, jade), 莹 (yíng, jade-like stone), 玺 (xǐ, royal seal), 国 (guó, country).

Remember that the internal component of 国 (country) is 玉 (jade) and not simply 王 (king).

22) 氐 **vs.** 氏

Characters with component 氐 (Dī, an ancient nationality in China) are generally also related to di in pronunciation, while those which include the component 氏 (shì, surname) are mostly related to the -i ending.

氏——纸 (zhǐ, paper), 舐 (shì, lick), 祇 (qí, earth deities), 芪 (qí, milk vetch), 扺 (zhǐ, clap).

氐——底 (dǐ, bottom), 抵 (dǐ, support), 砥 (dǐ, whetstone), 柢 (dǐ, root), 低 (dī, low), 邸 (dǐ, official residence), 祗 (zhī, venerate).

23 斥 **vs.** 斤

There are only a few characters which use 斥 (chì, scold) as a side component. Therefore if one can remember these, the remainder will all be written with 斤 (jīn, catty) as side component.

斥——拆 (chāi, disassemble), 柝 (tuò, watchman's clapper), 坼 (chè, split open), 诉 (sù, tell).

斤——折 (zhé/shé, snap, break), 析 (xī, analyze), 听 (tīng, hear), 暂 (zàn, temporary), 浙 (Zhè, Zhejiang Province), 所 (suǒ, place), 撕 (sī, rip), 斫 (zhuó, hack), 沂 (yí, Yihe River), 靳 (jìn, stingy).

24) 卬 **vs.** 卯

Characters taking the character 卯 (mǎo, mortise) as a component generally rhyme with -ao (with the exception of 柳 (liǔ, willow), whereas those containing 卬 do not.

卬——昂 (áng, hold one's head high), 仰 (yǎng, admire), 迎 (yíng, welcome), 抑 (yì, repress).

卯——铆 (mǎo, rivet), 昴 (mǎo, name of a constellation), 峁 (mǎo, hills), 贸 (mào, trading), 聊 (liáo, merely), 柳 (liǔ, willow).

25) 友, 𠂢 **vs.** 发

Note that 友 (yǒu, friend) only occurs as a component as the lower part of the character 爱 (ài, love). Most commonly occurring characters which use𠂢as a component are pronounced bá. By contrast, characters which take the simplified character 发 (fā, emit) as a component are not pronounced fá, but never the less will have labial initial consonants.

友——爱 (ài, love), 嗳 (ai, oh!), 暧 (ài, dim), 媛 (ài, [your] daughter), 瑷 (ài, a place name).

𠂢——拔 (bá, pull out), 跋 (bá, trek), 菝 (bá, a plant name), 魃 (bá, monster), 𪕲 (bá, part of 𪕲 ("marmot").

发——拨 (bō, poke), 泼 (bō, the jumping of fish), 泼 (pō, splash), 废 (fèi, abandon).

26) 小、氺、水 **and** 朩

These four components all occur at the bottom of characters or side components in which they appear. 小 is a variant of the "heart radical" 心, while both 朩 and 水 are variants of the character for water 水. 小 only appears in a very few characters.

小——恭 (gōng, respectful), 慕 (mù, admire), 忝 (tiǎn, unworthy), 添 (tiān, add), 舔 (tiǎn, lick).

桼——泰 (tài, safe), 漆 (qī, lacquer), 膝 (xī, knee), 黎 (lí, multitude), 滕 (téng, a surname), 藤 (téng, rattan), 黍 (shǔ, millet), 黏 (nián, sticky).

求——求 (qiú, beg), 球 (qiú, ball), 隶 (lì, subordinate), 棣 (dì, younger brother), 录 (lù, record), 禄 (lù, official preferment), 绿 (lù, green), 碌 (lù, mediocre).

杀——鳏 (guān, wifeless), 瘝 (guān, ill).

27) 圣 vs. 圣

The problem of the confusion of these two components arose only after the simplification of the characters. 圣 is the simplified form of 巠 (jīng, waterway), and characters which take it as a side component generally are related in prouunciation to -ing. There are only a few characters which take 圣 (shèng, sage) as a side component, and these are not related to -ing.

圣——经 (jīng, warp), 泾 (Jīng, Jinghe River), 茎 (jīng, stalk), 颈 (jǐng, neck), 痉 (jìng, spasm), 径 (jìng, path), 轻 (qīng, light), 氢 (qīng, hydrogen), 劲 (jìn, strength).

圣——怪 (guài, strange), 蛏 (chēng, razor clam), 柽 (chēng, tamarisk tree).

28) 东 vs. 柬

东 is the simplified form of 東 (dōng, east), while 柬 is the simplified form of 柬 (jiǎn, note). As they are both used as right hand components, they are often confused. Note that with the exception of 陈 (chén, display), most of the characters containing 东 as a component are related to dong in pronunciation, while most of those containing 东 as a component rhyme with -ian.

东——冻 (dòng, freeze), 栋 (dòng, ridgepole), 陈 (chén, display).

东——炼 (liàn, smelting), 拣 (jiǎn, select), 练 (liàn, practice).

29) 未 vs. 末

Note that characters taking 未 (wèi, not yet) as a component usually rhyme with -ei, while those taking 末 (mò, end) as a component usually rhyme with -o (with the exception of 袜 [wà, stocking]).

未——味 (wèi, flavor), 妹 (mèi, younger sister), 寐 (mèi, sleep), 昧 (mèi, conceal), 魅 (mèi, demon).

末——抹 (mǒ, smear on), 沫 (mò, foam), 茉 (mò, part of 茉莉 "jasmine"), 秣 (mò, fodder), 袜 (wà, stocking).

30) 癶 vs. 癶

These two components are very easily confused. Note that 癶 only appears on the top of the tenth Heavenly Stem 癸 (guǐ) and 登 (dēng, climb), while ... only appears on top of 祭 jì, sacrifice).

癶——癸 (guǐ, the last of the ten Heavenly Stems), 葵 (kuí, sunflower), 睽 (kuí, stare), 闋 (què, cease), 登 (dēng, mount), 蹬 (dēng, step on), 澄 (dèng, settle), 瞪 (dèng, stare), 凳 (dèng, stool), 橙 (chén/chéng, orange).

癶——祭 (jì, sacrifice), 察 (chá, examine), 擦 (cā, rub), 嚓 (cā, screech), 蔡 (Cài, a surname).

31) 戊, 戍, 戌, and 戎

戊 (wù, the fifth Heavenly Stem), 戍 (shù, garrison), 戌 (xū, the eleventh of twelve Earthly Branches), and 戎 (róng,

134

army) all differ in both meaning and pronunciation. Because
of their similarity of form they are most easily confused. While
not many characters employ these as components, they must
be carefully distinguished in meaning and pronunciation.

戊——茂 (mào, luxuriant).

戌——蔑 (miè, disdain), 篾 (miè, thin bamboo strip).

戎——绒 (róng, velvet), 贼 (zéi, thief).

32) 朿 vs. 束

The original meaning of 朿 is "thorn", so many of the characters which employ this as a component are related in at least
one of their meanings to this idea. The remainder of characters
employ 束 (shù, bind) as a side component.

朿——刺 (cì, sting), 策 (cè, whip), 枣 (zǎo, jujube), 棘 (jí,
bramble).

束——速 (sù, speed), 喇 (lǎ, part of 喇叭 "trumpet"),
辣 (là, peppery), 剌 (là, perverse), 瘌 (là, part of 瘌痢
"favus"), 悚 (sǒng, terrified), 赖 (lài, rely), 敕 (chì,
edict) 簌 (sù, rustle).

One should pay particular attention to distinguishing the two
characters 刺 (cì, sting) and 剌 (là).

33) 臣 vs. 臣

Note the very slight difference in form between these two
characters. Those which take 臣 as a side component generally
rhyme with -i.

臣——臣 (chén, feudal official), 卧 (wò, lie down), 宦 (huàn,
eunuch).

臣——颐 (yí, cheek), 姬 (jī, concubine), 熙 (xī, bustling).

135

34) 𠂤, 𣥐, **and** 辰

To distinguish these characters, remember that 𠂤 only occurs in the character 旅 (lǚ, travel), and other characters of which that is a part. 𣥐 only occurs in the character 派 (pài, send/sect). All other characters use 辰 (chén, the fifth Earthly Branch) as side component.

𠂤——旅 (lǚ, travel), 膂 (lǚ, backbone).

𣥐——派 (pài, send/sect).

辰——振 (zhèn, shake), 赈 (zhèn, aid), 娠 (shēn, pregnant), 晨, (chén, morning), 震 (zhèn, quake), 蜃 (shèn, clam), 唇 (chún, lip), 宸 (chén, house).

35) 免 **vs.** 兔

Although 免 (miǎn, avoid) and 兔 (tù, rabbit) are very different in both meaning and pronunciation, yet because they differ in their forms only by one "dot" stroke, characters containing them as side components are often confused or wrongly written. In fact, only a few characters such as 冤 (yuān, injustice) and 逸 (yì, leisure) employ 兔 as a side component, while many characters take 免 with no extra "dot" as a component part.

兔——冤 (yuān, injustice), 逸 (yì, leisure), 菟 (tù, dodder plant), 堍 (tù, ramp).

免——勉 (miǎn, strive), 冕 (miǎn, crown), 娩 (miǎn, childbirth), 鮸 (miǎn, cod croaker), 挽 (wǎn, pull), 晚 (wǎn, late), 搀 (chān, support with hand), 馋 (chán, greedy), 谗 (chán, slander).

36) 豖 **vs.** 豕

Most characters which contain 豕 as a side component are

136

pronounced zhuó, with the exception of 冢 (zhǒng, tomb),
while this is not true of those characters containing 豕 (shǐ,
pig) as a side component.

豖——逐 (zhú, pursue), 豚 (tún, suckling pig), 噱 (jué/xué,
　　　loud laughter), 遽(jù, hurriedly), 豢(huàn, groom)
　　　遂 (suì, fulfill), 隧 (suì, tunnel), 燧 (suì, flint).

豕——啄 (zhuó, peck), 琢 (zhuó, chisel) 诼 (zhuó, slander),
　　　冢 (zhǒng, tomb).

37) 亨 vs. 享

All characters which employ 亨 (hēng, go smoothly) as a
side component rhyme with -eng, while all of those employing
享 (xiǎng, enjoy) as a side component rhyme with -un.

亨——哼 (hēng, groan), 烹 (pēng, cook).

享——淳 (chún, pure), 醇 (chún, wine), 鹑 (chún, quail),
　　　谆 (zhūn, earnestly).

38) 舀 vs. 臽

All characters which use 舀 (yǎo, ladle) as a side component
rhyme with -ao, and those using 臽 generally rhyme with -an
(except for 掐 (qiā, pinch).

舀——蹈 (dǎo, tread), 稻 (dào, paddy), 滔 (tāo, flood),
　　　韬 (tāo, sheath).

臽——馅 (xiàn, filling), 陷 (xiàn, pitfall), 阎 (yán, gate of a
　　　lane), 焰 (yàn, flame), 谄 (chǎn, flatter), 菡 (dàn,
　　　part of 菡萏 "lotus"), 掐 (qiā, pinch).

39) 叚 vs 段

Characters using … rhyme with -ia, while those using 段
(duàn, section) rhyme with -uan.

叚——葭 (jiā, reed shoot), 假 (jiǎ, false), 蝦 (xiā, shrimp),

霞 (xiá, rosy clouds), 瑕 (xiá, flaw), 暇 (xiá, leisure).

段——煅 (duàn, forge), 锻 (duàn, forge), 缎 (duàn, satin),
椴 (duàn, linden plant).

40) 商 **vs.** 啇

Characters which employ the character 商 (shāng, commerce/ the Shāng Dynasty) as a side component are read shāng, while those using 啇 are generally pronouced di (with the exception of 摘 [zhāi, pluck]).

商——墒 (shāng, soil moisture), 熵 (shāng, entropy).

啇——滴 (dī, drip), 嘀 (dí, whisper), 嫡 (dí, wife's)
摘 (zhāi, pluck).

4. THE PRONUNCIATION OF CHINESE CHARACTERS

All characters have fixed pronunciations. In most cases, a character has only one pronunciation; characters with multiple pronunciations are in the minority. Although all pronunciations are fixed, they are usually not accurately represented by the form of the characters. This fact greatly increases the difficulty of learning characters. In Chapter One we discussed the gradual development of characters from meaning-representational into sound-representational symbols through a great increase in the number of picto-phonetic characters. While such picto-phonetic characters are capable of indicating their own pronunciations, the evolution of the sound system and of the forms of characters over time has resulted in a serious decrease in the accuracy of the phonetic components in such characters. Research shows that phonetic components in modern Chinese picto-phonetic characters only represent the character's pronunciation accurately in under 30 percent of all cases. Because of this, the method of 秀才识字读半边 (A scholar can pronounce a character by merely looking at half of it.) has become highly undependable and has even become a source of jokes. Moreover, a considerable number of characters have multiple pronunciations for different meanings or usages. The existence of these multiple pronunciations further increases the degree of difficulty experienced in learning characters. People accustomed to alphabetic writing systems must devote considerable effort to learning both the form and the pronunciation of characters. This chapter will introduce several major issues pertaining to the pronunciation of characters.

4.1 METHODS OF PHONETIC NOTATION

Since characters cannot of themselves accurately represent their pronunciation, we must seek another means to help us pronounce them correctly — namely, phonetic notation 注音. Many methods of phonetic notation have been applied to characters; the three principal methods are introduced below.

1) Zhíyīn 直音

Zhíyīn is the representation of a character's pronunciation through a homophonic character. One of the earliest Chinese dictionaries, Xǔ Shèn's Shuōwén Jiězì, discussed in the previous chapter, makes use of this method. For example, the character 珣 (xuān, jade implement) is noted by its homophone 宣; the character 勼 (jiū, gather) is noted by its homophone 鳩, etc. In the Shuōwén Jiězì this method is expressed as 读若 dú ruò, meaning "to be pronounced like", e.g. 珣读若宣 (珣 is pronounced like 宣.) 勼读若鳩 (勼 is pronounced like 鳩), etc.

The zhíyīn method is extremely simple and is still used in some dictionaries today. However, it has numerous shortcomings:

140

a) The zhíyīn method cannot show a character's actual, standard pronunciation in Putonghua 普通话. Given "A is pronunced like B", we know only that A and B are homophones, but still do not know how they should be pronounced in Putonghua. Thus, the zhíyīn method is of no direct assistance in learning the exact pronunciation of characters in Putonghua.

b) A large number of characters lack homophones. For example, based on their standard Putonghua pronunciations, the following characters have no homophones:

白 bái, 北 běi, 蹭 cèng, 揣 chuǎi, 寸 cùn, 打 dǎ, 摁 èn, 发 fā, 放 fàng, 粉 fěn, 给 gěi, 乖 guāi, 恨 hèn, 口 kǒu, 冷 lěng, 俩 liǎ, 溜 liū, 卵 luǎn, 乱 luàn, 嫩 nèn, 牛 niú, 拗 niù, 怒 nù, 跑 pǎo, 盆 pén, 捧 pěng, 品 pǐn ... The zhíyīn method is unable to cope with such characters.

c) A considerable number of characters have as their only homophones characters which are rarely used. For example, the common character 海 (hǎi, sea) has as its only homophone the rare character 醢 (a kind of sauce); 热 (rè, hot) has only two homophones, 爇 heating and 焫, heating both of which are rarely seen. If a person, who does not know the pronunciations of 海 and 热, looks them up in the dictionary and finds 海读成醢 (海 is pronounced like 醢) and 热读成爇(或焫)(热 is pronounced like 爇 or 焫), he is bound to end up even more confused than before. If he then in desperation looks up 醢 and finds 醢读成海 (醢 is pronounced like 海), he will be as unenlightened as ever.

Since the zhíyīn method possesses the above defects, it can only serve as a secondary, not as the principal, method of phonetic notation.

2) Fǎnqiè 反切

Because of the numerous defects inherent in the zhíyīn method, particularly for those characters that lack homophones, another and better method of phonetic notation, called fǎnqiè, was created around the end of the Hàn Dynasty.

In Chinese, each character represents a phonetic syllable 音节. Each syllable may be analyzed into two parts: an initial 声母 and a final 韵母. In modern Putonghua, the initial is generally a simple consonant; the final is either a simple or compound vowel, or a vowel plus a nasal consonant (-n or -ng). For example:

发 (fā, produce)   ⟶ f (initial) + ā (final)

飞 (fēi, fly)   ⟶ f (initial) + ēi (final)

翻 (fān, turn over) ⟶ f (initial) + ān (final)

In these examples, *a* is a simple vowel, *ei* a compound vowel, and *an* a vowel plus a nasal consonant. The bar symbol " − " over the main vowel in the final indicates tone 声调 (to be discussed below). A small number of syllables (such as 爱 [ài, love])possess a final but lack an initial consonant; these may be said to have a zero-initial 零声母. Every syllable, however, must have a final; that is, every syllable must have at least a vowel.

Now we return to the question of fǎnqiè. The fǎnqiè method takes two characters and, by joining the initial of the first and the final (including the tone) of the second together, forms a new syllable. For example, from the two characters 图 (tú, chart) and 翻 (fān, turn over), we take the initial t- of the first and the final -ān of the second and join them together to ex-

142

press the correct pronunciation of the character 贪 (tān, corrupt). This process is expressed in old dictionaries such as the Kāngxī Zìdiǎn by the formula: 贪，图翻切 (tān, tú fān qiè), indicating that the fǎnqiè of the two characters 图 and 翻 will give the correct pronunciation of the character 贪. Another example is 同，徒红切(The pronunciation of the character 同 ([tóng, harmony])may be derived from the characters 徒 tú and 红 hóng by the fǎnqiè method), that is:

徒 (tú)　　　　　红 (hóng)

⋯t　+　óng⋯　=　tóng (同)

Using this fǎnqiè method, we can provide phonetic notations for all characters; in this respect, fǎnqiè is superior to zhíyīn. Fǎnqiè, however, also has its problems:

a)　For every fǎnqiè notation, one must find two appropriate characters and break them up into initial and final. This is a lot of trouble to go to just to find the pronunciation of one character.

b)　Like the zhíyīn method, fǎnqiè cannot indicate the exact Putonghua pronunciation of a character. Because Chinese characters are not true sound-representational symbols, readers who speak different dialects may pronounce the two characters which undergo fǎnqiè differently. Naturally, there is no guarantee that the result of such variant fǎnqiè readings will be the standard Putonghua pronunciation of the characters in question.

3)　Phonetic Spelling　拼音

The simplest and most scientific method of supplying accurate phonetic notations for characters to aid in the study of modern Chinese Putonghua is to establish a phonetic alphabet system in accordance with the initials, finals and tones of modern Chinese Putonghua. To date, the most widely used such systems have been the Zhùyīn Zìmǔ 注音字母 (Mandarin Phonetic Symbols [MPS]), promulgated in 1918, and the Hanyu Pinyin System 汉语拼音方案 or the Scheme for the Chinese Phonetic Alphabet, promulgated in 1958. Since the MPS system makes use of symbols based on Chinese characters, it is far less convenient for international use than Hanyu Pinyin, which employs the letters of the Latin alphabet. Hanyu Pinyin has already become an important and widely used tool throughout the world for the study of Chinese and for noting the correct pronunciation of Chinese characters.

The following is a brief introduction to the Hanyu Pinyin System. Zhùyīn Zìmǔ (MPS), International Phonetic Symbols, and the approximate English pronunciations are included for reference.

THE CHINESE PHONETIC ALPHABET

HP Symbol	Name of Symbol	Name in MPS	Approx. Engl. Pron. (as in)	Name in IPA
A a	a	ㄚ	a (aha)	[a]
B b	bê	ㄅㄝ	b (boy)	[pɛ]
C c	cê	ㄘㄝ	ts (rats)	[ts'ɛ]
D d	dê	ㄉㄝ	d (dog)	[tɛ]
E e	ê	ㄜ	u (uh)	[ɤ]
F f	êf	ㄝㄈ	f (fire)	[ɛf]
G g	gê	ㄍㄝ	g (gay)	[kɛ]

144

H h	ha	ㄏㄚ	h (here)	[xa]
I i	i	ㄧ	ee (eel)	[i]
J j	jie	ㄐㄧㄝ	j (jeep)	[tɕiɛ]
K k	kê	ㄎㄝ	k (kite)	[kʻɛ]
L l	êl	ㄝㄌ	l (lay)	[ɛl]
M m	êm	ㄝㄇ	m (may)	[ɛm]
N n	nê	ㄋㄝ	n (night)	[nɛ]
O o	o	ㄛ	o (or)	[o]
P p	pê	ㄆㄝ	p (pay)	[pʻɛ]
Q q	qiu	ㄑㄧㄡ	ch (cheek)	[tɕʻiou]
R r	ar	ㄚㄦ	r (pleasure)	[ar]
S s	ês	ㄝㄙ	s (song)	[ɛs]
T t	tê	ㄊㄝ	t (take)	[tʻɛ]
U u	u	ㄨ	oo (ooze)	[u]
V v	vê	ㄪㄝ	v (vain)	[vɛ]
W w	wa	ㄨㄚ	w (want)	[wa]
X x	xi	ㄒㄧ	sh (sheep)	[ɕi]
Y y	ya	ㄧㄚ	y (yard)	[ja]
Z z	zê	ㄗㄝ	ds (beds)	[tsɛ]

(Note: "V" is used only in writing words of dialect, minority language or foreign origin.)

Initials:

The first part of a Chinese syllable is called the initial 声母.
Putonghua has twenty-one initials, which are represented in
Hanyu Pinyin as follows:

b (ㄅ) d (ㄉ) g (ㄍ) j (ㄐ) zh (ㄓ) z (ㄗ)

p (ㄆ) t (ㄊ) k (ㄎ) q (ㄑ) ch (ㄔ) c (ㄘ)

    m (ㄇ)   n (ㄋ) h (ㄏ) x (ㄒ) sh (ㄕ) s (ㄙ)
    (ㄈ)   l (ㄌ)   r (ㄖ)

Finals:

The remaining part of a Chinese syllable is called the final 韵母. Finals may be divided into three types: simple finals, compound finals, and nasal finals.

A final composed of a simple vowel is called a simple final 单韵母. Hanyu Pinyin has six principal simple finals: a (ㄚ), o (ㄛ), e (ㄜ), i (ㄧ), u (ㄨ), and ü (ㄩ). Ü does not appear in the alphabet chart; it is pronounced similarly to French u or German ü. The vowel i is pronounced as [ʅ] after retroflexed initials, as in the four syllables zhi (知), chi (痴), shi (诗), ri (日), and is pronounced [ɿ] after palatal initials, as in zi (资), ci (雌), and si (思). (In phonetics these are called homorganic apical vowels.) In addition to the six simple finals above, there is also a retroflex final er (ㄦ). This final, written er when it represents an independent syllable (e.g. 儿童, értóng, children), is written -r when it is added on to an existing final (e.g. 花儿 huār, flower).

Finals with two and three vowels are called compound finals 复韵母. Hànyǔ Pīnyīn has thirteen compound finals: ai (ㄞ), ao (ㄠ), ei (ㄟ), ou (ㄡ), ia (ㄧㄚ), ie (ㄧㄝ), iao (ㄧㄠ), iou (ㄧㄡ), ua (ㄨㄚ), uo (ㄨㄛ), uai (ㄨㄞ), uei (ㄨㄟ), and üe (ㄩㄝ). Note that the vowel e in ie and üe is pronounced ㄝ (similar to the [ɛ] in English "bed"). In addition, the compound finals iou and uei are always written iu and ui respectively when preceded by an initial: e.g. niú ⟨牛, cow⟩, guī (归, return).

146

A final composed of a vowel plus either of the nasal endings -n or -ng is called a nasal final 鼻韵母. Hànyǔ Pīnyīn has sixteen nasal finals: an (ㄢ), ang (ㄤ), en (ㄣ), eng (ㄥ), ong (ㄨㄥ), ian (ㄧㄢ), iang (ㄧㄤ), in (ㄧㄣ), ing (ㄧㄥ), iong (ㄩㄥ), uan (ㄨㄢ), uang (ㄨㄤ), un (ㄨㄣ), ueng (ㄨㄥ), üan (ㄩㄢ), and ün (ㄩㄣ). Note that uen is uniformly written as un when preceded by an initial: e.g. lùn (论, discuss).

The finals which begin with i, u, and ü, when independently forming a syllable, are written as follows:

yi (i), ya (ia), ye (ie), yao (iao), you (iou), yan (ian), yang (iang), yin (in), ying (ing), yong (iong); wu (u), wa (ua), wo (uo), wai (uai), wei (uei), wan (uan), wang (uang), wen (uen), weng (ueng); yu (ü), yue (üe), yuan (üan), yun (ün).

In addition, when ü, üe, üan, and ün follow the palatalized initials j, q, and x, the two dots of the ü are always omitted: e.g. ju (居), qu (区), xu (需), jue (决), que (缺), xue (学), juan (捐), quan (全), xuan (宣), jun (军), qun (群), and xun (训). However, the two dots must not be omitted when ü is used with n or l: e.g. nü (女), lü (吕), etc.

Syllables and Tones:

Generally, initials and finals combine to form syllables (with the exception of a small number of syllables which lack initials). The changes in pitch that occur within a syllable are called **tones**. In Chinese, tones are extremely important, serving to differentiate meaning among what would otherwise be homophones. There are four tones in modern Chinese Putonghua:

Name of Tone	Tone Marker	Pronunciation	Example
First tone (阴平 yīn píng)	¯	high and level	mā (妈, mother)
Second tone (阳平 yáng píng)	´	rising from mid to high	má (麻, hemp)
Third tone (上声 shǎng shēng)	ˇ	falling, then rising	mǎ (马, horse)
Fourth tone (去声 qù shēng)	`	falling from high to low	mà (骂, scold)

The tone marker 声调符号 is placed over the main vowel 主要元音 of each syllable: e.g. jī（鸡），fēi（飞），xiǎo（小），hóng（红），chuán（船）. When the main vowel is not written, as in iu and ui, the tone marker is placed over the last vowel: e.g. jiù（就），huí（回）.

Apart from the four fundamental tones, there is also a neutral tone 轻声. No tone marker is used with the neutral tone: e.g. xiānsheng, nǐ hǎo ma?（先生，你好吗? How are you, sir?)

The Apostrophe:

There are two ways of using Hanyu Pinyin to transcribe characters — character by character and transcription into words. When the latter method is used, it sometimes happens that a syllable beginning with *a*, *o*, or *e* follows immediately after another syllable within a word. In such a case, confusion can easily arise as to the boundaries of each syllable. To prevent this confusion, an **apostrophe** "'" 隔音符号 must be used to separate the syllables. For example:

pí'ǎo（皮袄, fur-lined jacket）   cháng'é（嫦娥, Moon Goddess）
Xī'ān（西安, Xi'an [city]）   hǎi'ōu（海鸥, seagull）

4.2 POLYPHONIC CHARACTERS

Most characters have only one pronunciation, while a relatively small number have two or more pronunciations. The phenomenon of one character having different pronunciations is called polyphony 多音字.

A humorous example of polyphony is a curious couplet inscribed at the entrance to the Temple of Mèng Jiāngnǚ 孟姜女 in Shānhǎiguān 山海关, China. The first line of the couplet is: 海水朝朝朝朝朝朝朝落; the second is: 浮云长长长长长长长消. Many visitors to the temple do not understand these lines, which contain two characters repeated over and over again. The key to the puzzle is that the character 朝 has two pronunciations and two meanings, cháo (rising tide) and zhāo (morning, day), while the character 长 also has two pronunciations and two meanings, cháng (long) and zhǎng (grow). Thus, the couplet should be read as follows:

Hǎishuǐ cháo, zhāozhāo cháo, zhāo cháo zhāo luò;

Fúyún zhǎng, chángcháng zhǎng, cháng zhǎng cháng xiāo.
(The sea tide rises; it rises every day; it rises and falls once a day. Floating clouds gather; they always gather; they gather and disperse forever.)

The phenomenon of polyphony is of course not limited to Chinese. In English, for example, "lead" has two pronunciations: [led] the element, and [li:d] to conduct; "wind" also has two pronunciations: [wind] the meteorological phenomenon, and [waind] to wrap around. In Chinese, however, the problem of polyphony is far more serious. For example:

One character with two pronunciations:

行 {
háng ——银行 yínháng (bank), 行列 hángliè, (ranks), 同行 tóngháng (of the same trade)

xíng ——流行 liúxíng (popular), 行走 xíngzǒu (to walk 同行 tong xíng (to walk together)
}

One character with three pronunciations:

強 {
qiáng ——强大 qiángdà (powerful), 强盛 qiángshèng (mighty)

qiǎng ——勉强 miǎnqiǎng (reluctantly), 强辞夺理 qiǎngcí duólǐ (sophistry)

jiàng ——倔强 juéjiàng (stubborn), 强嘴 jiàngzuǐ (reply defiantly)
}

One character with four pronunciations:

差 {
chà ——成绩太差 chéngjì tài chà, (Results are poor.), 差不多 chàbuduō (almost)

chā ——差别 chābié (difference), 差错 chācuò (error) 相差 xiāngchā (differ)

chāi ——出差 chūchāi (away on assignment), 差遣 chāiqiǎn (assign) 差人, chāirén (corvée)

cī ——参差不齐 cēncī bù qí (uneven)
}

Statistics show that of the 11,834 characters listed in the Cí Hǎi dictionary, 2,603, or 22 percent, are polyphonic characters. The most extreme case is the one character 那 with eight pronunciations: nā, nǎ, nà, né, něi, nèi, nuá, nuò. There are about 700 polyphonic characters that actually come into use; of these, about 300 are frequently used — still not an insignificant number. The phenomenon of polyphonic characters constitutes one of the difficulties of learning characters.

Polyphonic characters are divided into two main types: heteronymic and heterophonic.

1) Heteronymic Characters 多音多义字

A heteronymic character is a polyphonic character whose different pronunciations distinguish different meanings, as

151

in the English word "bow" which may be pronounced as [bou], meaning "a weapon for shooting arrows", or as [bau], meaning "to bend at the neck or waist". As used here, the phrase "different meanings" also includes different parts of speech, different ranges of use, etc. For example, the character 弹 has two pronunciations: dàn when used as a noun (子弹 zǐdàn, bullet; 炮弹 pàodàn, shell), and tán when used as a verb (弹琴 tán qín, to play an instrument). Another example: 华 is usually pronounced huá (中华 Zhōnghuá, China; 华丽 huálì, dazzlingly beautiful), but when used as a surname it must be pronounced Huà. Heteronymic characters frequently embrace different meanings, different parts of speech, and different usages. Heteronymic characters are a difficult but important aspect of learning Chinese characters, requiring conscientious study. For reference purposes, some of the most commonly used heteronymic characters are arranged below in alphabetical order.

阿：ā——阿姨、阿哥
　　ē——阿谀

拗：ào——拗口令
　　niù——执拗

把：bǎ——把持，把守
　　bà——刀把儿

耙：bà——耙 (harrow)
　　pá——铁耙

刨：bào——刨床，刨子
　　páo——刨一个坑

背：bèi——背后，背诵
　　bēi——背包，背带

奔：bēn——奔跑，奔走
　　bèn——投奔

辟：bì——复辟
　　pì——开辟，精辟

便：biàn——方便，随便
　　pián——便宜

别：bié——分别，特别，别人
　　biè——别扭

152

泊：bó——停泊，飘泊
　　pō——湖泊

卜：bǔ——卜卦，占卜
　　bo——萝卜

参：cān——参加，参考
　　cēn——参差不齐
　　shēn——人参，海参

藏：cáng——埋藏，矿藏、躲
　　　　　　藏
　　zàng——宝藏，西藏

曾：céng——曾经
　　zēng——曾祖父，姓曾

差：chā——差别，相差
　　chà——差不多，差一点儿
　　chāi——差遣，出差
　　cī——参差不齐

刹：chà——一刹那，古刹
　　shā——刹车

场：cháng——场地，一场雨
　　chǎng——市场，会场，场合

长：cháng——长短，长久
　　zhǎng——生长，团长

朝：cháo——朝代，朝向
　　zhāo——朝夕，朝霞

称：chèn——对称，称心
　　chēng——称呼，称赞

匙：chí——汤匙
　　shi——钥匙

冲：chōng——冲突，冲锋
　　chòng——味儿很冲

臭：chòu——很臭
　　xiù——无色无臭

处：chǔ——处理，处分
　　chù——处所，办事处

畜：chù——牲畜，家畜
　　xù——畜牧，畜养

传：chuán——宣传，传播
　　zhuàn——自传

创：chuāng——创伤
　　chuàng——创造，创立

大：dà——大小，大哥
　　dài——大夫 (doctor)

担：dān——担水，担任
　　dàn——担子，重担

单：dān——简单，单身
　　shàn——姓单
　　chán——单于 (title for
　　　　　　the ruler of the
　　　　　　Huns)

弹：dàn——子弹，弹药
　　tán——弹琴，弹性

当：dāng——担当，应当，当
　　　　　　然
　　dàng——恰当，上当

倒：dǎo——打倒，摔倒
　　dào——倒水，倒退

153

得：dé——得奖，得意

　　děi——你得去(You should go)

　　de——好得很，办得到

的：dí——的确

　　dì——目的

　　de——好的，美丽的

地：dì——土地，地方

　　de——慢慢地走

调：diào——调查，调动，腔调

　　tiáo——调解，调和，调皮

钉：dīng——钉子

　　dìng——钉钉子

都：dōu——都去，都很好

　　dū——首都，都市

斗：dǒu——一斗米，烟斗

　　dòu——斗争，奋斗

度：dù——长度，程度

　　duó——揣度，猜度

囤：dùn——粮囤

　　tún——囤积

恶：è——恶劣，凶恶

　　ě——恶心

　　wù——可恶，厌恶

发：fā——发展，出发

　　fà——头发

分：fēn——分开，分析

　　fèn——水分，身分

缝：féng——缝衣服

　　fèng——门缝，缝隙

干：gān——干柴，干涉

　　gàn——骨干，干工作

更：gēng——五更，更换

　　gèng——更好，更加

供：gōng——提供，供给

　　gòng——供词，口供

勾：gōu——勾销，勾结

　　gòu——勾当

冠：guān——衣冠，花冠

　　guàn——冠军

还：hái——还是，还不来

　　huán——归还，偿还

号：háo——呼号，号叫

　　hào——口号，记号

好：hǎo——好坏，好处

　　hào——爱好，好奇

喝：hē——喝水，喝茶

　　hè——喝彩，喝问

和：hé——和气，和平，你和我

　　hè——和诗，一唱一和

　　huó——和泥，和面

　　huò——和药

荷：hé——荷花

　　hè——负荷，电荷

154

横：héng——横竖，横冲直撞
　　hèng——蛮横，横财
哄：hōng——哄动，哄堂大笑
　　hǒng——哄骗，哄小孩
　　hòng——起哄，一哄而散
划：huá——划船，划火柴
　　huà——划分，计划
会：huì——会面，开会
　　kuài——会计
几：jī——几乎，茶几
　　jǐ——几个，几时
纪：jì——纪念，纪律
　　jǐ——姓纪
夹：jiā——夹子，夹攻
　　jiá——夹袄，夹裤
贾：jiǎ——姓贾
　　gǔ——商贾
假：jiǎ——真假，假如
　　jià——假期，放假
间：jiān——中间，夜间
　　jiàn——间接，间谍
监：jiān——监察，监视
　　jiàn——太监
将：jiāng——将来，将军
　　jiàng——将官，将士
降：jiàng——降落，下降
　　xiáng——投降，降服
教：jiāo——教书，教唱歌

教：jiào——教育，宗教
角：jiǎo——牛角，墙角
　　jué——角色，主角，角斗
觉：jiào——睡觉
　　jué——觉悟，感觉
解：jiě——解剖，解释
　　jiè——解送，押解
　　xiè——姓解
禁：jīn——禁受，不禁
　　jìn——禁止，禁烟
尽：jǐn——尽管，尽快
　　jìn——尽力，无穷无尽
劲：jìn——干劲，劲头
　　jìng——劲敌，刚劲
圈：juàn——猪圈，羊圈
　　quān——圆圈，铁圈
卷：juǎn——卷起袖子，
　　juàn——试卷，卷宗
卡：qiǎ——卡车，卡片
　　kǎ——关卡，卡住了
看：kàn——看见，观看
　　kān——看守，看门
空：kòng——空白，天空
　　kōng　——空隙，闲空
乐：lè——快乐，乐观
　　yuè——音乐，乐器
累：léi——累赘
　　lěi——积累，连累

155

　　　　lèi——我累了

了：liǎo——了解，直截了当

　　　　le——走了，上课了

笼：lóng——竹笼，蒸笼

　　　　lǒng——笼罩，笼络

率：lǜ——效率，百分率

　　　　shuài——率领，坦率

落：luò——降落，落实

　　　　lào——落色，落枕

　　　　là——丢三落四

没：méi——没有，没关系

　　　　mò——沉没，没收

闷：mēn——闷热，闷气

　　　　mèn——愁闷，闷闷不乐

蒙：mēng——蒙骗，蒙蒙亮

　　　　méng——承蒙，蒙蔽，

　　　　měng——蒙古

秘：mì——秘密，秘书

　　　　bì——　秘鲁（国名）

磨：mó——磨刀，磨擦

　　　　mò——石磨，磨坊

模：mó——模范，模糊

　　　　mú——模子，模样

哪：nǎ——哪个，哪里

　　　　na——真难哪！

难：nán——困难，难题

　　　　nàn——灾难，难民

呢：ní——呢子，毛呢

　　　　ne——好不好呢

宁：níng——安宁，宁静

　　　　nìng——宁可，宁愿

炮：páo——炮制

　　　　pào——炮兵，大炮

漂：piāo——漂流，漂泊

　　　　piǎo——漂白

　　　　piào——漂亮

屏：píng——屏风，画屏

　　　　bǐng——屏除，屏弃

仆：pū——前仆后继

　　　　pú——仆从，仆人

铺：pū——铺路，铺设

　　　　pù——床铺，店铺

奇：qí——奇怪，惊奇

　　　　jī——奇数 (odd number)

强：qiáng——强大，强调

　　　　qiǎng——勉强，强词夺理

　　　　jiàng——倔强，强嘴

切：qiē——切开，切西瓜

　　　　qiè——一切，切身

茄：qié——茄子

　　　　jiā——雪茄烟

曲：qū——弯弯曲曲

　　　　qǔ——歌曲，曲调

塞：sāi——堵塞，塞子

　　　　sài——边塞，塞外

　　　　sè——闭塞，阻塞

散：sǎn——松散，散文

　　　sàn——散会，散布，分散

丧：sāng——丧事，吊丧

　　　sàng——丧失，丧命

扇：shàn——扇子，电扇

　　　shān——扇风

少：shǎo——多少，少数

　　　shào——少年，少女

舍：shě——舍弃

　　　shè——宿舍，校舍

什：shén——什么

　　　shí——家什，什锦

省：shěng——省略，节省，四
　　　　　　　川省

　　　xǐng——反省，省悟

盛：shèng——强盛，盛大

　　　chéng——盛饭，盛得下

石：shí——石头，石灰、岩石

　　　dàn———石米

数：shǔ——数钱，数一数二

　　　shù——数目，代数

说：shuō——说话，学说

　　　shuì——游说

伺：sì——伺机，窥伺

　　　cì——伺候

提：tí——提高，提问

　　　dī——提防

挑：tiāo——挑选，挑水

tiǎo——挑战，挑拨

帖：tiē——妥帖，伏伏帖帖

　　　tiě——请帖

　　　tiè——字帖，碑帖

拓：tuò——开拓，拓荒

　　　tà——拓本，拓片

为：wéi——成为，为难

　　　wèi——为了，为什么

系：xì——系列，系统，关系

　　　jì——系鞋带

相：xiāng——相对，相信

　　　xiàng——宰相，真相

校：xiào——学校，校官

　　　jiào——校对，校正

兴：xīng——兴盛，兴奋

　　　xìng——高兴，兴趣

行：xíng——行走，发行，行
　　　　　　　了

　　　háng——行列，银行

要：yào——重要，我要去

　　　yāo——要求，要挟

应：yīng——应该，应允

　　　yìng——应用，答应

晕：yūn——头晕，晕倒

　　　yùn——晕车，月晕

载：zǎi——记载，登载

　　　zài——装载，载重

脏：zāng——肮脏

zàng——心脏

凿：záo——凿子，凿了一口井

zuò——确凿

扎：zhā——扎针，扎实

zhá——挣扎

zā——扎彩，扎起裤腿

炸：zhá——油炸，炸鸡蛋

zhà——爆炸，炸弹

占：zhān——占卜，占卦

zhàn——霸占，占据

着：zháo——着急，着火

zhuó——穿着，着手

zhe——为着，坐着吃饭

折：zhē——折腾

zhé——曲折，折断

shé——折本，折耗

症：zhēng——症结

zhèng——病症，症状

挣：zhēng——挣扎

zhèng——挣脱，挣钱

只：zhǐ——只有，只好，只是

zhī——只身，一只鸡，两只手

中：zhōng——中间，中心，中华，中学

zhòng——中毒，中意，射中

种：zhǒng——种类，品种，各种

zhòng——种田，种花

重：zhòng——重量，轻重，尊重

chóng——重复，重演

转：zhuǎn——转身，转变，转弯

zhuàn——旋转，转动，转圈子

钻：zuān 钻研，钻探

zuàn——钻石，钢钻

作：zuō——作坊

zuò——工作，写作，作风

(Total: 152 characters)

2) Heterophonic Characters　异读字

A heterophonic character is a polyphonic character whose different pronunciations express the same meaning. For example, the character 血 has two pronunciations, xuè and xiě, both of which mean "blood"; the character 指 has three pronunciations, zhǐ, zhī, and zhí, all of which mean "finger".

There are various complicated reasons for the existence of heterophonic characters. A principal reason is the phenomenon of 文白异读 (wén bái yì dú, different literary and vernacular pronunciations), which indicates any character with a literary (written form) pronunciation different from its vernacular(oral) one. To take for example, the character 血 for "blood" just mentioned: xuè is the literary and xiě the vernacular pronunciation. To take another example, the character 薄, meaning "thin", has the literary pronunciation bó and the vernacular pronunciation báo.

The different pronunciations of heterophonic characters express the same meaning, but through long-established habits of use, they cannot be substituted for each other in most situations. These different pronunciations generally appear in different linguistic environments which cannot be casually altered. Some pronunciations, for instance, can only be used as one-syllable words, while others can only be used as morphemes in compound words; some can only appear as morphemes in one group of words, others only in another; etc. A few examples are given below for the readers' examination.

剥：bāo—— only when used as an independent word, as in 剥花生 (bāo huāshēng, to shell peanuts);

bō—— only when used as a bound morpheme, as in 剥削 (bōxuē, to exploit); 剥夺 (bōduó, to deprive).

血：xiě—— only when used as an independent word, as in 流了一点血 (liúle yīdiǎnr xiě, just a little bleeding);

xuè—— only when used as a bound morpheme, as in
血管 (xuèguǎn, blood vessel); 血统 (xuètǒng, blood relationship).

给：gěi—— only when used as an independent word, as in
给你一本书 (gěi nǐ yī běn shū, give you a book);

jǐ—— only when used as a bound morpheme, as in
供给 (gōngjǐ, to supply); 给予 (jǐyǔ, to give).

嚼：jiáo—— in words such as 嚼舌 (jiáoshé, to gossip),
咬文嚼字 (yǎowén-jiáozì, to pay excessive attention to wording);

jué—— only when used in the word 咀嚼 (jǔjué, to chew).

壳：ké—— only in vernacular or spoken words, such as 蛋壳儿 (dànkér, egg shell), etc.

qiào—— only in literary or formal words, such as 地壳 (dìqiào, the earth's crust), etc.

色：sè—— only in literary or formal words, such as 颜色 (yánsè, colors), 色彩 (sècǎi, color), etc.

shǎi—— used only in vernacular or spoken words, such as 掉色 (diào shǎi, to fade), etc.

指：zhī—— only in the word 指甲 (zhījiǎ, finger nail);

zhí—— only in the word 指头 (zhítou, finger);

zhǐ—— in all other words, such as 手指 (shǒuzhǐ, finger), 指导 (zhǐdǎo, to guide), 指挥 (zhǐhuī, to command).

Some heterophonic characters have different pronunciations even in the same linguistic environment. These may be called pure heterophonic characters. Usually these different pronunciations arise from people´ pronouncing the same character differently, or from different pronunciations arising at different periods of time. Of course, among several different pronunciations of one character, some are more generally used and some less so. A few examples are given below:

傍 (close to): pronounced bàng by some, páng by others

胞 (womb): pronounced bāo by some, pāo by others

触 (to contact): pronounced chù by some, zhù by others

逮 (to catch): pronounced dài by some, dí by others

档 (files): pronounced dàng by some, dǎng by others

堤 (dike): pronounced dī by some, tí by others

冈 (ridge): pronounced gāng by some, gǎng by others

鹤 (crane): pronounced hè by some, háo by others

谬 (false): pronounced miù by some, niù by others

披 (to drape): pronounced pī by some, pēi by others

Whereas heteronymic characters have a legitimate existence and must be learned, heterophonic characters merely increase the difficulty and confusion associated with pronunciation. This is a problem of character pronunciation requiring further research and resolution.

4.3 STANDARDIZATION OF CHARACTER PRONUNCIATION

The standard for the pronunciation of modern Chinese characters is modern Chinese Pǔtōnghuà. The divergence and confusion associated with the pronunciation of characters can be nearly eliminated by specifiying a standard Pǔtōnghuà pronunciation for each character. This is what is meant by the standardization of character pronunciation.

The great majority of characters have a fixed, generally agreed upon Pǔtōnghuà pronunciation, so the main object of standardization is the remaining minority—polyphonic characters. Among polyphonic characters, the main objects of standardization are the heterophonic characters, those which express the same meaning with different pronunciations. As discussed above, many heterophonic characters have different pronunciations when used in different words (e.g. 嚼 is pronounced jiáo in 嚼舌 (jiáoshé, to gossip), jué in 咀嚼 (jǔjué, to chew), because of this, the question of heterophonic characters must be linked to the question of heterophonic words 异读词 in order to be resolved.

In 1956 the Chinese Academy of Sciences established a committee to standardize pronunciations for Pǔtōnghuà. Between 1957 and 1962, the committee published in three parts the "First Draft of a List of Authorized Pronunciations for Heterophonic Words in Pǔtōnghuà". This list standardized pronunciations for approximately 2,000 words. In 1963 the three parts were compiled into a "First Draft of the Three Combined Lists of Authorized Pronunciations for Heterophonic Words in Pǔtōnghuà". In 1982 a new committee to standardize pronunciation for Pǔtōnghuà was formed from among members of the State Language Commission, the State Education Commission and the Ministry of Radio and Television. This committee subjected the "First Draft" to examination and revision,

162

and in late 1985 promulgated the "List of Authorized Pronunciations for Heterophonic Words in Pǔtōnghuà" 普通话异读词审音表. This revision was made in accordance with the development of the Pǔtōnghuà phonetic system and had the goal of facilitating Pǔtōnghuà study for the great mass of the people.

The revisers accepted existing realities, adopting generally accepted pronunciations and usages. For example, the character 荨 in 荨麻疹, (nettle rash or urticaria), is assigned the pronunciation qián in dictionaries, but the masses—including doctors—pronounce it xún (possibly a misreading of the character). Because this pronunciation has been generally accepted by people, the committee could only accept the situation and authorize xúnmázhěn as the pronunciation of 荨麻疹. Another example is the character 曝 in 曝光 (exposure); according to dictionaries, it should be pronounced pù, but since it is now universally pronouced bào, the only solution is to follow the masses and authorize the pronunciation bào.

The characters in the "List of Authorized Pronunciations for Heterophonic Words in Pǔtōnghuà" may be divided into two types, according to whether their multiple pronunciations were abolished or retained.

1) Characters Whose Divergent Pronunciations Have Been Abolished

For characters which had no need to be split into multiple pronunciations, one of the more common pronunciations was fixed upon as the standard pronunciation, while the others were abolished. For example, of the three pronunciations zhǐ, zhī and zhí of 指 (finger), zhǐ was taken as the standard pronunciation, and zhī and zhí were abolished. In the List these characters are classified as having unified pronunciation 统读; such characters are to be pronounced the same way uniformly wherever they occur. A total of 588 characters are fixed with unified pronunciations in the List—almost 70 percent of all those that came under the committee's investigation. A few of the most commonly used are listed below.

	Divergent Pronunciations	Unified Pronunciation	Examples of Usage
隘	ài, ǎi	ài	狭隘，关隘
凹	āo, yāo	āo	凹凸不平
傍	bàng, páng	bàng	傍晚，依山傍水
胞	bāo, pāo	bāo	同胞，胞兄
庇	bì, pì	bì	包庇，庇护
波	bō, pō	bō	波浪，水波
埠	bù, fù, fǔ	bù	商埠，外埠
惩	chéng, chěng	chéng	惩罚
弛	chí, shǐ	chí	松弛
触	chù, zhù	chù	接触，触电
呆	dāi, ái（呆板）	dāi	发呆，呆板
档	dàng, dǎng	dàng	档案，归档
堤	dī, tí	dī	堤岸，大堤
缚	fù, fó	fù	束缚
冈	gāng, gǎng	gāng	山冈，景阳冈
鹤	hè, háo	hè	白鹤，仙鹤
壑	hè, huò	hè	沟壑
脊	jǐ, jí	jǐ	脊梁，脊背

164

酵	jiào, xiào	jiào	发酵
俊	jùn, zùn	jùn	英俊，俊俏
括	kuò, guā	kuò	包括，括弧
劣	liè, liě, lè	liè	恶劣
络	luò, lè	luò	联络，脉络
谬	miù, niù	miù	谬论，荒谬
盟	méng, míng（盟誓）	méng	盟国，盟誓
琶	pá, bá	pá	琵琶
披	pī, pēi	pī	披露，披星戴月
坯	pī, pēi	pī	土坯，砖坯
剖	pōu, pāo	pōu	解剖，剖析
洽	qià, qiā	qià	融洽，洽商
嵌	qiàn, kān	qiàn	镶嵌，嵌入
挈	qiè, xié, xiè	qiè	提纲挈领
侵	qīn, qǐn	qīn	侵犯，侵略
雀	què, qiāo, qiǎo	què	麻雀，雀斑，雀盲眼
绕	rào, rǎo（缠绕）	rào	绕弯儿，缠绕，围绕
森	sēn, shēn	sēn	森林，阴森
硕	shuò, suò	shuò	硕果，丰硕
溪	xī, qī	xī	小溪，溪流
淆	xiáo, yáo	xiáo	混淆，淆惑
挟	xié, xiá	xié	要挟，挟持
械	xiè, jiè	xiè	机械，器械
谑	xuè, nüè	xuè	戏谑，谐谑
寻	xún, xín（寻思）	xún	寻找，寻思，寻开心

崖	yá, ái	yá	山崖，悬崖
杳	yǎo, miǎo	yǎo	杳无音信
跃	yuè, yào	yuè	跃进，飞跃
暂	zàn, zhàn	zàn	暂时，短暂
质	zhì, zhí	zhì	本质，质量
指	zhǐ, zhī（指甲）, zhí（指头）	zhǐ	手指，指导，指甲，指头
诌	zhōu, zōu	zhōu	胡诌，瞎诌
骤	zhòu, zòu	zhòu	步骤，骤然
逐	zhú, zhù	zhú	驱逐，逐渐

2) Characters Whose Divergent Pronunciations Have Been Retained

Heterophonic characters (including a number of heterony-mic characters) of which it is generally accepted that they must retain different pronunciations in different linguistic environments are clearly laid out in the List. Some commonly used characters are given below as examples (文 indicates a literary pronunciation; 语 a vernacular pronunciation):

剥：bō（文）剥削	bāo（语）剥花生
臂：bì 手臂，臂膀	bei 胳膊
薄：bó（文）薄弱，稀薄	báo（语）纸很薄
澄：chéng（文）澄清	dèng（语）把水澄清了
答：dá 报答，答复	dā 答应，答理
逮：dài（文）逮捕	dǎi（语）逮蚊子
坊：fāng 牌坊	fáng 粉坊，磨坊，碾坊
给：jǐ（文）供给，补给	gěi（语）给他一本书
骨：gǔ 骨头，骨骼	gū 骨碌，骨朵儿

虹：hóng（文）彩虹，虹吸　　　　jiàng（语）天上出虹了

壳：qiào（文）地壳，甲壳　　　　ké（语）蛋壳儿，脑壳

溃：kuì 溃烂，崩溃　　　　　　　huì 溃浓（only used in
　　　　　　　　　　　　　　　　　　　　this word）

量：liàng 量力，量体裁衣　　　　liáng 打量，商量

露：lù 揭露，露天　　　　　　　　lòu 露面，露马脚

绿：lù 绿林，鸭绿江　　　　　　　lù 绿色，绿化，绿油油

片：piàn 唱片，相片　　　　　　　piān 纸片儿，画片儿，
　　　　　　　　　　　　　　　　　　　　唱片儿

色：sè（文）颜色，色彩　　　　　shǎi（语）掉色，退色

杉：shān（文）紫杉，水杉　　　　shā（语）杉木，杉篙

似：sì 相似，近似，似乎　　　　　shì 似的（only used in
　　　　　　　　　　　　　　　　　　　　this word）

遂：suì 遂心，不遂　　　　　　　　suí 半身不遂（only used
　　　　　　　　　　　　　　　　　　　　in this word）

尾：wěi 尾巴，末尾　　　　　　　　yǐ 马尾巴（only used in
　　　　　　　　　　　　　　　　　　　　this word）

吓：hè（文）恐吓，威吓　　　　　xià（语）吓唬，吓了一
　　　　　　　　　　　　　　　　　　　　跳

巷：xiàng 小巷，街巷　　　　　　　hàng 巷道（only used in
　　　　　　　　　　　　　　　　　　　　this word）

削：xuē（文）剥削，削减　　　　　xiāo（语）切削，削铅笔

血：xuè（文）贫血，呕心沥血　　　xiě（语）流了点儿血

轧：yà 倾轧，轧棉花　　　　　　　zhá 轧钢，轧辊

择：zé 选择，不择手段　　　　　　zhái 择菜，择不开

4.4 MISREADING OF CHARACTERS

It is easy not only to write characters incorrectly, but often also to read them incorrectly. There are three main situations in which characters are apt to be misread:

1) Polyphonic characters. If a character has several pronunciations, it is easy to misread the less common for the more common pronunciation. For example, the character 度 has two pronunciations: dù is used as a noun, as in 长度 (chángdù, length), 温度 (wēndù, temperature), and 程度 (chéngdù, degree); duó is used as a verb, as in 揣度 (chuǎiduó, to conjecture), 猜度 (cāiduó, to surmise). Dù is more commonly used than duó, so that it is easy to misread 揣度 as chuǎidù and 猜度 as cāidù. We will say no more here about polyphonic characters, as they have already been discussed in the preceding two sections.

2) Characters which are similar in form. When two characters are very similar in form, it is easy to misread the less common for the more common one: e.g. to read 祟 (suì, evil spirit) as 崇 (chóng, to esteem), the more commonly used of the two, or to read 侯 (hóu, marquis) as the more common 候 (hòu, await). With regard to the forms of characters, see Chapter 3.

3) Characters with misleading phonetic components. Over 80 percent of all characters are of the semantic-phonetic or picto-phonetic type. The phonetic component of this type of character is used to show the character's pronunciation, e.g.:

胡 hú, phonetic component ——→湖, 糊, 瑚, 葫, 蝴, 猢, 醐, 鹕 (all pronounced hú)

皇 huáng, phonetic component ——→湟, 惶, 煌, 遑, 蝗, 篁, 隍, 徨, 凰 (all pronounced huáng)

If the phonetic components of all picto-phonetic characters were as accurate in indicating pronunciation as 胡 and 皇, then the problem of pronunciation would be solved for the great majority of characters. Unfortunately, just the opposite is the case; continuous changes in the language and the writing system have made the vast majority of phonetic components ineffective in indicating pronunciation. For example:

各 gè phonetic component ⟶ 格，骼，胳，袼，铬，阁 ge

客，恪 ke
貉 he
烙，酪，络 lao
咯 ka
洛，珞，骆，硌，雒，络， 烙， luo
路，赂，辂 lu
略 lüe

If one phonetic component can indicate so many proununciations—ge, ke, he, lao, ka, luo, lu, and lüe, it may be said that it has altogether lost its usefulness in indicating pronunciation. Moreover, as some phonetic components accurately indicate pronunciation while others do not, the inconsistency of the system makes mispronunciation even more likely. For example, it is correct to pronounce 锭 and 碇 according to their phonetic component 定 dìng, but 淀 and 靛 are pronounced diàn, and 绽 is pronounced zhàn. If one believes that the phonetic 定 dìng is an accurate indicator of pronunciation, then one is bound to mispronounce 淀，靛 and 绽. To take an example of the opposite case: 帝 dì in the common characters 啼 and 蹄 (both pronounced tí) does not accurately give the pronunciation. When one comes across the seldom used character

缔 (dì; here the phonetic component is accurate), however, through the influence of 啼 and 蹄, one will tend to mispronounce 缔 as tí. Misleading phonetic components such as these are frequently the basis of jokes about the misreading of characters.

Of the three situations in which characters are liable to be misread, this drawing of false analogies from the phonetic component is the most common cause of mispronunciation—though the other two causes are by no means insignificant. For general reference, examples of the characters most commonly mispronounced due to false analogy from the phonetic component are given below.

Correct Pronunciation		Incorrect Pronunciation	Examples of Usage
皑	ái	kǎi （凯）	皑皑白雪
隘	ài	yì （益）	关隘，狭隘
愎	bì	fù （复）	刚愎自用
濒	bīn	pín （频）	濒于破产
哺	bǔ	fǔ（甫），pǔ（浦）	哺乳动物
阐	chǎn	chán, shàn （禅）	阐述，阐明
谄	chǎn	xiàn （陷）	谄媚
伥	chāng	zhàng （帐）	为虎作伥
掣	chè	zhì （制）	掣肘，风驰电掣
嗔	chēn	zhēn （真）	嗔怪
瞠	chēng	táng （堂）	瞠目结舌
骋	chěng	pìn （聘）	驰骋
笞	chī	tái （台）	鞭笞
啻	chì	dì （帝）	不啻如此
黜	chù	zhuō （拙）	罢黜

170

绌	chù	zhuō（拙）	相形见绌
蹴	cù	jiù（就）	一蹴而就
眈	dān	chén（忱）	虎视眈眈
涤	dí	tiáo（条）	洗涤
淀	diàn	dìng（定）	沉淀，淀粉
玷	diàn	zhān（沾）	玷污
恫	dòng	tóng（同）	恫吓
咄	duō	zhuō（拙）	咄咄逼人，咄咄怪事
踱	duó	dù（度）	踱来踱去
蜚	fēi	péi（裴）	流言蜚语
沸	fèi	fó（佛），fú（弗)	沸腾
讣	fù	bǔ（卜），pū（扑.)	讣告
觥	gōng	guāng（光），	觥筹交错
梏	gù	gào（告），hào（浩)	桎梏
犷	guǎng	kuàng 矿	粗犷
刽	guì	kuài（会）	刽子手
聒	guō	guā（刮）	聒噪
皓	hào	gào（告）	皓月
涸	hé	gù（固）	干涸
囫	hú	wù（勿）	囫囵吞枣
怙	hù	gǔ（古）	怙恶不悛 (quān)
徊	huái	huí（回）	徘徊
讳	huì	wěi（伟）	忌讳，直言不讳
肓	huāng	máng（盲、忙)	病入膏肓
畸	jī	qí（奇）	畸形
汲	jí	xī（吸）	汲取
菅	jiān	guǎn（管）	草菅人命

歼	jiān	qiān（千）	歼灭
酵	jiào	xiào（孝）	发酵
厩	jiù	jì（既）	马厩
狙	jū	zǔ（阻）	狙击
沮	jǔ	zǔ（阻）	沮丧
谲	jué	jú（橘）	谲诈
忾	kài	qì（气）	同仇敌忾
瞰	kàn	gǎn（敢）	鸟瞰
犒	kào	gǎo（搞）	犒赏
恪	kè	gè(各), luò(洛)	恪守，恪遵
脍	kuài	huì（会）	脍炙 (zhì) 人口
喟	kuì	wèi（胃）	喟然长叹
廓	kuò	guō（郭）	轮廓
岚	lán	fēng（风）	山岚
赂	lù	luò（洛）	贿赂 (huìlù)
缕	lǚ	lǒu（搂）	千丝万缕
赁	lìn	rèn（任）	租赁
裸	luǒ	kē(棵), guǒ(果)	裸体
霾	mái	lí（狸）	阴霾
袂	mèi	jué(决), quē(缺)	分袂（分别）
懑	mèn	mǎn（满）	愤懑
娩	miǎn	wǎn（挽）	分娩
挠	náo	ráo（饶）	百折不挠
匿	nì	ruò（若）	匿名信
酿	niàng	ràng（让）	酝酿 (yùnniàng)
懦	nuò	rú（儒）	懦夫，懦弱
湃	pài	bài（拜）	澎湃
庖	páo	bāo（包）	庖厨

172

畔	pàn	bàn（半）	河畔，湖畔
抨	pēng	píng（平）	抨击
毗	pí	bǐ（比）	毗邻，毗连
骈	pián	bìng（并）	骈体文，骈肢
瀑	pù	bào（暴）	瀑布
畦	qí	guī（圭）	菜畦
憩	qì	xī（息）	少憩
悭	qiān	jiān（坚）	悭吝
堑	qiàn	zhǎn（斩）	天堑
倩	qiàn	qīng（青）	倩影
惬	qiè	xiá（侠），jiá（颊）	惬意
沁	qìn	xīn（心）	沁人心脾
龋	qǔ	yǔ（禹）	龋齿
觑	qù	xū（虚）	面面相觑
悛	quān	jùn（俊）	怙（hù）恶不悛
茸	róng	ěr（耳）	鹿茸，毛茸茸的
阮	ruǎn	yuán（元）	姓阮
腮	sāi	sī（思）	腮帮子
缫	sāo	cháo（巢），	缫丝
赡	shàn	zhān（瞻）	赡养父母
摄	shè	niè（聂）	摄影
枢	shū	qū（区）	中枢，枢纽
娠	shēn	zhèn（振）	妊娠（rènshēn）
墅	shù	yě（野）	别墅
涮	shuàn	shuā（刷）	涮羊肉
吮	shǔn	yǔn（允）	吮吸
怂	sǒng	cóng（从）	怂恿

173

溯	sù	shuò （朔）	追溯，溯流而上
塑	sù	shuò （朔）	塑造，塑料
獭	tǎ	lài （赖），lǎn（懒）	水獭
挞	tà	dá （达）	鞭挞
恬	tián	guā （刮）	恬静，恬不知耻
迢	tiáo	zhāo （招）	千里迢迢
彤	tóng	dān （丹）	红彤彤
湍	tuān	chuǎn （喘）	湍急，湍流
臀	tún	diàn （殿）	臀部
唾	tuò	chuí （垂）	唾弃，唾沫
娲	wā	wō （窝）	女娲
韪	wěi	huì （讳）	冒天下之大不韪
斡	wò	dǒu （斗）	斡旋
葸	xǐ	sī （思）	畏葸不前
膝	xī	qī （漆）	膝盖，屈膝
呷	xiā	jiǎ （甲）	呷茶
峡	xiá	jiá （夹）	海峡
黠	xiá	jí （吉），jié (洁)	狡黠
罅	xià	hū （乎）	罅隙
纤	xiān	qiān （千）	纤维
涎	xián	yán （延）	垂涎三尺
骁	xiāo	ráo （饶）	骁勇
楔	xiē	qì （契）	楔子
偕	xié	jiē （皆）	偕同
屑	xiè	xiāo （肖）	琐屑，不屑
栩	xǔ	yǔ （羽）	栩栩如生
酗	xù	xiōng （凶）	酗酒

绚	xuàn	xún （旬）	绚烂
揠	yà	yàn.（堰）	揠苗助长
肴	yáo	xiáo （淆）	酒肴
谒	yè	jiē （揭）	谒见，拜谒
沂	yí	qí （祈）	沂蒙山（山东省）
诣	yì	zhǐ （旨）	造诣，苦心孤诣
屹	yì	qǐ （气）	巍然屹立
映	yìng	yāng （央）	反映，放映
莠	yǒu	xiù （秀）	良莠不齐
隅	yú	ǒu （偶）	墙隅，向隅而泣
峪	yù	gǔ （谷）	嘉峪关（甘肃省）
伛	yǔ	ōu （讴）	伛偻 (lǚ)
垣	yuán	héng （恒），	城垣，断垣残壁
苑	yuàn	wǎn （宛）	文苑，艺苑
愠	yùn	wēn （温）	面有愠色
蕴	yùn	wēn （温），	蕴藏
绽	zhàn	dìng （定）	破绽，皮开肉绽
湛	zhàn	shèn （甚）	精湛，湛江（广东省）
砧	zhēn	zhān （沾）	砧板
箴	zhēn	xián （咸），	箴言
		jiān （缄）	
圳	zhèn	chuān （川）	深圳（广东省）
拯	zhěng	chéng （丞）	拯救
帧	zhèng	zhēn （贞）	装帧
峙	zhì	shì （恃），	对峙
		chí （持）	
滞	zhì	dài （带）	滞留，停滞

栉	zhì	jié（节）	鳞次栉比，栉风沐雨
瞩	zhǔ	shǔ（属）	瞩目，高瞻远瞩
幢	zhuàng	tóng（童）	一幢楼房
惴	zhuì	chuǎi（揣）	惴惴不安
谆	zhūn	chún（淳），dūn（敦）	谆谆教导
灼	zhuó	sháo（勺），shuò（妁）	灼热，真知灼见
滓	zǐ	zǎi（宰）	渣滓
梓	zǐ	xīn（辛）	梓里，吴敬梓（人名）
眦	zì	cǐ（此）	目眦尽裂

There is also a small number of characters which, despite their appearance, are not picto-phonetic characters at all, but associative compound characters. If one tries to use the semantic-phonetic method and pronounce them by their seeming "phonetic" component, the result will inevitably be a mispronunciation. For example:

陟 (zhì, to ascend or mount) must not be pronounced like its component 步 (bù, step) nor like 涉 (shè, to wade) which is also an associative compound character;

劓 (yì, a form of punishment in which the nose is cut off) must not be pronounced like its component 鼻 (bí, nose);

筮 (shì, to use milfoil in divination) must not be pronounced like its component 巫 (wū, shaman).

5. THE SEMANTICS OF CHINESE CHARACTERS

Every Chinese character has form, pronunciation, and meaning, which we may call the three essential elements of a Chinese character. Complicated though the forms may be, they are distinguishable. Similarly, complex as the pronunciations may be (especially in the case of characters which have more than one reading), nevertheless they are still identifiable by sound as well. But the meanings of the characters are not immediately visible or audible, but are rather intertwined with the shapes and pronunciations of the characters, so they must be carefully studied and distinguished.

In ancient times, almost all Chinese characters represented independent, monosyllabic words. Nowadays, about half of contemporary Chinese characters can be used as independent, monosyllabic words, while the other half only represent bound morphemes which can no longer occur as independent words. But whether they represent morphemes or words, each morpheme and therefore each character which represents it has meaning. The meaning of words or morphemes, and the characters which represent them, include three types of meaning: (1) conceptual meaning 概念意义, which refers to the expression of the meanings of certain things, actions, and conditions; (2) grammatical meaning 语法意义, such as the functions of parts of speech (noun, verb, adjective, etc.) which a word or morpheme may perform; (3) rhetorical meaning 修辞意义, which includes all sorts of connotations, emotional coloring, stylistic flavor, etc. in addition to the narrow denotative meaning. In general, when we speak of the meaning of a word or character, we usually refer to its basic conceptual or denotative meaning, to which the other meanings are appended.

In learning a Chinese character, it is essential to master its meaning or meanings in different contexts. In terms of reading, we cannot fully comprehend a piece of writing if we do not understand the meanings of some of the characters in it, and sometimes we may even misinterpret the meaning. To give an example if the meaning of the character 亡 (wáng) in the fixed four-character proverbial expression 亡羊补牢 (wáng yáng bǔ láo) is not correctly understood as "to lose", rather than in its usual sense of "to die", then one cannot correctly understand the true meaning of the entire phrase, which is "to mend the fold after the sheep is lost" (with the implication that it is still not too late to prevent further losses), rather than that the sheep has died. Conversely, in writing, if one does not distinguish carefully between the exact meanings of certain Chinese characters (especially characters which represent homophones in the spoken language), then one may mistakenly write the wrong character, often with a ridiculous effect. Thus, for example, some people— instead of writing biānji (editor) correctly with the characters

编辑 — may mistakenly write the second character as 缉 (jí, arrest), or — instead of asking to be 上调 (shàng diào, transfered to a higher position), — may request to 上吊 (shàng diào, hang oneself), both with ridiculous results.

5.1 THE SEMANTIC EVOLUTION OF CHINESE CHARACTERS

As the Chinese language and society have evolved over the centuries, so Chinese characters have constantly changed in their forms, pronunciations, and meanings. Let us examine these changes under the following three headings.

1) Original Meaning and Present Day Meaning

The original meaning 本义 of a character is its meaning at the time when it was coined. The present day meaning 今义 is the meaning of a character in modern Chinese. The commonly accepted source for original meanings is the Shuō Wén Jiě Zì by Xǔ Shèn of the Eastern Hàn Dynasty (see 8.4), although there are in fact some characters that have been shown to be incorrectly interpreted in that work in the light of later discoveries of oracle bone inscriptions and bronze inscriptions.

For many Chinese characters, their original and present day meanings are quite distant from each other, and some are completely different. For example, the original meaning of the character 走 (zǒu, now "to walk" or "depart") was "to run," as may be seen in a line of poetry written by the famous Táng Dynasty poet Dù Fǔ, in his poem entitled 《石壕吏》 (Shí Hào Lì, An Official at Shí Háo Village). The line is:

老翁逾墙走 (Lǎo wēng yú qiáng zǒu), which means "the old man ran away over the wall". Similarly, the original meaning of the character 汤 (tāng) was "hot (or warm) water", rather than its present day meaning of "soup". The original meaning of the character 涕 (tì) was "tears" and not "mucus", as it is today. It is often useful to learn these older meanings because, although they no longer have their older senses in present day language, nevertheless they may preserve some of their older meanings in compounds, or in fixed literary expressions which remain as set phrases or idioms in the contemporary language. Without an understanding of the original meanings of these characters, we cannot correctly comprehend such idioms and phrases, and may in fact distort them. Let us look at a couple of examples:

赴汤蹈火 (fù tāng dǎo huǒ, literally "Going into boiling water and dancing in fire"), means "fearing no difficulties". If the character 汤 (tāng, hot water) is taken in its modern meaning of "soup", the phrase becomes ridiculous.

痛哭流涕 (tòng kū liú tì), means "to weep bitterly" or "cry one's heart out" (literally "painfully crying with flowing tears"). If the original meaning of the character 涕 "tears" is misunderstood in its modern sense of "mucus", then the image becomes less attractive (although it is easy to see how the semantic shift could have occurred over the years).

Because the original meaning of a character is defined as its meaning at the time of its coinage, often the easiest way to understand its original sense is in conjunction with the method of coinage of that character. Here are a few examples:

止 (zhǐ): The original meaning of this picto-graphic character is (as it appears in oracle bone inscriptions in the shape of ⼦ a "foot". Now that meaning has become obsolete and the present day meaning is "to stop".

行 (xíng): The original meaning of this character was "road". In the oracle bone inscriptions and bronze inscriptions it appears as a picto-graphic character 卝 looking like an intersection of two roads. Nowadays the meaning has changed from the noun "road" to the verb "walk".

干 (gān): This originally appears to have been some sort of forked weapon, as it was written in the oracle bone inscriptions as Ƴ, another pictographic character. Although no longer used in this sense, the original meaning of this character may be seen in the set phrase 大动干戈 (dà dòng gān gē, to resort to arms).

兵 (bīng, soldier): The original meaning of this character was "weapon". In the oracle bone inscriptions it was written as 𠬝...showing two hands holding a huge axe, an "associative" character (see 1.2). Although the character no longer has this meaning when used independently, the meaning of "weapon" may still be seen in such set phrases as 短兵相接 (duǎn bīng xiāng jiē, hand to hand combat) and 秣马厉兵 (mò mǎ lì bīng, preparing for war).

为 (爲) (wéi): The original meaning of this character was to "work while leading an elephant (by hand)", as may be seen in its ancient complex from 爲, originally written as ...象... with a hand above and an elephant with its long nose and tusks below.

Now its meaning has been broadened into the more general meaning of "work" or "do".

治(zhì) : The original meaning of this character was "to control rivers or water", an important concept in feudal agricultural China. Looking at it today as a picto-phonetic character (see 1.2) it is not obvious why this character, now pronounced zhì and meaning simply "control", should have a "water" radical, unless we understand its historical background.

理 (lǐ): The original meaning of this character was "working with jade". As a picto-phonetic character, while it is still clear why it has the phonetic component lǐ, it is not clear why a character having its present day meaning of "arrange, manage, order" should have a "jade" (玉) semantic radical, unless its original meaning is known.

There are two types of evolution in the meaning of a character. In the one case, the original meaning has been completely replaced by the present day meaning, as in the cases of 止, 行, and 为 just noted. We may describe this kind of change as resembling the evolution of a butterfly from a caterpillar, in which the former completely replaces the latter. The other case is that of the simultaneous co-existance of both the new and old meanings, as in the case of 兵 noted just above. This second type may be said to resemble a mother giving birth to a child, which continues to coexist with her. It is often the case, however, that the present meaning becomes the dominant sense of the character and the original sense is not used as much anymore.

182

2) Basic Meanings and Extended Meanings

The basic meaning基本义of a Chinese character is its primary and most frequently used meaning. Note that the terms "basic meaning" and "original meaning" are not necessarily synonymous. For some characters such as 山 (shān, mountain) and 手 (shǒu, hand) the original meaning and the basic meaning are still the same. But for others, such as the character 兵 (bīng) just discussed, the original meaning (weapon) has been replaced by a new basic meaning (soldier).

An extended meaning 引申义 is a meaning that has developed and expanded beyond the basic one. For example, the *original* meaning of the character 绝 (jué) is that of a "thread or wire broken into two pieces". This is why it has a "silk thread" radical (系). Its present-day *basic* meaning is "cut off" or "sever". The *extended* meanings which have evolved from its original and basic meanings include:

    a) "exhausted, used up, finished", as in 弹尽粮绝 (dàn jìn liáng jué, have run out of ammunition and provisions).

    b) "desperate, hopeless", as in 绝境 (jué jìng, "hopeless situation).

    c) "unique, superb, matchless", as in 绝技 (jué jì, unique and incomparable skill).

    d) "extremely, most", as in 绝妙 (jué miào, excellent, extremely clever), 绝密 (jué mì, extremely confidential).

Another example of an extended meaning is that of the character 浅 (qiǎn), whose original meaning, as may be seen from its semantic "water" (氵) radical, is "shallow water". At present its basic meaning is like the English word "shallow", in which it can be used literally (of water, etc.) or abstractly (as of thought). In this way have arisen its extended meanings, such as "simple, plain", as in 浅近 (qiǎnjìn, easy to understand); "superficial", as in 浅见 (qiǎnjiàn, superficial view); "not intimate", as in 交情很浅 (jiāoqíng hěn qiǎn, not on familiar terms); "light in color", as in 浅黄 (qiǎn huáng, light yellow); "not long in time", as in 相处的日子还浅 (xiāng chǔ de rìzi hái qiǎn, time together not long); etc.

Some extended meanings are based on rhetorical devices such as simile 比喻 and borrowed 借代 meaning. For example, the character 射 (shè) is an associative character whose original meaning referred to 射箭 (shè jiàn), "shooting arrows" or "archery". Based on this original meaning, similar "shooting" actions are now expressed by the word 射, as in 机枪扫射 (jī-qiāng sǎoshè, machine gun strafing); 射球门 (shè qiúmén, to score a [field] goal); 泉水喷射 (quánshuǐ pēnshè, a fountain spurting water); 阳光四射 (yángguāng sì shè, sunlight cast in all directions); 电波发射 (diànbō fāshè, transmit electric waves); etc., and thus the meaning of the character 射 has been extended rhetorically.

As an example of "borrowed meaning", the character 鳞 (lín) originally refers specifically to the scales of fish. But as writers such as Fàn Zhòngyān 范仲淹 have used that character in expressions such as 锦鳞游泳 (jǐn lín yóu yǒng), in which 锦鳞 (jǐn lín) — which literally means "colorful scales" — is a metaphor for "pretty fish", the meaning of the character has been

184

"borrowed" through the rhetorical device of metonymy and thus has had its meaning extended.

Such extensions of meaning may not only change the meaning of a character, but may also change its part of speech as well. For instance, the original meaning of the character 将 (jiàng) is "to lead". But in the sense of "general" or "high-ranking military officer", as in 大将 (dàjiàng) or 将官 (jiàngguān), both of which are nouns, the character 将 changes its part of speech.

As another example, both the original and basic meaning of the character 白 (bái) is "white", an adjective, as in 白菜 (báicài, Chinese cabbage), etc. But in many of its extended meanings of "clear, pure, plain, in vain", etc. it becomes more of an adverbial modifier: e.g., 明白 (míngbái, be clear about, understand); 空白 (kòng bái, blank); 交白卷 (jiāo báijuàn, hand in a blank examination paper); 白开水 (báikāishuǐ, plain hot water); 白费力气 (bái fèi lìqì, to makes efforts in vain); 白忙（乎）(bái máng [hū], be pointlessly busy); 白吃 (bái chī, to eat without paying), etc.

A character which has only one basic meaning may be called a monosemic character 单义字, while one which has more than one meaning may be termed a polysemic character 多义字. One should pay particular attention to such polysemic characters when learning Chinese and using Chinese dictionaries.

3) The Four Types of Semantic Evolution

We may say that there are four ways in which the meanings of Chinese characters have evolved over time: preservation, expansion, reduction, and transference of meaning. Let us examine each of these.

a)   Preservation means that the original meaning of a character has remained basically unchanged and is still its basic meaning today. Such characters are almost always drawn from the "root vocabulary" or "root words" of the Chinese language, for example, 人 (rén, human being); 山 (shān, mountain); 水 (shuǐ, water); 树 (shù, tree), 手 (shǒu, hand); 马 (mǎ, horse); 牛 (niú, cow/ox); 羊 (yáng, sheep); 鸡 (jī, chicken); etc.

b)   Expansion refers to the enlargement of the meaning of a character, usually from denoting a specific thing, action, or condition, to denoting a more generalized set of such things, actions, or states. This is an important mechanism for the evolution of meanings in Chinese characters. For example:

-江   Originally referring only to the Yangtze River 长江 (Cháng Jiāng), this character now refers to all large rivers in general.

-河   Originally referring only to the Yellow River 黄河 (Huáng Hé), it now means "rivers" in general.

-琴   Originally referring to one specific type of ancient Chinese zither with fifty strings, 琴 (qín) now may refer to any stringed instrument, as well as pianos 钢琴 (gāngqín), organs 风琴 (fēngqín), harmonicas 口琴 (kǒuqín), etc.

-皮   Originally referring only to animal skins or furs, 皮(pí) now refers to any kind of "skin", including tree bark 树皮 (shùpí), dried soybean milk skin 豆腐皮 (dòufupí), buckwheat husks 荞麦皮 (qiáomàipí), etc.

-牙   Originally the molar teeth at the back of the mouth,

today 牙 (yá) refers to any type of tooth, or anything relating to teeth, dentistry, etc.

-脸 The original meaning of 脸 (liǎn) referred to facial cheeks only, while today it refers to the entire face. Therefore in ancient times people had two 脸, while today people have only one.

-种 The original meaning of the character was "kinds of grain", which explains why it has a semantic "grain" radical 禾. Nowadays, when read zhǒng, it simply means "kind(s)", "type(s)", or "variety" of anything in general.

- 类 The original meaning of 类 (lèi) was "category of animals", which explains the "dog" 犬 component in its old complex form 類. Now it simply means "kind", "type", or "sort" of anything.

- 灾 Originally referring only to naturally occurring fire disasters, (hence its "fire" 火 component), now 灾 (zāi) refers to any type of natural disaster or calamity, including 水灾 (shuǐzāi, floods), 旱灾 (hànzāi, droughts), and 虫灾 (chóngzāi, insect plagues).

- 双 The original meaning of this character was "two birds", as may be seen from its original complex form 雙. Nowadays 双 shuāng may refer to anything in a "pair", such as 一双鞋 (yī shuāng xié), a pair of shoes, 一双手套 (yī shuāng shǒutào, a pair of gloves), 一双筷子 (yī shuāng kuàizi, a pair of chopsticks), etc.

- 洗 The original meaning of 洗 (xǐ) referred specifically

187

to "washing feet" only, but now it has become the general word for any type of washing, e.g. 洗脸 (xǐ liǎn, to wash one's face), 洗衣服 (xǐ yīfu, to wash clothing), etc.

- 取 The original meaning of 取 (qǔ) referred particularly to "cutting off the ears of captives". Now it simply means to "attain" or "acquire" in general, as in 取款 (qǔ kuǎn, to withdraw funds), 取名 (qǔ míng, to adopt a name), etc.

c) Narrowing of meaning is the opposite of expansion of meaning. There are only a few examples of Chinese characters narrowing their meanings. For example:

- 瓦 wǎ originally referred to all types of household utensils made from baked clay, but now it refers only to roof tiles.

- 坟 fén originally referred to any large earthen mound, but today its meaning is limited to that of "graves".

- 谷 gǔ originally referred to all sorts of grains in general, but now it generally refers to rice.

- 禽 qín was originally the collective term for all animals, but now it refers to birds only.

- 子 zǐ originally included both sons and daughters, but now refers only to sons.

- 殿 diàn originally referred to all tall buildings, but now refers only to palaces or Buddhist halls.

- 枚 méi formerly was a measure word for a wide range of things, e.g., 鸟一枚 (niǎo yī méi, one bird), 鲍鱼百枚 (fùyú bǎi méi, a hundred fishes); 竹简一枚

(zhújiǎn yī méi, one bamboo slip), 剑二枚 (jiàn èr méi, two swords), etc. Now it is rarely used and is limited only to small items such as 一枚奖章 (yī méi jiǎngzhāng, one medal).

- 臭 chòu originally included all odors, but now refers specifically only to unpleasant ones.

d) Transference refers to replacement of the original meaning of a character by a different one. The original meaning in some cases is completely lost, or else is preserved only in a few compound words or set literary phrases or idioms. For example:

- 涕 Although the present meaning of 涕 (tì) refers to nasal mucus, its original meaning was "tears", as may still be seen in the set phrases 痛哭流涕 (tòngkū liú tì, painfully whipped to tears) and 感激涕零 (gǎn-jī tì líng, moved to tears by gratitude).

- 闻 The old meaning of this character 闻 (wén, to hear) may be seen in its inclusion of the "ear" component 耳, although it is now generally used in the sense of "to smell". Yet the older meaning still survives in a word such as 新闻 (xīnwén, news), or a set phrase such as 耳闻目睹 (ěr wén mù dǔ, what one sees and hears).

- 脚 The original meaning referred to the calf or shank of the leg, but now 脚 (jiǎo) refers primarily to the foot, as in 脚印 (jiǎoyìn, foot print), etc.

- 权 quán originally referred to the sliding weight of steel-yard scales, although it now occurs primarily in such

189

words as 权利 (quánlì, right) or 权力 (quánlì, power). The older meaning of this character may still be seen in an expression such as 权衡利弊 (quánhéng lì-bì, weigh and balance the advantages and disadvantages), wherein 权 (quán) refers to the sliding weight of a steelyard, and 衡 (héng) refers to the steelyard beam itself.

- 玄 The old meaning of this character was "black-colored", as in 玄狐 (xuán hú, black fox), 玄鸟 (xuán niǎo, black bird), etc., but now it means "profound" or "abstruse", as in 玄妙 (xuánmiào, mysterious, abstruse).

- 穷 Although 穷 (qióng) today means "poor", its original meaning was the "extreme end", or "to search to the root of the matter", as may be seen in the set phases 山穷水尽 (shān qióng shuǐ jìn, at the end of one's tether), and 穷追猛打 (qióng zhuī měng dǎ, vigorously pursue and fiercely attack).

- 信 The original meaning of the character 信 (xìn) was "messenger", i.e., the one who delivers a letter, but later its meaning was transferred to the letters themselves.

5.2 THE RELATIONSHIP BETWEEN THE MEANINGS OF INDIVIDUAL CHARACTERS AND THE MEANINGS OF WORDS

In modern spoken and written Putonghua, apart from a minority of Chinese characters which are used to represent monosyllabic words (i.e. words of only one syllable which can occur independently), most Chinese characters are now used to represent morphemes in polysyllabic "compound" words such as 知道 (zhīdào, to know). A compound word usually consists of two, three, or four syllables, and each syllable is represented by one Chinese character. While it may be true in the case of the monosyllabic words that to know the meaning of the character is to know the meaning of the word, this is not always the case with the large majority of polysyllabic words. Thus Chinese delight in telling the story of the foreign missionary who came to China having assiduously memorized the forms, pronunciations, and meanings of hundreds of independent Chinese characters out of a dictionary, and proceeded to interpret Chinese texts character by character, much to the amusement of his Chinese listeners. Thus his interpretation of the word 先生 (xiānsheng, Mister, teacher) based on the independent meanings of the two characters was "born first"! Similarly his interpretation of 东家 (dōngjia, landlord) was "the eastern family", and of 帝国主义 (dìguózhǔyì, imperialism) he made out "emperor's country advocating the code of chivalry", again provoking much amusement.

Of course, there are many such polysyllabic words which can be understood as the sum total of their individual characters; e.g., if one knows the meanings of 牛 (niú, cow), 肉 (ròu, meat), and 奶 (nǎi, milk), then the meanings of 牛肉 (niúròu, beef) and 牛奶 (niúnǎi, cow's milk) are obvious. However, even if one knows that the basic meaning of the character 娘 (niáng) is "mother", this will not help in such compound words as 姑娘 (gūniang, girl), 娘娘 (niángniang), used to address an empress, or 娘子 (niángzi), used in classical novels and plays to mean "wife". Similarly, 老板 (lǎobǎn, boss) cannot be understood literally as "old board", 小说 (xiǎoshuō, fiction) cannot be understood literally as "small talk", 大家 (dàjiā, everyone) cannot be taken literally as "big family", and 坏蛋 (huàidàn, scoundrel) cannot always be understood literally as "bad egg". Thus in learning Chinese characters, we must be aware of their meanings in compound words as well as their basic meanings as independent characters, and not — like the missionary in the story — 出洋相 (chū yángxiàng) "make a spectacle of ourselves" by mistakenly assuming the whole word always to be equal to the sum of its parts.

Let us examine in detail the following five different relationships between the meanings of individual characters and the meaning of words.

1) The Whole Is Equal to the Sum of Its Parts.

The easiest type of compound word to learn is that in which the meaning of the entire word is basically equal to the combined meanings of the individual characters which compose it. However, note that different types of relations may hold between the meanings of the various component characters:

a) The first character modifies the second one: as in 木床 (mùchuáng, wooden bed), 饭碗 (fànwǎn, rice bowl), 牛肉 (niúròu, beef), 电灯 (diàndēng, electric lamp), 狂欢 (kuánghuān, wildly cheer), 雪白 (xuěbái, snow white), 轻信 (qīngxìn, credulous).

b) The meanings of the two characters are basically the

same, as in 道路 (dàolù, road), 朋友 (péngyou, friend), 牙齿 (yáchǐ, teeth), 人民 (rénmín, the people), 学习 (xuéxí, study), 帮助 (bāngzhù, help), 美丽 (měilì, beautiful), 刚才 (gāngcái, just now).

c) The meanings of the two characters are interrelated, as in 钢铁 (gāngtiě, "steel & iron", steel), 姓名 (xìngmíng, "surname & personal name", name), 针线 (zhēnxiàn, "needle & thread", needlework), 书刊 (shūkān, "books & periodicals", reading matter), 教学 (jiàoxué, "teach & study", teaching), 批改 (pīgǎi, "criticize & correct", correcting), 简明 (jiǎnmíng, "simple & clear", concise), 热闹 (rè nào, "hot & noisy", lively).

d) The meanings of the component characters are opposite as in 天地 (tiāndì, "heaven & earth", world), 左右 (zuǒyòu, "left & right", approximately), 收发 (shōufā, "receive & send out", dispatching), 出纳 (chūnà, "receive & pay out", cashier), 高低 (gāodī, "tall & low", height), 轻重 (qīngzhòng, "light & heavy", weight), 冷热 (lěngrè, "cold & hot", temperature), 开关 (kāiguān, "open & shut", switch).

e) The two characters are in a verb- object structure, as in 说话 (shuōhuà, "speak a language", talk, speak), 唱歌 (chàng-gē, "sing a song", sing), 吃饭 (chīfàn, "eat a meal", eat), 跳舞 (tiàowǔ, "perform a dance", to dance), 报名 (bàomíng, "register a name", register).

f) The two characters stand in a verb plus complement relation, as in 提高 (tígāo "raise higher", raise), 改善 (gǎishàn, "change better", improve), 听懂 (tīngdǒng, "hear & understand", understand), 学会 (xuéhuì, "study — able to", master), 讲明 (jiǎngmíng, "talk-clear", explain), 放大 (fàngdà, "make bigger", enlarge).

g) The two characters stand in a subject plus verb relation, as in 心疼 (xīnténg, "heart hurts", love dearly), 地震 (dìzhèn, "earth quakes", earthquake), 胆怯 (dǎnqiè, "gallbladder is timid", timid, cowardly), 性急 (xìngjí, "disposition is nervous", impatient, short-tempered), 山崩 (shānbēng, "mountain collapses", landslide), 人为 (rénwéi, "man makes", artificial), 头晕 (tóuyūn, "head is dizzy", giddy), 市立 (shìlì, "city-manage", municipally-managed), 手软 (shǒuruǎn, "hand is soft", softhearted).

2) The Meaning of the Word Is Only Equal to a Part of the Meanings of the Characters Which Comprise It.

The original meaning of the modern word 国家 (guójiā), which now means "country, state, nation", may be seen from its component characters 国 (guó, country) and 家 (jiā, family, household), meaning something like the "national family", but now this original meaning has disappeared. Similarly, 睡觉 (shuìjiào), which now means simply "to sleep", originally meant "to sleep and to wake up", as may be seen from its two component characters. Words such as these in which one character carries the primary meaning and the other has no semantic function are called 偏义词 (piānyìcí), or "semantically biased words". Here are some further examples:

兄弟 (xiōngdi) Not "older brother" and "young brother", but only the latter.

人物 (rénwù) Not "person" and "thing", but only "personage".

窗户 (chuānghu) Not "window" and "door", but only "window".

干净 (gānjìng) Not "dry" and "clean", but only the latter.

忘记 (wàngjì) Not "forget" and "remember", but only the former.

好歹 (hǎodǎi) Not "good" and "bad", but only "mishap".

Note that the characters which do not carry the principal meaning in these words are not dispensible: 人物 (rénwù, personage) is different from 人 (rén, person) in modern Chinese, single characters such as 弟 (dì, younger brother) or 净 (jìng, clean) cannot be used alone to represent indopendent words.

3) **The Meaning of the Word Equals the Sum of Its Parts Plus Additional Connotations.**

From its two component characters 安 (ān, peace) and 息 (xī, rest) we might conclude that the word 安息 (ānxī) means "to rest peacefully", but in fact it can be used (as in English) as an expression of comfort for deceased persons. Thus if one were to understand this word purely on the basis of its two consitituent characters and conclude a letter to one's parents telling them to "rest in peace", one would be making a definite mistake. Therefore rather than simply attempting to understand such compound words purely on the basis of their component characters, we must be on the lookout for additional meanings and connotations, which are usually clearly explained in good word dictionaries. Here are a few more examples:

补正 (bǔzhèng) Not simply "supplement and correct", but rather "errors caused by negligence".

保重 (bǎozhòng) Not merely "protect" and "care", but used in the sense of "take care of yourself".

出落   (chūluò) Not "drop out", but rather "to grow (prettier)", usually of young women.

出院   (chūyuàn) Not to "come out of a courtyard", but rather to "leave hospital".

宽宏   (kuānhóng) Not simply "broad" and "great", but "magnanimous".

亲善   (qīnshàn) Not simply "close" and "kind", but "close and friendly (between countries)".

硬朗   (yìnglang) Not simply "strong" and "bright", but "hale and hearty", usually of older people.

作文   (zuòwén) More than just to "produce writing"; it refers specifically to students writing compositions in school.

To attempt to guess the meanings of such words purely on the basis of their component characters without taking such implied meanings or restricted usages into account will lead to many errors. One cannot write that a room is 宽宏 (kuānhóng, magnanimous) when one means 宽大 (kuāndà, spacious), and one cannot describe relations between friends as 亲善 (qīnshàn, close and friendly [between nations]), instead of 亲密 (qīnmì, intimate). Literal readings of the characters which are used to form words are often the source of misunderstandings in reading and wrong word choice in writing.

4) The Meaning of the Word Is a Metaphorical Extension of the Meanings of Its Component Characters.

From its component characters 铁 (tiě, iron) and 窗 (chuāng, window), we might understand the word 铁窗 (tiěchuāng) to to mean something like "iron window". In fact, by extension this word refers to "jail" or "prison". 桃 (táo, peaches) and 李 (lǐ, plums) together form an expression which refers metaphorically to a teacher's students or disciples. Thus the true meaning of such compound words comes not from the meanings of the characters which compose them but from an extension of their meaning(s). This goes beyond the type of additional connotations discussed in section (c); in this type of example, the word has a meaning which is totally different from its component characters. There are many examples of this type of extended meaning or metaphorical extension:

虎口 (hǔkǒu) Literally "tiger's mouth", meaning a dangerous situation, as in the expression 虎口余生 (hǔkǒu yú shēng, escaped from the jaws of disaster; a narrow escape).

骑墙 (qíqiáng) Literally, "straddle a wall"; by analogy, to take an indefinite position on.some issue; "fence-straddling".

失足 (shīzú) Literally, to "lose one's footing", meaning to become corrupted or to commit serious misdemeanors, as in 一失足成千古恨 (yī shīzú chéng qiāngǔ hèn, one slip and you'll regret it forever)

裙钗 (qúnchāi) Literally "skirts and hairpins", formerly used as a metaphorical term for women.

风雨 (fēngyǔ) Literally "wind and rain", but figuratively meaning difficulties and misery, as in the expression 经风雨，见世面 (jīng fēngyǔ, jiàn shìmiàn, having weathered the storms, to know the nature of the world).

手足 (shǒuzú) Literally "hands and feet", but meaning "brothers", from an old expression for brothers 情同手足 (qíng tóng shǒuzú), literally "close as hands and feet".

爪牙 (zhǎoyá) Literally "paws and teeth", meaning the underlings or confederates of evil people.

江山 (jiāngshān) Literally "rivers and mountains", but often used to mean a state or the state's power.

骨肉 (gǔròu) Literally "bones and flesh", but referring (as in English) to one's own "flesh and blood" (i.e., close relatives).

鱼肉 (yúròu) Literally "fish and meat", or things to be cut up and killed. By extension this word is used as a verb meaning to suppress by violence, as in the expression 鱼肉百姓 (yúròu bǎixìng, to suppress the common people).

5) The Meaning of the Word Bears No Relationship to Its Component Characters.

There are some words whose semantic meaning seems to have no relation whatsoever to the meanings of the characters which are used to represent its component syllables. Here are some examples:

东西 (dōngxi) does not mean "east-west", but rather "thing".

三七 (sānqī) does not mean "three-seven", but rather "pseudo-ginseng", a type of herbal medicine.

马虎 (mǎhu) does not mean "horses and tigers", but rather "careless, slapdash"

198

八哥　(bāgē) does not mean "eighth older brother", but rather "myna bird".

推敲　(tuīqiāo) does not mean "pushing and knocking", but rather to "ponder or deliberate over".

矛盾　(máodùn) does not mean literally "spear and shield", but rather metaphorically "contradiction".

In such cases, when it is impossible to guess the meaning of a word from either of its constituent characters, it is often necessary to know some classical allusion or story 典故 in order to understand the source of the meaning, as e.g., the story of the unbreakable spear and the impenetrable shield in the last example just given.

Another source of such non-analyzable compounds is of course transliteration of foreign words, as in 沙发 (shāfā) which uses the characters for "sand" and "produce" purely for their sound values in order to imitate the sound of the borrowed English word "sofa".

5.3 SYNONYMOUS AND ANTONYMOUS CHARACTERS

In terms of their meanings, Chinese characters may be viewed as synonyms and antonyms, which can sometimes be useful in learning them.

Characters which are the same or close in meaning are often called synonyms 同义. In fact, true synonymy — that is, a situation where two characters mean exactly the same thing — is quite rare, as generally characters (like words) usually have some slight differences at least in connotation and usage, if not in denotation, between them. Thus strictly speaking, such characters are not truely synonymous, but merely close in mean-

199

ing 近义· To give but one example, both 看 (kàn) and 望 (wàng) may be glossed as "to look", but while 看 (kàn) is the most common modern term for "looking", 望 (wàng) is more often used to mean "to look afar; to gaze into the distance" (either literally, or metaphorically, as into the future: "to expect").

Synonymous characters generally differ in the following three ways, often with some overlapping.

1) Differences in Denotation

a) 革 vs. 皮 The character 革 (gé) refers specifically to animal skins which have been processed and had their hair removed. This character is not used alone in modern Chinese. 皮 (pí), on the other hand, is generally used to refer to the outer layer of tissue on the bodies of humans and other living things, e.g. 树皮 (shùpí, tree bark), etc., as well as other things with an outer covering, e.g., 饺子皮 (jiǎozi pí, dumpling wrappings), etc.

b) 仓 vs. 库. The character 仓 (cāng) primarily refers to places used for storing grains, while 库 (kù) may refer to a place for storing other types of goods or materials, such as gold, silver, etc. Cf. 谷仓 (gǔcāng, grain warehouse), 粮仓 (liáng-cāng, granary) vs. 国库 (guókù, national treasury), 金库 (jīnkù, gold depository), etc.

c) 孔 vs. 洞. The character 孔 (kǒng) usually refers to small holes, as in 鼻孔 (bíkǒng, nasal orifice), 毛孔 (máokǒng, pores), etc., while 洞 (dòng) refers to bigger holes, as in 山洞 (shāndòng, cave), 防空洞 (fángkōngdòng, air raid shelter), etc.

d) Both 冷 (lěng) and 凉 (liáng) denote a low temperature, but 冷 (cold) is lower in temperature than 凉 (cool).

e) 呆 vs. 傻. The character 呆 (dāi) means mentally slow or dull as opposed to being mentally quick or sharp, as in the expression 呆若木鸡 (dāi ruò mùjī, dumbstruck). 傻 (shǎ), on the other hand, means "stupid" or "muddle-headed", as in 傻瓜 (shǎguā, simpleton), or 傻孩子 (shǎ háizi, stupid child).

f) While both 拼 (pīn) and 凑 (còu) mean "to combine", the former character connotes combining things in some sort of order, as in 拼音 (pīnyīn, spelling) or 拼版 (pīnbǎn, to make up or lay out a page, etc.), whereas 凑 (còu) means to combine without any particular order and usually refers to people (or money), as in 凑热闹 (còu rènào, to join the fun), 凑人数 (còu rénshù, to get people together), 凑分子 (còu fènzi, to go in together [to present a gift]), etc.

2) Differences in Style

a) Both 舟 (zhōu) and 船 (chuán) refer to boats, but they are used in different styles of writing. The former is used in the 文言 (wényán) literary style, while the latter represents the word most often used in speech and modern colloquial writing. Compare 小舟 (xiǎozhōu, small vessel) vs. 小船 (xiǎo chuán, small boat); 一叶扁舟 (yī yè piān zhōu, a skiff) vs. 一只小船 (yī zhī xiǎo chuán, a small boat).

b) Both 佳 (jiā) and 好 (hǎo) may mean "good", but they differ similarly to the previous pair in their style level; compare 身体不佳 (shēntǐ bù jiā) vs. 身体不好 (shēntǐ bù hǎo). In addition, the character 好 may also be used as a verb in the fourth tone hào meaning "love, like, be fond of", while 佳 also

201

has other connotations, as in 才子佳人 (cáizǐ jiārén, gifted scholars and beautiful ladies), or 佳宾 (jiābīn, most welcome guests).

c) 窃 (qiè) and 偷 (tōu) both basically mean "to steal", but again differ in style level. While the latter is now the common term used in the spoken language, the former is now used only as a bound form in the literary wényán style. This distinction was employed by the famous writer Lu Xun to satirize the bankrupcy of intellectuals of the old scholarly class in his famous short story about one of them, 孔乙己 (Kǒng Yijǐ):

"... What do you mean you're clean? The day before yesterday I saw with my own eyes that you stole (偷 tōu) a book from the Hé family, and they hung you up and beat you for it." Kong Yiji's face flushed and the blue veins on his forehead stood out: "To pilfer (窃 qiè) a book is not the same as stealing (偷 tōu) one ... pilfering (窃 qiè) books... concerns intellectuals; how can you equate it with stealing (偷，tōu)?..."

3) Differences in Usage

While both 红 (hóng) and 赤 (chì) may refer to the color red, the former may be used independently, while the latter may not. Thus one may say 这朵花很红 "This flower is very red" (... hěn hóng), but never 这朵花很赤 "This flower is very chì". These characters also have differing secondary meanings. Thus 赤 (chì) may also mean "loyal" or "bare", as in the fused-phrase idiom 赤胆忠心 (chìdǎn zhōngxīn, utter devotion), or 赤脚医生 (chìjiǎo yīsheng, barefoot doctor).

b) The character 胖 (pàng) is usually used to describe people, while 肥 (féi) is used for animals. Thus a child may be described as quite 胖 (pàng), while a pig (or its meat) would only be described as 肥 (féi).

c) Both 二 (èr) and 两 (liǎng) mean "two", but they are quite different in usage. 二 (èr) is used for the number "two" in isolation, while the bound form 两 (liǎng) is required before measure words, as in 两个人 (liǎng gè rén, two people), etc. This usage is conventionalized, however, as may be seen from the following examples: 第二个 (dì-èr gè, the second one), not 第两个 (dì liǎng gè); 二分之一 (èr fēn zhī yī, one-half), not 两分之一 (liǎng fēn zhī yī); 两点钟 (liǎng diǎn zhōng, two o'clock), not 二点钟 (èr diǎn zhōng).

d) While both 停 (tíng) and 止 (zhǐ) convey the meaning of "to stop", the former is used to express a state or change of state, as in 雨停了 (yǔ tíng le, The rain stopped), or 我在北京停了三天 (wǒ zài Běijīng tíngle sān tiān, I stopped over in Beijing for three days). 止 (zhǐ), on the other hand, is used more in a causative sense of "to make something stop", as in 止血 (zhǐ xuè, to stop the bleeding), 止痛 (zhǐ tòng, to stop the pain), etc.

Antonymous characters are those whose meanings are opposite or contrary. Thus pairs of adjectives such as the following express opposite meanings of characteristics or state: 大 (dà, big) vs. 小 (xiǎo, small), 深 (shēn, deep) vs. 浅 (qiǎn, shallow), 真 (zhēn, true) vs. 假 (jiǎ, false), etc.

Pairs of verbs such as the following ones express opposite actions or behaviors: 出 (chū, exit) vs. 入 (rù, enter), 生 (shēng, live) vs. 死 (sǐ, die), 开 (kāi, open) vs. 关 (guān, close), etc.

Other such pairs express opposite meanings referring to

things, positions, and times: 古 (gǔ, ancient) vs. 今 (jīn, present day), 上 (shàng, above) vs. 下 (xià, below), 天 (tiān, heaven/sky) vs. 地 (dì, earth); 男 (nán, male) vs. 女 (nǔ, female), etc.

Two points concerning such antonymous pairs should be noted. The first is that because of the existence of synonyms just discussed, a character may not have only one antonym, but rather more than one synonymous antonym. Thus, for example, the opposite of 死 (sǐ, to die/dead) is not only 生 (shēng, to live), but also the character 活 (huó, living). Similarly the opposite of 冷 (lěng, cold) can be both 热 (rè, hot) or 暖 (nuǎn, warm). Antonyms of 高 (gāo), tall/high) are both 低 (dī, low) and 矮 (ǎi, short),

The other point is because of the existence of polysemy, or a number of different meanings represented by the same character, one or more characters may be the antonyms of one sense of a character, while another character (or characters) may represent the opposite of another of its meanings. Thus, for example, the opposite of the character 生 (shēng) in its sense of "to live" is the character 死 (sǐ, to die/dead), but the opposite of the same character 生 (shēng) in its sense of "raw, uncooked", is 熟 (shú, cooked, ripe). To give another example, the opposite of the character 正 (zhèng) in its sense of "obverse" is the character 反 (fǎn, reverse), but the antonym of the character 反 in its sense of "upright" is 斜 (xié, slanting).

Synonymous and antonymous characters play a very important rhetorical function in Chinese. Thus, for example, in many four-character fused-phrase idioms (成语 chéngyǔ), such pairs of characters are often used to achieve stylistic parallelism or antithesis.　Here are some examples of such chéngyǔ employing pairs of synonyms:

四分五裂　(sì fēn wǔ liè,　completely rent by disunity), literally "divided into fours and split into fives".

行尸走肉　(xíng shī zǒu ròu, a walking corpse; one who vegetates; an utterly worthless person), literally "walking corpse, walking flesh".

Here are some examples of chéngyǔ employing antonymous opposition:

积少成多　(jī shǎo chéng duō, many a little makes a mickle), literally "accumulate little becomes much".

七上八下　(qī shàng bā xià, helter-skelter; at sixes and sevens), literally "seven up, eight down".

Finally, here are some examples employing both synonymous and antonymous oppositions:

同甘共苦　(tóng gān gòng kǔ, to share weal and woe), literally, "together sweetness, communal bitterness".

大惊小怪　(dà jīng xiǎo guài, to be surprised at something perfectly normal), literally "great surprise, small wonder".

Note:　"．" = synonymous; "。" = antonymous.

This type of stylistic parallelism and antithesis is also found in many popular sayings, proverbs, and maxims; for example:

远水救不了近火　(yuǎn shuǐ jiù bù liǎo jìn huǒ, a slow remedy cannot meet an urgent need), literally "distant water cannot put out a fire close at hand".

兼听则明，偏听则暗　(jiān tīng zé míng, piān tīng zé àn)

205

"Listen to both sides and you will be enlightened; listen to only one side and you will be benighted".

5.4 CHARACTERS OFTEN WRONGLY USED

The two most common types of errors made when writing Chinese characters are called cuòzì 错字 and biézì 别字. The term cuòzì refers to characters which in fact do not exist; that is to say, that the writer has miswritten or malformed the character he or she intended to write in such a way that the resulting form is in fact not a real Chinese character at all. (see 3.4).

The other most common type of mistake in writing Chinese characters is to substitute a character which does exist for another one by mistake. This type of error is called 别字 biézì, or 白字 báizì which we may understand to mean an inappropriately used character. There are three common reasons for this type of error:

1) The two characters are the same or close in pronunciation, as for example, when the word 诡计 (guǐjì, plot) is miswritten as 鬼计 (guǐjì), not in fact a real word, but a homophone which seems to mean something like a "devilish plan".

2) The two characters look alike, as when the character 荼 (tú, a bitter fruit), which is most commonly seen in the fused-phrase idiom 如火如荼 (rú huǒ rú tú, spreading like wildfire), is miswritten as the more commonly encountered character 茶 (chá, tea), which it closely resembles.

3) The two characters both look and sound alike, as when the word 精悍 (jīnghàn, concise) is miswritten as 精捍 (jīnghàn), which is in fact a non-existent word.

The best way to avoid these types of errors is to study carefully the differences in meaning and usage of different characters. For example, many people miswrite the word 欢度 (huāndù), which is most commonly encountered in such phrases as 欢度佳节 (huāndù jiājié, to celebrate a festival with jubilation), as 欢渡 (huāndù). Now as verbs, both 度 (dù) and 渡 (dù) mean to "pass through" or to "go by", but 度 is usually used to express the idea of passing or experiencing a period of time, while 渡 (with a "water" radical) means to "cross or pass over water", and by extension, to "tide over difficulties, etc". If these differences are understood, then the chances of miswriting the one character for the other will be greatly reduced. Of course, this confusion does not usually arise with the other senses and uses of the character 度 (dù), as for example, when it is used as a noun in such words as 温度 (wēndù, temperature) or 一度电 (yī dù diàn, one degree of electricity; one kilowatt/hour). Thus we should best focus on those occasions or circumstances where certain characters are most likely to be confused.

The following alphabetical list presents a brief analysis of fifty of the most frequently and most easily confused characters.

1) 辨 vs. 辩 (biàn)

The character 辨 (biàn), with a "knife" component at its centre, means to "differentiate, discern, or discriminate", and is frequently used in such compounds as 辨认 (biànrèn, to recognize), 辨析 (biànxī, to distinguish and analyze), and the expression 明辨是非 (míng biàn shì-fēi, to distinguish right from wrong). The character 辩 (also pronounced biàn), with a "speech" radical at its centre, means "to argue, justify, or rationalize", and is often used in such words as 辩论 (biànlùn, to debate), 辩驳 (biànbō, to refute), 雄辩 (xióngbiàn, eloquence), and the expression 能言善辩 (néng yán shàn biàn, to have a glib and argumentative tongue).

2) 查 vs. 察 (chá)

The core meanings of the character 查 (chá) are to "examine, investigate, or look for", as in such words as 搜查 (sōuchá, to ransack, to search), 查帐 (chá zhàng, to audit accounts), 查问 (cháwèn, to interrogate), or 查字典 (chá zìdiǎn, to consult a dictionary). The character 察 (also chá), on the other hand, means principally "to look at carefully", "to make a thorough inquiry", as in 观察 (guānchá, to look into, to observe), 视察 (shìchá, to inspect), or the expression 察颜观色 (chá yán guān sè, to feel someone out by watching his moods and studying his words). Note that the word 考查 (kǎochá) means "to examine and weigh according to certain standards", as in 考查学生成绩 (kǎochá xuéshēng chéngjī, to examine students' achievements), while the word 考察 (kǎochá) means "to settle down in a certain place for profound and careful research on something", as in 出国考察 (chūguó kǎochá, to go abroad for research).

3) 斥 vs. 叱 (chì)

Both of these homophones carry a sense of blaming, but 斥 means to "censure harshly", while 叱 means to "rebuke loudly or vociferously", with an emphasis on the loudness of the voice (cf. its "mouth" radical). For example, 驳斥 (bóchì) means "to refute an erroneous statement", and 怒斥 (nùchì) is to "rebuke angrily", while 怒叱 (nùchì) is to "scold loudly in anger".

4) 纯 vs. 淳 (chún)

While both of these characters are pronounced chún and may be glossed as "pure", they are different in their connotations and usage. The character 纯 is used to describe the pure, unamixed, unadulterated nature of things, and by extension as a metaphor for a person's character, manner, or disposition. Thus the word 纯粹 (chúncuì, pure, sheer) could be used to describe both a "pure waste of time" as well as a "pure (and simple) person". The homophonous character 淳, however, is used only in the second sense of "pure, honest, simple, unsophisticated" when describing manners, and customs, as in 淳厚 (chúnhòu, pure and honest, simple and kind). This being the case, the word 淳朴 (chúnpǔ, honest, simple) is often written either as 纯朴 or 淳朴.

5) 词 vs. 辞 (cí)

These two homonyms now both generally refer to "words", that is independent units in the Chinese language, often of more than one syllable. In this general sense the two characters are now often used interchangeably, as in 词典 and 辞典 (cídiǎn, word dictionary), 发刊词 or 发刊辞 (fākāncí, foreword [or introduction] to a periodical), 义正词严 or 义正辞严 (yìzhèng cíyán, to speak with the force of justice). In discussing classical Chinese literature, however, these two terms refer to two very different types of literary forms. In this context the character 词 refers to a type of poetry written to certain tunes with strict tonal patterns and rhyme schemes, in fixed numbers of lines and words, which originated in the Tang Dynasty and continued into the Song, while the character 辞 refers to another type of

209

classical Chinese literature which employs dialect and rhymes to describe local happenings. Thus the two characters must be carefully distinguished in these technical senses. In addition, in modern linguistic discussions, where the character 词 is used to refer to the word as a linguistic unit, or in other such technical terms such as 词句 (cí-jù, words and phrases), 词组 (cízǔ, word group), 词类 (cílèi, parts of speech), 名词 (míngcí, noun), 动词 (dòngcí, verb), etc., only this character may be used.

6) 订 vs. 定 (dìng)

The character 订 (with the "speech" radical) means to "fix" in the sense of "to conclude, draw up, or agree on", while its homophone 定 has a basic meaning of "stable" or "fixed", also used as a verb to mean to "fix, set, or decide". Thus the two characters are sometimes interchangeable, as in such expressions as "to make an appointment beforehand", or "being settled after research and discussion". For example, the character 定 may be substituted for 订 in such expressions as 订购 (dìnggòu, to place an order), 订货 (dìnghuò, to order goods), 订阅 (dìngyuè, to subscribe to a periodical), 订婚 (dìnghūn, to become engaged), 订计划 (dìng jìhuà, to settle on a plan), and 订条约 (dìng tiáoyuē, to conclude a treaty), but in fact the character 订 is preferred. The character 定, on the other hand, is more widely used and is the only possibility in such words as 稳定 (wěndìng, stable, steady), 决定 (juédìng, decide), 规定 (guīdìng, rules, regulations), 定论 (dìnglùn, conclusive evaluation), 定案 (dìng'àn, pass a verdict), 定额 (dìng'é, quota, norm), and 定局 (dìngjú, forgone conclusion), while only 订 may be used in 订正 (dìngzhèng, to emend a text) and 修订 (xiūdìng, to revise).

7) 烦 vs. 繁 (fán)

The basic meaning of the character 烦 is "irritated" or "annoyed," and therefore this character is often employed in words describing psychological states, as in 烦闷 (fánmèn, unhappy, worried), 烦恼 (fánnǎo, vexed, worried), or 烦躁 (fánzào, fidgety, agitated). The meaning of the character 繁, on the other hand, is "numerous, complicated", and thus it is usually found in words describing objective states of affairs, as in 繁复 (fánfù, large and complicated), 繁华 (fánhuá, flourishing, busstling), 繁难 (fánnán, troublesome), or 繁重(fánzhòng, strenuous, onerous). Both characters, however, can refer to something multifarious, thus 烦冗 and 繁冗 (fánrǒng, tedious, complicated) are interchangeable and so are 烦琐 and 繁琐 (fánsuǒ, over-elaborate, tedious).

8) 奋 vs. 愤 (fèn)

The basic meaning of the character 奋 is to "exert or rouse onself to vigorous action", as in 奋斗 (fèndòu, struggle, strive), 奋勇(fènyǒng, summon up all one's courage and energy), and 奋不顾身(fèn bù gù shēn, dash ahead regardless of one's safety). The character 愤, on the other hand, means to be indignant or resentful, as in 愤恨 (fènhèn, to resent indignantly), 愤慨 (fènkǎi, righteous indignation), and 愤怒 (fènnù, indignant wrath). 发奋 and 发愤 (both fāfèn), though sometimes interchangeable, are different in that the former means to "work energetically" while the latter means "to make a firm resolution".

9) 工 vs. 功 (gōng)

The basic meaning of the character 工 is "work", while that of 功 is "merit", "achievement", or "skill", so the two should not easily be confused. Where they are often confused, however, are in the two words 工夫 and 功夫, both pronounced gōngfu. The former word is used to refer to the amount of time or effort expended, often to achieve a skill, e.g. 她三天工夫就学会了游泳, while the latter term should refer only to a certain level of skill or art, but the terms are sometimes used interchangeably.

10) 鬼 vs. 诡 (guǐ)

The basic meaning of 鬼 may be said to be "devil" or "devilish", while that of 诡 is "deceitful, tricky, cunning". This slight difference may be seen when both are used as adjectival modifiers, as in 鬼话 (guǐhuà, nonsense, lit. "devilish speech", 鬼点子 (guǐdiǎnzi, wicked ideas), and 鬼鬼祟祟 (guǐguǐ-suìsuì, sneaky), as opposed to 诡诈 (guǐzhà, crafty, treacherous), 诡辩 (guǐbiàn, sophistry), and 诡计 (guǐjì, trick, crafty plot). Note that this last word should not be written as 鬼计.

11) 含 vs. 涵 (hán)

The original meaning of the character 含 is to "hold in the mouth" (cf. its "mouth" component) and thus it has been extended to mean "to contain", in the sense of holding something back, as may be seen in the words 含泪 (hánlèi, to hold back one's tears), 含怒 (hánnù, to harbor anger or indignation), and the expression 含情脉脉 (hánqíng mòmò, to look at someone with eyes brimming with affection). The character 涵 (with the "water" radical), on the other hand, means both "to contain", and "culvert", so that it occurs in words and expressions suggesting containment or discipline, as in 涵养 (hányǎng, self-restraint), or 望你海涵 (wàng nǐ hǎihán, please be magnanimous enough to forgive our shortcomings). Because both characters thus have a sense of "contain", they are used interchangeably in the words 含蓄/涵蓄 (hánxù, to contain/implicit), and 含义/涵义 (hányì, meaning, implication). But the two characters are used differently in words 包含 (bāohán, contain) and 包涵 (bāohán, excuse, forgive).

12) 洪 vs. 宏 (hóng)

While both of these characters convey the sense of "great", the character 洪, which can also literally mean "a flood", is generally used in the sense of "big" or "vast" to describe such concrete things as volume, capacity, or voice, while 宏 is used in the sense of "great" or "grand" to describe more abstract concepts, such as degree or quality. Please note the following examples: 洪水 (hóngshuǐ, flood), 洪流 (hóngliú, mighty torrent, current), 洪亮 (hóngliàng, sonorous), 洪钟 (hóngzhōng, a large bell), as opposed to 宏大 (hóngdà, grand, great), 宏伟 (hóngwěi, magnificent, grand), 宏图 (hóngtú, great plan), and 宏观 (hóngguǎn, macroscopic).

13) 会 vs. 汇 (huì)

Both of these homophonous characters have the meaning of "converge" or "come together", but 会 (with the "person" radical on the top) refers to the meeting of people, while 汇 (with the "water" radical) refers to a coming-together of things, including words. Examples of words containing the character 会 are 会餐 (huìcān, dine together), 会师 (huìshī, join forces), 开会 (kāihuì, hold a meeting), 会诊 (huìzhěn, group consultation), etc., while examples of words containing 汇 are 汇流 (huìliú, flow together), 汇集 (huìjí, collect, compile), 汇编 (huìbiān, compilation, collection) and 词汇 (cíhuì, vocabulary glossary). 会合 and 汇合 sometimes can be used interchangeably, but only in similes and metaphors.

14) 积 vs. 绩 (jī)

The basic meaning of the character 积 is to "store up" or "accumulate", while the most commonly encountered meaning of the character 绩 (which almost never occurs initially in polysyllabic words) is "achievement, accomplishment, or merit", as in 成绩 (chéngjī, achievement), 战绩 (zhànjī, military achievement), or the expression 丰功伟绩 (fēng gōng wěi jī, great achievements). People who substitute the character 绩 for 积 in such combinations (thus creating nonsense words) should keep in mind these basic differences in meaning.

15) 即(jí) vs. 既 (jì)

The meaning of the character 即 (jí, rising tone) is similar to that of the character 就 (jiù, then) when used as an adverb, or to its meaning when it occurs in the word 就是 (jiùshì, even, even if) as a conjunction. The character 既 (jì, falling tone) on the other hand, has a meaning of "already" as an adverb, or of "since, now that" when used as a conjunction. Obviously it is because the two characters are so similar in shape, pronunciation, and abstract meaning that they are so often confused. The character 即 (jí) is most often seen in the function words 即使 (jíshǐ), 即或 (jíhuò), and 即便 (jíbiàn), all meaning "even, even if, even though", as well as 即将 (jíjiāng) "be about to", while 既 (jì) occurs in 既然 (jìrán) or 既是 (jìshì), both meaning "since, now that".

16) 记 vs. 纪 (jì)

As both of these homophonous characters may have

214

the meaning of "record, write down", there are some words in which they may be used interchangeably: e.g. 记录/纪录 (jìlù, take notes/record), 记要/纪要 (jìyào, summary). But in some words, only 记 may be used, e.g. 记载 (jìzài, record/account), 记帐 (jìzhàng, keep accounts), 记事 (jìshì, keep a record of events), 记工 (jìgōng, record workpoints). Only 纪 may be used in the terms 纪年 (jìnián, a way of numbering the years in a sixty-year cycle), and 纪元 (jìyuán, epoch, era). 纪念 (jìniàn, commemorate, souvenir) is sometimes also written as 记念 when used in the sense of "memory", but 记忆 (jìyì, remember/memory) must be written with 记, as must the word 记者 (jìzhě, reporter), and the word 记诵 (jìsòng, learn by heart).

17) 嘉 vs. 佳 (jiā)

As both of these homophonous characters mean "good, fine", they are interchangeable in the expression 嘉宾/佳宾 (jiābīn, honored guest), but only 佳 may be used in 佳话 (jiāhuà, a much-told tale), 佳节 (jiājié, joyous festival), 佳境 (jiājìng, a beautiful place), 佳音 (jiāyīn, joyous tidings). On the other hand, 嘉 also means "to praise or commend", and thus only that character may occur in the verbs 嘉奖 (jiājiǎng, commend) and 嘉许 (jiāxǔ, praise, approve).

18) 坚 vs. 艰 (jiān)

The character 坚 basically means "hard, solid, firm, strong", as in such compounds as 坚硬 (jiānyìng, hard, solid), 坚定 (jiāndìng, firm, staunch, steadfast), 坚持 (jiānchí, persist, persevere), 坚固 (jiāngù, firm, solid, strong), 坚决 (jiānjué, firm, resolute), 坚强 (jiānqiáng, firm, staunch), 坚忍 (jiānrěn, steadfast and perservering), and 坚实 (jiānshí, solid, substantial). The homophonous character 艰, on the other hand, has a basic meaning of "difficult, hard", as in such words as 艰巨 (jiānjù, arduous), 艰难 (jiānnán, difficult), 艰深 (jiānshēn, abstruse), and 艰险 (jiānxiǎn, perilous). Note also that while 艰苦 (jiānkǔ) means "arduous, difficult", 坚苦 (jiānkǔ) means "tenacious, showing the utmost fortitude", and thus these two should be distinguished.

19) 捡 vs. 拣 (jiǎn)

The basic meaning of the character 拣 is to "choose, select, or pick out", while that of its homophone 捡 is "pick up, collect, or gather". Thus in the sense of picking up or collecting, they may be used interchangeably, so that 捡柴 (jiǎn chái, gather firewood), 捡粪 (jiǎn fèn, collect manure), and 捡破烂儿 (jiǎn pòlànr, scavenging) may also be written as 拣柴, 拣粪 and 拣破烂儿, respectively. However, in its sense of "select, choose" only the character 拣 may be used in such expressions as 拣选 (jiǎnxuǎn, select, choose), or 挑肥拣瘦 (tiāo féi jiǎn shòu, choose whichever is to one's personal advantage). When the character 捡 is being used in its secondary sense of "to tidy up or put things in order", however, as in 捡漏 (jiǎnlòu, to fix leaks in the roof), etc., only 捡 may be used.

20) 截 vs. 节 (jié)

These two homophonous characters may both be used as qualifiers or measure words which refer to a part or piece of something, and hence are easily confused. The character 截 refers to a section, chunk, or length or something which has been cut out or extracted from the entire body, as in 一截木头 (yī jié mùtou, a section or length of wood), or 话说了半截儿 (huà shuōle bàn jiér, to break off halfway and say nothing more".

The character 节, on the other hand, is used to describe parts of sections of things as they occur naturally, as in 竹节 (zhújié, bamboo joint), 两节车厢 (liǎng jié chēxiāng, two railway cars), 三节课 (sān jié kè, three class periods), 第一章第五节 (dì-yī zhāng, dì-wǔ jié, Chapter One, Section Five), etc

21) 绝 vs. 决 (jué)

Both of these homophonous characters may be used as adverbs before such negatives as 不 (bù, not), 无 (wú, haven't), or 非 (fēi, not) to intensify the negative, as in 绝不 (jué bù, absolutely not), 决不 (jué bù, certainly not), etc. The character 决 carries a sense of "certainly" or "surely", while 绝 signifies "absolutely, without any conditions whatsoever, no matter what". Therefore, a negative intensified by 绝不 is much stronger in tone that one modified by 决不.

22) 卷 (juàn) vs. 券 (quàn)

When used as a noun, the character 卷 (juàn) refers to books, documents, or examination papers, etc., as in 卷宗 (juànzōng, folder, file), 考卷 (kǎojuàn, test paper), 手不释卷 (shǒu bù shì juàn, never seen without book in hand). The character 券 (quàn), on the other hand, refers to a certificate or ticket, as in 入场券 (rùchǎngquàn, admission ticket), 国库券 (guókùquàn, treasury bonds), or 稳操胜券 (wěn cāo shèng quàn, sure to win). As their shapes and pronunciations are so similar and both are semantically related to paper, they are easily confused in reading and writing.

23) 棵 vs. 颗 (kē)

Both of these homophonous characters are measure words. 棵 is the measure word for plants of any size with one main stem, as in 一棵树 (yī kē shù, one tree), 一棵草 (yī kē cǎo, a blade of grass), 几棵牡丹 (jǐ kē mǔdān, several stems of peonies), etc. 颗, on the other hand, is used for anything small and roundish, as in 一颗珠子 (yī kē zhūzi, a pearl), 一颗黄豆 (yī kē huángdòu, one soybean grain), 一颗子弹 (yī kē zǐdàn, one bullet), etc.

24) 刻 vs. 克 (kè)

The character 刻 basically means to "carve" or "engrave", and by extension "deeply" as in 深刻 (shēnkè, profound, penetrating), and 刻苦 (kèkǔ, hard-working, assiduous). The basic meaning of 克, on the other hand, is to "conquer" or "capture", as in 攻克 (gōngkè, capture), and 克服 (kèfú, overcome). Note that 刻苦 (kèkǔ, hard-working) must not be written as 克苦, but 克日完成 (kè rì wán chéng, finish within the deadline) can be written as 刻日完成 and has the same meaning.

25) 滥 vs. 烂 (làn)

There are only two commonly used characters pronounced làn in contemporary Chinese, and both may be used as adjectives with derogatory meanings. The original meaning of the character 滥 is to "overflow" or "flood", with an extended meaning of "excessive", as in 滥用职权 (lànyòng zhíquán, to abuse one's authority), 滥交 (lànjiāo, to make friends lavishly), 陈词滥调 (chén cí làn diào, hackneyed phrases, banalities). The homophonous character 烂, on the other hand, means "rotten, spoiled, worn-out", as in 烂苹果 (làn píngguǒ, rotten apple), 破铜烂铁 (pò tóng làn tiě, iron and bronze scrap, junk), and 烂摊子 (làn tān zi, an awful mess).

26) 连 vs. 联 (lián)

These two homophonous characters are also quite close semantically when used as verbs. 连 means to "link, join, connect", while 联 means "to ally oneself with, unite with, join". They are sometimes interchangeable, as most frequently seen in the words 连接/联接 (liánjiē, join, link), and 连绵/联绵 (liánmián, continuous, unbroken). They are not interchangeable in the following compounds: 连带 (liándài, related), 连贯 (liánguàn, link up, coherent), 连续 (liánxù, successive, continuous), 连夜 (liányè, that very night; several nights running), 连用 (liányòng, use together), 连缀 (liánzhuì, join together, cluster), vs. 联合 (liánhé, unite, alliance), 联欢 (liánhuān, have a get-together), 联结 (liánjié, bind, tie, join), 联络 (liánluò, contact), 联盟 (liánméng, coalition), 联系 (liánxì, contact, link), 联想 (liánxiǎng, connect in the mind).

27) 练 vs. 炼 (liàn)

These two homophonous characters are quite close in meaning when used as verbs. The most commonly encountered senses of 练 are "to practice", as in 练兵 (liànbīng, troop training), 练习 (liànxí, practice), 训练 (xùnliàn, training), 操练 (cāoliàn, drill), and "experienced, seasoned", as in 熟练 (shúliàn, skilled, proficient), 老练 (lǎoliàn, seasoned, experienced). The homophonous character 炼 (with the "fire" radical) literally means to "refine" or "extract", as in 炼钢 (liàn gāng, steel-making), 炼铁 (liàn tiě, iron-smelting). In its senses of "forge", "temper", or "steel", 炼 is extended to mean mental or physical training, as in 锻炼 (duànliàn, have physical training, toughen), 锤炼 (chuíliàn, hammer into shape, temper [oneself]), and 磨炼

(móliàn, temper or steel oneself). They are interchangeable in 精练 and 精炼 (jīngliàn, succinct), but they cannot replace one another in any of the above mentioned cases.

28) 蜜 vs. 密 (mì)

The character 蜜 (with the "insect" radical) refers to honey, and is extended semantically to "sweet", as in 甜蜜 (tiánmì, sweet and happy), 蜜月 (mìyuè, honeymoon), and 甜言蜜语 (tián yán mì yǔ, honeyed words). The homophonous character 密 (with the "mountain" radical), on the other hand, has a basic meaning of "close, dense, thick", and an extended meaning of "close" in the sense of "intimate, friendly", as in 亲密 (qīnmì, intimate), 密切 (mìqiè, close, intimate), etc.

29) 脑 vs. 恼 (nǎo)

The character 脑 (with the "flesh" radical) refers to the brain in the sense of the physical organ in the body. The homophonous character 恼 (with the "heart" or "mind" radical), on the other hand, refers to the psychological state of being angry, irritated, or annoyed. The first character 脑 is often mistakenly substituted for the second 恼 in such expressions as 苦恼 (kǔnǎo, distressed), 烦恼 (fánnǎo, vexed), 懊恼 (àonǎo, annoyed), 恼恨 (nǎohèn, resent), 恼火 (nǎohuǒ, irritated), and 恼羞成怒 (nǎo xiū chéng nù, to fly into a rage out of humiliation).

30) 曲 vs. 屈 (qū)

Semantically, both of these homophonous characters are related to "bend". 曲 is used as an adjective meaning "bent" as opposed to straight in such words as 曲折 (qūzhé, tortuous, winding), 曲线 (qūxiàn, curve). 屈, on the other hand, is primarily used as a verb "to bend", as in 屈服 (qūfú, surrender, yield), 屈膝 (qūxī, bend one's knees), 屈指一算 (qū zhǐ yī suàn, count on one's fingers), etc. Note that 委曲 (wěiqū) refers to something "winding", "tortuous", whereas 委屈 (wěiqū) means "to feel wronged".

31) 溶 vs. 熔 vs. 融 (róng)

The character 溶 (with the "water" radical) means to dissolve solid material into a liquid, as salt into water. The character 熔 (with the "fire" radical), on the other hand, refers to metal solids changing into a liquid state after being heated to a high temperature, i.e., melting, smelting, as in 熔铁 (róng tiě, smelting iron). The character 融 refers to the natural melting of things like snow, candles, etc. at normal temperatures, as for example in 雪已经融化了 (Xuě yǐjīng rónghuà le, The snow has melted), etc.

32) 申 vs. 伸 (shēn)

The character 申 has the basic meaning of "express" or "explain" (often to someone in authority), as in 申请 (shēnqǐng, apply for), 申报 (shēnbào, report to a higher authority, customs, etc.) and 申诉 (shēnsù, appeal). The homophonous character 伸, on the other hand, literally means to "stretch, extend (from a bending state)", as in 伸手 (shēn shǒu, stretch out one's hand), 伸展 (shēnzhǎn, spread, extend), and 伸张 (shēnzhāng, uphold, enhance). 伸冤 and 申冤 (shēnyuān, right a wrong) can be used interchangeably.

33) 诵 vs. 颂 (sòng)

The character 诵 basically means to read aloud or recite, with a secondary meaning of "to praise", as in 朗诵 (lǎngsòng, read aloud with expression), 背诵 (bèisòng, recite from memory), 传诵 (chuánsòng, on everyone's lips), or 称诵 (chēngsòng, praise, extoll, eulogize).   The homophonous character 颂, on the other hand, only has the latter meaning of "to praise", as in 颂扬 (sòngyáng), 赞颂 (zànsòng), and 歌颂 (gēsòng), all of which mean "to sing someone's praises, to extoll, to eulogize".

3） 提 vs. 题 (tí)

The character 提 (with a "hand" radical on the left) is usually used as a verb with a core meaning of "to raise, to lift", as in 提倡 (tíchàng, advocate, promote), 提问 (tíwèn, raise questions), 提议 (tíyì, propose), 提示 (tíshì, point out), etc. The homophonous character 题, on the other hand, has a core meaning of "topic, subject, problem", i.e., it may be used as a noun, as in 题目 (tímù, subject, topic), 题材 (tícái, subject matter, theme), 题解 (tíjiě, explanatory notes), and 问题 (wèntí, question, problem), although some expressions can be either noun or verbs, as in 题字 (tízì, inscribe/inscription), 题词 (tící, [write a] dedication).   Lastly, note that the expression 提钢 (tígāng) is a noun referring to an outline of keypoints (e.g., of an article) and should not be miswritten with the character 题.

35) 玩 vs. 顽 (wán)

The meaning of the character 玩 is "to play with" and "enjoy", as in 玩笑 (wánxiào, joke), 游玩 (yóuwán, amuse oneself, go sight-seeing) 玩赏, (wánshǎng, enjoy, take pleasure in), and 玩月 (wán yuè, to enjoy looking at the moon).   A secondary meaning of this character is to trifle with or treat lightly, as in 玩忽 (wánhū, neglect, trifle with), or 玩弄 (wánnòng, dally with, play with).   The character 顽, on the other hand, means "stupid, dense, stubborn, or mischievous,"as in 愚顽 (yúwán, ignorant and stubborn), 顽固 (wángù, stubborn, obstinate), 顽皮 (wánpí, naughty), 顽童 (wántóng, a naughty child).

36) 勿 (wù) vs. 毋 (wú)

Both of these characters have a sense of "forbid", and are usually used only in written style as the equivalent of the colloquial "don't". The character 勿 is usually used as a negative admonition, as in 请勿吸烟 (Qing wù xī yān, Please do not smoke), etc. The character 毋, on the other hand, is usually not used alone, but rather combines with other characters to create negative formula expressions used in literary Chinese style, such as 毋宁 (wúnìng), an adverbial expression meaning "would rather, had better", 毋庸 (wúyōng, need not), and 宁缺毋滥 (nìng quē wú làn, rather have nothing at all than a substandard substitute).

37) 线 vs. 限 (xiàn)

The character 线 means "thread, wire", or "line", while 限 when used as a noun means "bounds" or "limit" as in 界限 (jièxiàn, dividing line), 期限 (qīxiàn, time limit, deadline), 权限 (quánxiàn, limits of power), and 限度 (xiàndù, limit, limitation). Note also that these two characters are interchangeable in the word 界限/界线, meaning "dividing line" when describing things other than land boundaries.

38) 像 vs. 相

The character 相 refers to the looks or appearance of people, as in 相貌 (xiàngmào, facial feature, looks, appearance), 相片 (xiàngpiàn, photograph), 照相机 (zhàoxiàngjī, camera), 可怜相 (kěliánxiàng, pitiful appearance), etc. The character 像

(with the "person" radical), on the other hand, means a likeness, portrait, or picture, as in 画像 (huàxiàng, [draw a] portrait), 塑像 (sùxiàng, statue), 佛像 (fóxiàng, image of the Buddha), etc. It is easy to see why these characters are so often confused, but they must be distinguished properly.

39) 斜 vs. 邪 (xié)

While both of these homophonous characters have the meaning of not straight, not upright, they refer to different types of things. The character 斜 refers primarily to concrete things, as in 倾斜 (qīngxié, tilt, slope, slant), 歪斜 (wāixié, slanting, crooked), 斜坡 (xiépō, slope), 斜线 (xiéxiàn, oblique line), etc. The character 邪, on the other hand, usually describes human affairs, indicating something irregular, heretical, or evil, as in 邪说 (xiéshuō, heresy), 邪念 (xiéniàn, wicked ideas), 邪恶 (xié'è, evil, wicked), or 改邪归正 (gǎi xié guī zhèng, give up evil ways and return to righteousness).

40) 泄 vs. 泻 (xiè)

As may be seen from their "water" radicals, both of these characters are related to liquids. The character 泻 basically means "to flow swiftly or to pour out", as in 倾泻 (qīngxiè, come down in torrents), 一泻千里 (yī xiè qiān lǐ, flow for thousands of miles), 泻肚子 (xiè dùzi, have diarrhoea), etc. The character 泄, on the other hand, means "to let out, discharge, or release", as in 排泄 (páixiè, drain, excrete), or 水泄不通 (shuǐ xiè bù tōng, No drops of water could trickle through; to be jam-packed). 泄 can also be used metaphorically to mean "to release, to let out, or give vent to", as in 泄气 (xièqì, lose heart), 泄密 (xièmì, to give away a secret), or 泄恨 (xièhèn, give vent to one's anger), etc.

41) 形 vs. 型 (xíng)

Both of these homophonous characters can describe people and things. The basic meaning of the character 形 is the form, shape, or structure of people or things, as in 形象 (xíngxiàng, image, form, figure), 形态 (xíngtài, form, shape, pattern), 形式 (xíngshì, form, shape), 图形 (túxíng, graph, figure), 圆形 (yuánxíng, round or circular shape), 方形 (fāngxíng, square shape), and 地形 (dìxíng, terrain), etc. The character 型, on the other hand, refers to a model, pattern or type, as in 模型 (móxíng, model), 类型 (lèixíng, type), 典型 (diǎnxíng, exemplar), 血型 (xuèxíng, blood type), 脸型 (liǎnxíng, facial shape), 新型 (xīnxíng, new type), and 型号 (xínghào, model, type).

42) 须 vs. 需 (xū)

The character 须 means "to have to do something", while the character 需 means "indispensible or necessary". The difference between the two words 须要 and 需要 is that the former is an auxiliary verb, meaning that something has to be done, as in 国家的法律，人人须要遵守 (Guójiā de fǎlù, rénrén xūyào zūnshǒu, Everyone must obey the nation's laws); 需要, on the other hand, acts either as a principal verb or a noun, as in 他需要一本字典 (Tā xūyào yī běn zìdiǎn, He needs a dictionary), or 从群众的需要出发 (cóng qúnzhòng de xūyào chūfā, start out with a consideration of the needs of the masses). The difference between 须要 and 需要 is that the former is also an auxiliary verb meaning "to have to do something", while the latter is a verb which means "to be essential or indispensible".

43) 应 vs. 映 (yìng)

As a verb, the character 应 means "to answer, respond, or echo", as in 答应 (dāyìng, answer, respond), 反应 (fǎnyìng, reaction, response), 应征 (yìngzhēng, respond to the call, enroll, enlist), and 应付 (yìngfù, cope with, handle). The verb 映 means "reflect, mirror, shine", as may be seen in 反映 (fǎn-yìng, reflect), 映射 (yìngshè, shine on), and 水天相映 (shuǐ tiān xiāng yìng, water and sky reflecting each other). The difference between 反应 and 反映 (both fǎnyìng) is that 反应 is a noun, "reaction, response", referring to the reaction of organic bodies to stimulation, and by extension to reactions to things or events. 反映, on the other hand, is a verb, "to reflect", which may be used to mean "reflect a state of affairs", as in "reflecting the development of Chinese industry", or "reflecting (i.e., reporting) the true state of affairs to the leadership", etc.

44) 由 vs. 尤 (yóu)

In fact the two characters 由 (cause, reason) and 尤 (especially) are quite different in their meanings and usage, but because they are homophones and both used as function words inherited from the literary (wényán) language, they are often confused. The character 由 is often used as a preposition meaning "because" or "(starting) from", while 尤 is used as an adverb, meaning "especially, extremely", as in 尤为 (yóuwéi, particularly), 尤甚 (yóushèn, extremely), and 尤其 (yóuqí, especially, particularly).

45) 在 vs. 再 (zài)

The character 在 represents the most frequently used preposition in contemporary Chinese, and is usually combined with place words or locatives in the pattern 在 … plus position word, as 在 … 上 (zài … shàng, on [top of] …), etc. 在 is also used preverbally to indicate continuous or pro gressive aspect, as in 她在吃饭 (Tā zài chī fàn, She is eating), etc. The character 再, on the otherhand, represents an adverb meaning "again", as in 再见 (zàijiàn, See you again, good-bye), 再说一次' (zài shuō yī cì, Say it once more), 再三再四 (zài sān zài sì, repeated again and again), or meaning "later", as in 想好了再写 (xiǎng-hǎole zài xiě, write it after one has made up one's mind), 明天再说吧 (míngtiān zài shuō ba, Let's talk about it tomorrow).

46) 振 vs. 震 (zhèn)

The original meaning of the character 振 is to rise with great vigor, as in 振奋 (zhènfèn, rouse oneself, be inspired with enthusiasm), 振作 (zhènzuò, bestir or exert oneself). This character 振 also means "to shake", as in 振动 (zhèndòng, vibration), 振荡 (zhèndàng, vibration, oscillation), and 振臂高呼 (zhèn bì gāo hū, raise one's arm and shout loudly). The character 震 also has the meaning of "shake", but in the sense of a violent shock or quake, and in 地震 (dìzhèn, earthquake), 震动 (zhèndòng, shake, shock), 震荡 (zhèndàng, shake, shock, quake), 震天动地 (zhèn tiān dòng dì, earth-shaking). This character may also by extension refer to a person's being greatly "moved" emotionally by some outside stimulus, as in 震惊 (zhènjīng, shock, amaze, astonish), 震怒 (zhènnù, be furious), 震撼人心 (zhènhàn rénxīn, to convulse people with excitement and amazement).

47) 支 vs. 只 (zhī)

These two characters are easily confused in that they are

homonyms and are both used as classifiers or measure words. The character 支 is often used to quantify things in the shape of sticks or stems (its original meaning), as in 一支枪 (yī zhī qiāng, a gun), 一支笔 (yī zhī bǐ, a writing instrument), 一支香烟 (yī zhī xiāngyān, one cigarette), etc. (In this sense, it may also be written as 枝.) This character may also be used to quantify soldiers as in 一支军队 (yī zhī jūnduì), a contingent of soldiers, or to quantify songs, as in 一支歌 (yī zhī gē) or 一支曲 (yī zhī qǔ, a song). The character 只 (which is used as the simplified form of the complex character 隻) is used to refer to one of a pair of things, as in 一只鞋 (yī zhī xié, one shoe), 两只手 (liǎng zhī shǒu, two hands), etc. It also refers to some animals which are thought to occur in pairs, as in 一只鸟 (yī zhī niǎo, one bird), 两只兔子 (liǎng zhī tùzi, two rabbits) and to quantify some common articles, such as 一只箱子 (yī zhī xiāngzi, a suitcase, trunk), 一只手表 (yī zhī shǒubiǎo, a wrist watch), as well as for boats, as in 一只小船 (yī zhī xiǎo chuán, a small boat).

48) 至 vs. 致 (zhì)

The character 至 has basic meanings of "arrive, until, as far as", as in 至于 (zhìyú, as far as ... is concerned), 至今 (zhìjīn, up to now), 自始至终 (zì shǐ zhì zhōng, from beginning to end), 以至 (yǐzhì, so that), 甚至 (shènzhì, even), zhìshǎo, 至少 (zhì shǎo, at least). The basic meaning of the character 致, on the other hand, is "to cause to reach", as in 致富 (zhìfù, become rich), 学以致用 (xué yǐ zhì yòng, study in order to use), etc. It also means "to send, extend, or deliver to another party", as in 致敬 (zhìjìng, pay one's respects to), 致欢迎词 (zhì huānyíng cí, make welcoming remarks), as well as "to devote one's efforts

228

to", as in 致力 (zhìlì, devote oneself to), or 专心致志 (zhuānxīn zhìzhì, concentrate one's attention on wholeheartedly). Note that both 以至 (yǐzhì) and 以致 (yǐzhì) can be used in the sense of "so that; with the result that", but 以致 usually implies a bad outcome. Compare: 他专心看书，以至忘了吃饭 (Tā zhuānxīn kàn shū, yǐzhì wàngle chīfàn, He concentrated on his reading so much that he forgot to eat) vs. 她没有认真研究，以致作出了错误的结论 (Tā méiyǒu rènzhēn yánjiū, yǐzhì zuòchūle cuòwù de jiélùn, She did not study seriously and thus drew an erroneous conclusion).

49) 妆 vs. 装 (zhuāng)

The character 妆 (which contains the "woman" component on the right) specifically refers to female adornment and the action of putting on make-up, as in 梳妆 (shūzhuāng, to dress and make-up), 红妆 (hóngzhuāng, gay feminine attire), 化妆 (huàzhuāng, put on make up), and 嫁妆 (jiàzhuāng, dowry), 妆奁 (zhuānglián, trousseau), etc. The character 装 may be used as a verb to mean "to decorate, to dress up, to beautify, or to overdo unnaturally". It can be used not only for people, but also for things, as in 装饰 (zhuāngshì, decorate, adorn), 装点 (zhuāngdiǎn, bedeck, decorate), 化装 (huàzhuāng, make up, disguise), 假装 (jiǎzhuāng, pretend), 装模作样 (zhuāngmú zuòyàng, put on an act), 装腔作势 (zhuāngqiāng zuòshì, be affected and pretentious), 装潢 (zhuānghuáng, decorating, mounting, packaging), 装订 (zhuāngdìng, book-binding), and 装裱 (zhuāngbiǎo, to mount [a picture, etc.]).

50) 作 vs. 做 (zuò)

These two characters are most often confused when used

as transitive verbs with objects. The character 作 is used in 作曲 (zuòqǔ, compose music), 作文 (zuòwén, write compositions [for practice]), 作弊 (zuòbì, cheat), 作对 (zuòduì, oppose), 作怪 (zuòguài, make trouble), 作假 (zuòjiǎ, counterfeit), 作客 (zuòkè, sojourn), 作乱 (zuòluàn, rise in revolt), and 作呕 (zuò'ǒu, to feel sick). The character 做, on the other hand, is used in such expressions as 做诗 (zuò shī, write poems), 做文章 (zuò wénzhāng, write essays), 做衣服 (zuò yīfu, make clothes), 做伴 (zuòbàn, keep company), 做工 (zuògōng, engage in manual labor), 做事 (zuò shì, engage in work), 做梦 (zuòmèng, dream), 做人 (zuòrén, conduct oneself [properly]), 做生日 (zuò shēngrì, celebrate a birthday), 做声 (zuòshēng, make a sound), and 做主 (zuòzhǔ, make decisions for, be master of). Note that 作法 and 做法, (both zuòfǎ), are different in that the former refers particularly to the way a composition is done, while the latter refers to the way something is dealt with or produced.

6. THE ORDERING OF CHINESE CHARACTERS

In a warehouse, there are all kinds of goods; in a pharmacy, there are all kinds of medicines. Obviously, if these things were all mixed up together, then looking for something would be very troublesome. But if things are arranged in an orderly manner according to some system, then it will always be easy to find what one is looking for. It is the same with Chinese characters. There are thousands, even tens of thousands, of Chinese characters; if they are thrown together without any order, then finding a certain character from among them all will be like looking for a needle in a haystack. We need to arrange characters according to set rules in order to be able to find them easily. This is what is meant by the ordering of Chinese characters 汉字的排序.

Character ordering is important not only for referencing 检索 (looking up characters in dictionaries, lexicons and indexes) but also for Chinese-language data processing 中文信息处理. With the rapid development of computer technology, the ordering of Chinese characters for input has become a crucial problem, urgently awaiting a solution. Some people describe it as the "bottleneck" problem; if things are slowed down by the bottleneck of inputting the characters, then everything else has to stop and wait. In this chapter, we will focus on these two problems of character referencing methods and Chinese-language computer input. Before going on to these topics, however, we must first discuss the problem of criteria for ordering the elements of a writing system.

6.1 STANDARDS FOR ORDERING ELEMENTS OF WRITING

The elements of any writing system can be placed in order according to fixed rules. There are, however, good orderings and bad ones. By what rules may one produce an ideal arrangement? To answer this question we must ask another: what is an ideal arrangement? Experience has taught us that an ideal arrangement is one that will satisfy the four criteria listed below.

1) Uniqueness Standard 唯一性标准

The uniqueness standard requires that there be only one allowable ordering for any list of items to be arranged. If our ordering system fails to fix absolutely the position of each item in a list, then it has not met the uniqueness standard. Consider the alphabetical word ordering system of English, which does satisfy this standard. The following ten words: find, basis, player, voyage, able, iron, test, comfort, play, comedy, arranged in alphabetical order, give us this ordering:

able
basis
comedy
comfort

find
iron
play
player
test
voyage

The position of each word in this ordering is unique — no word could occupy any other position and still obey the rules of alphabetical order. If any other word is added into the list, for example, "cone", it can only go in one position, between "comfort" and "find"; its position is uniquely determined.

Now let us take an example using Chinese characters. Take for instance the ten characters 课，群，秀，妹，圆，默，矛，英，拿，and 追. Ordering them according to the number of strokes in each character, those with fewer strokes preceding those with more strokes, produces the following list.

矛 (5 strokes)　课 (10 strokes)
秀 (7 strokes)　拿 (10 strokes)
英 (8 strokes)　圆 (10 strokes)
妹 (8 strokes)　群 (13 strokes)
追 (9 strokes)　默 (13 strokes)

In this listing, the two characters 英 and 妹 both have eight strokes, and the three characters 课，拿，and 圆 all have ten. This method of ordering does not satisfy the uniqueness requirement, as it is equally correct to put 妹 before 英 or to put 英 before 妹, or to mix up the three ten-stroke characters in any order. Thus the method of ordering characters according to number of strokes fails to meet the uniqueness standard.

2) Single-rule Standard 单一性标准

This criterion is aimed at minimizing the number of rules needed to put items in order. It requires that one rule be enough to arrange all items into a fixed order. English alphabetization satisfies this standard. In English, the repeated application of just one rule — the rule of alphabetical order — is sufficient to order all words in the language in a unique order.

If Chinese characters are ordered according to number of strokes, the ordering of the majority of characters cannot be uniquely determined. Therefore another rule is still needed to supplement the number-of-stroke rule. For example, the three characters 课，拿，and 圆 all have ten strokes; there is no way to determine which should come first and which last. So we must supplement the rule with another one: characters with the same number of strokes are to be ordered by what type of stroke their first stroke is. We order the strokes thus: 1) horizontal stroke, 2) vertical stroke, 3) left-falling stroke, 4) dot, and 5) turning stroke. The first stroke of 圆 is a vertical stroke, so it should come first in order; the first stroke of 拿 is a left-falling stroke, so it should come second; and the first stroke of 课 is a dot, so it should come third. Because of the complexity of Chinese character structure, one must often apply three or four different rules successively just to set a group of characters in order. Sometimes, even after four rules are applied, characters still remain which cannot be set in a fixed order.

3) Transparency Standard 直观性标准

This standard requires that the relative ordering of two items be obvious at a glance, without excessive inspection or analysis. Taking as an example the two English words "conservation" and "conversation", one look is enough to tell us that "conservation" comes before " conversation" in a alphabetical ordering. Now consider the two Chinese characters 露 and 罐. Going by number of strokes, it is not immediately apparent which character has fewer strokes and so should come first. (On counting, we find that 露 has 21 strokes and 罐 23 strokes.) If these two characters are transcribed into Hanyu Pinyin, however, the correct alphabetical ordering of lù 露 and guàn 罐 becomes apparent. Hanyu Pinyin ordering is more "transparent" and in this respect superior to ordering by number of strokes.

The transparency of an ordering system is directly related to ease and efficiency of referencing. The more transparent the system, the easier it will be to look up items so arranged.

4) Simplicity standard　简易性标准

This standard requires that ordering rules be simple and easy to grasp. In particular, there should not be too many exceptions to the rules; exceptions must be memorized, and memorization wastes time and effort.

English alphabetic ordering requires only the memorization of twenty-six letters in their correct order. There are no exceptions to be memorized. Among the various ordering methods of Chinese characters, ordering according to number of strokes is relatively easy, while ordering according to radicals (see the following section) is the most troublesome. Ordering according to Hanyu Pinyin is the easiest of all methods. While ordering by strokes is relatively simple, as we have seen this method fails to satisfy the uniqueness and transparency standards. When looking at any criterion, one must take the other criteria into consideration as well.

Ordering methods which can satisfy the four standards described above are of course the best kind. While alphabetic writing systems, such as English and Russian, can satisfy these criteria completely with alphabetic ordering systems, writing systems which do not use an alphabet generally have great difficulty satisfying them completely. Especially for ideographic writing systems like Chinese characters, finding an ordering which will satisfy the four criteria is almost impossible. In the past few decades, many people have studied the problem of ordering Chinese characters. Each has tried to find an ideal ordering method that would satisfy all the criteria. However, though many have racked their brains and not a few have spent their entire lives engaged in research, no method has yet been developed which satisfies everyone. Some say that the problem of ordering Chinese characters is one of the most difficult problems in the world, and this statement is no exaggeration.

6.2 METHODS OF REFERENCING CHINESE CHARACTERS

Character referencing methods 查字法 are ways of arranging Chinese characters, as in dictionaries and indexes, according to fixed rules and with the aim of making them as easy as possible to look up. Since there is no ordering method which completely satisfies the criteria we have stipulated, we will have to be satisfied with any method that is relatively easy to learn and use. There are already numerous methods for referencing Chinese characters. Even today, people continue trying to develop new and better ones. The five most widely used methods are explained in the following paragaphs.

1) Character referencing by radicals　部首查字法

It was discussed in a preceding section that all picto-phonetic characters possess a semantic component, while all the components of associative characters are semantic in nature. In classifying Chinese characters by semantic components, all characters with a common semantic component will be classified together under one 部 or "part". The common semantic component is then called the radical 部首 of these characters. For example, the following characters are all classified under the semantic radical 木 (wood): 木, 本, 未, 末, 术, 札, 朽, 朴, 杂, 杆, 杠, 杜, 杖, 杨 and 李. Many radicals are not characters in their own right, but merely parts or variant forms of characters, such as 亻 (人, person), 冫 (冰, ice), 刂 (刀, knife), 巛 (川, river), 扌 (手, hand), 氵 (水, water), 犭 (犬, dog), 讠 (言, word), and 饣 (食, food).

The system of ordering by radicals is said to have been invented by Xǔ Shèn of the Eastern Hàn period. His Shuō Wén Jiě Zì was the first lexicon to be arranged according to radicals. Xǔ Shèn proposed a system of 540 "significs" or radicals. During the Míng Dynasty, Méi Yīngzuò's 梅膺祚 Zì Huì 字汇 (*Glossary*) reduced the number of radicals to 214; the later Kāngxī Zìdiǎn, Cí Yuán 词源 (*Source of Words*), Cí Hǎi, Zhōng-huá Dà Zìdiǎn 中华大字典 (*Zhonghua Unabridged Dictionary*) and other works retained the 214-radical classification. Modern lexicons and dictionaries published in mainland China, such as Xīnhuá Zìdiǎn (*Xinhua Dictionary*), Sìjiǎo Hàomǎ Xīn Cídiǎn 四角号码新词典 (*New Four-Corner Code Dictionary*), and Xiàndài Hànyǔ Cídiǎn use a system of 189 radicals. The new edition of Cí Hǎi and a few other dictionaries and lexicons use a system of 250 radicals. The 540 radicals of Shuō Wén Jiě Zì is useful for studying the origins of characters; this approach to radicals stresses the principle of character construction. The radicals of later lexicons stress the relation between radicals and character structure, which is convenient for referencing characters; this approach stresses the principle of character referencing. The goals of these two sorts of approach are not entirely alike. To take a few concrete examples:

The character 相 (xiàng, to look at), according to the principle of character construction, should be classified under the radical 目 eye), because looking at things requires the use of the eyes. According to the principle of character referencing, it should be classified under 木 (wood), because radicals are in principle located on the left side of a character, and reducing exceptions to this rule makes it easier to look up characters.

Another example: 磨 (mó, to grind), according to the principle of character construction, should be classified under 石 (stone), because 石 is the semantic component of this character i.e. grind stone. According to the principle of character referencing, it should be classified under 麻 (hemp) because radicals are often found in the upper part of a character (and because there are other characters with the same component, such as 摩，麾，糜 and 魔).

Again: 穎 (yǐng, grain husk), according to the principle of character construction, should be classified under 禾 (grain), because of the semantic connection. According to the principle of character referencing, however, it should go under 頁, because the left section 呆 is not a radical.

For the purpose of making it easier to look up characters, it is better to adhere to the principle of character referencing and not to worry excessively about the principle of character construction. The basic method of looking up a character by its radical is explained below.

a) Find the radical. For example, to look up the character 锵 (qiāng, clang), one must first determine that its radical is the leftmost 钅 (gold, metal) component. 钅 has five strokes, so we look it up in the "Five Strokes" section of the radical list and then turn to the section of the index listing the 钅-radical characters.

b) Count the remaining strokes. In the characters 锵, once the radical 钅 is split off, the left-over part 将 has nine strokes. We then look under the "Nine Strokes" subsection of the listing of the 钅-radical characters to find 锵, which turns out to be pronounced qiāng, representing the sound "clang".

c) For characters in which it is impossible to identify a radical, there is a special section of the radical index titled "Remainder". Characters such as 及, 也, 长, 凸, 够, and 酉, as well as many others, are to be found in this part of the index listed by total number of strokes. Many dictionaries contain a similar total stroke order listing of "Hard to Identify Characters" or "Characters with Obscure Radicals" following the regular radical listing.

Character referencing by radicals is the traditional method of looking up Chinese characters, and its applications are widespread. However, the radical method is plagued by more shortcomings than any other method. Many aspects of the radical method require unification and standardization. This issue will be discussed in greater detail in the next section.

2) Character Referencing by Number of Strokes 笔数查字法

Character referencing by number of strokes is the simplest method of all. In this type of ordering, characters with fewer strokes are placed in front, and those with more are placed in back.

When looking up characters by stroke number, the most important thing is to count the number of strokes correctly. The number of strokes is in turn related to whether or not the character is written in its standard form. For instance, the character 鬼 (guǐ, ghost, devil) so written (standard form) has nine strokes, but written 鬼 it has ten strokes. The number of strokes is also related to stroke order. For instance, the character 长 (cháng, long) written with the standard stroke order: ノ一上长 has four strokes, but written: ｜㇑上长 it has five strokes. For questions on the standard form, number of strokes, and stroke order of Chinese characters, it is best to consult the "List of Chinese Character Forms for General Printing" (see 3.3).

The greatest drawback to character referencing by number of strokes is that there are too many characters with the same

240

number of strokes. The Cí Hǎi dictionary provides us with the following statistics on the number of strokes of 11,834 Chinese characters:

No. of strokes:	No. of characters:	No. of strokes;	No. of characters:
1	3	19	201
2	22	20	162
3	72	21	93
4	160	22	78
5	247	23	57
6	445	24	3
7	788	25	24
8	1020	26	9
9	1164	27	5
10	1191	28	3
11	1199	29	2
12	1206	30	1
13	1000	31	1
14	770	32	1
15	654	33	0
16	562	34	0
17	407	35	0
18	256	36	1

If characters are ordered only according to number of strokes, then when one wants to look up a character with eight, nine, ten, eleven, twelve, or thirteen strokes, one must search among more than one thousand characters. This defeats the purpose of ordering characters in the first place. Therefore,

241

the stroke-numbering method must proceed in coordination with other methods (such as radicals or stroke order) in order to be practical for use in referencing. However, ordering characters by number of strokes is entirely practical when one is dealing with a limited number of characters. For example, a name list of a hundred or so entries can conveniently be ordered according to the number of strokes in each person's surname.

3) Character Referencing by Stroke Form 笔形查字法

The strokes that make up Chinese characters may be divided into five types. Their order and individual names are as follows:

Stroke Form	一（ノ）	l（J）	ノ（ ´ ）	丶（乀）	一（乚）
Name	Horizontal stroke	Vertical stroke	Left-falling stroke	Dot	Curving stroke
Order	1	2	3	4	5
Direction of Stroke	→	↓	↙	↘	↗ ↘

Characters may be arranged in sequence according to which of these five types of strokes their first stroke belongs to. There are two ways of arranging characters, depending on the number of strokes they contain:

If a character is made up of five or fewer strokes, then it is sequenced simply according to its first stroke. For example:

Four strokes：〔一〕比切扎支…〔丨〕止少中内…〔ノ〕仁仆从气…〔丶〕计订六方…〔一〕劝双引以尺水书…

If a character contains six or more strokes, then it is se-

242

quenced according to the first and second strokes together, always in the order given above. For example:

Eleven strokes: 〔——〕球彗… 〔—丨〕堆彬… 〔—丿〕硕厢 〔—丶〕雪…〔—→〕棒匭…〔丨—〕虚彪…〔丨丨〕斐…〔丨丶〕雀堂… 〔丨→〕唱帷…〔丿—〕银笛…〔丿丨〕做衅…〔丿丿〕得舶…〔丶丶〕领 盒…〔丿㇆〕猜馆…〔丶—〕族章…〔丶丨〕情阐…〔丶丿〕烽焊…〔丶 丶〕减着…〔丶→〕谋涛…〔→—〕弹屠…〔→丨〕隆蛋…〔→丿〕婚颅… 〔→丶〕颈翌…〔㇆㇆〕雏绩…

The "five-stroke" referencing method described above is also known as the "札 (zhá) method", because the character 札 contains all five of the basic strokes in the correct order. The method was developed in the 1950's by the Linguist Lí Jínxī 黎锦熙, and has been adopted for use in numerous reference works (including the encyclopedic dictionary Cí Hǎi).

4) Character Referencing by the Four-corner Code 四角 号码查字法

A) Stroke Configurations and Codes

This method of character referencing divides the stroke configurations of characters into ten types and represents them by the ten digits 0 through 9, as en page 244:

B) Character Referencing Method

(a) Order of corners. Each character is assigned four numbers corresponding to that character's 1) top left corner, 2) top right corner, 3) bottom left corner, and 4) bottom right corner, in that order. E.g.:

Stroke Name	Number	Configura-tion	Sample Characters	Explanation
Head （头）	0	亠	主病广言	dot over a horizontal stroke
Horizontal （横）	1	一（ㄟ ㄟ ㇀）	天办活培织 兄风	horizontal stroke; rising stroke, horizontal hook, right-falling hook
Hanging （垂）	2	丨（丿 ㇀ 丨）	旧山干顺力 则	vertical stroke; left-falling stroke, vertical hook
Dot （点）	3	丶丶丶（丶丶）	宝社军外去 亦造瓜	dot; right-falling stroke
Cross （叉）	4	十（ 十才 乂 扌 扌）	古草对式皮 猪	one stroke crossing through another
Insertion （插）	5	中（丰 戈 史 声 丰） 泰申	青本打戈史	one stroke crossing through two or more strokes
Box （方）	6	口口（口 口）	另扣国甲由 曲目四	full square enclosure
Corner （角）	7	フ乛乚乚 （厂 亅 」） 兵雪	刀写亡表阳	a stroke turning angularly down or to the right; angle formed by the heads of two strokes
Eight （八）	8	八八 ⺈ 丷	分共余佘央 羊午	form of the character or similar to 八
Small （小）	9	小忄小 丷 ⺌ 丷）	尖宗快木录 当兴组	form of the character 小, or similar to ...

244

(b) Method for determining codes of each corner

b-1. One stroke may be divided into several parts and used to obtain codes for more than one corner. E.g.:

以 乱 七 习 乙 几

b-2. The stroke configurations formed by the upper and lower ends of a single stroke in combination with other strokes can separately derive codes for two corners. E.g.:

半 大 木 耒 火 米

b-3. Where stroke configuration tends to a bottom corner of the character, give it a number according to the corner it actually occupies, and assign the empty corner a "0". E.g.:

产 户 亏 飞 弓 妒

However, when characters like 弓 or 亏 are used as character components, assign the lower left corner of the character the number "2".E.g.:

张 鄂

b-4. The lower left and right corners of characters enclosed by structures of the form 口, 门, or 鬥 are assigned numbers according to the lower corners of the enclosed portion. E.g.:

园 =6021   田 =6040   闲 =3724   鬨 =7744   鬮 =7721

This does not include, however, characters of this form that have additional stroke configurations on the top, bottom, or left or right side. E.g.:

苗 =4460   恩 =6033   泪 =3610   睦 =6401   简 =8822

b-5. If one corner of a stroke configuration has already been assigned a number, all subsequent corners occupied by the same configuration are assigned a "0". E.g.:

王　冬　之　直　中　全　卜
心　斗　持　时　一　十　口
八　小

(c) Additional symbols

c-1. To differentiate characters with the same four-corner code, take the stroke configuration just above the lower right (final) corner, obtain its code number, and add this onto the first four numbers. If this configuration has already been used for the upper right corner (as in 决 and 连), then take "0" as its code number. E.g.:

芒 =44710　喜　目　工　元　石　百　出　欠

令　公　玉　疳　西　固　宙　逢　单　子

都　豆　否　泰　决　连

c-2. For characters whose four-corner code and additional symbol are both identical, order them according to the number of horizontal strokes (一 丿 丶 乛) in each character. E.g.:

市　(two horizontal strokes)　帝　(three horizontal strokes)

C) Additional Rules

(a) The standard for stroke configuration is the "List of Chinese Character Forms For General Printing". E.g.:

Correct

住　言　路　比　反　禺　祚　户　卜

246

Incorrect

住 ¹言 ,路 比¹ 反¹ 禺 ¹祚 ¹户 卜

Correct

斥 ʼ业 ₂亦 ʼ灰 ʼ免 ʼ草 执 ,衣 ,么

Incorrect

斥 ʼ业 ₂亦 ⁷灰¹ ₂免 ¹草¹ 执 ₁衣 ₂么

(b) Points to be remembered when deriving stroke configurations:

b-1. Derive compound rather than simple stroke configurations wherever possible. E.g.:

Correct

₂庄 ₁寸 ₁扎 ⁷厂¹ ₂养 ₂介 ₂气 ₂少

Incorrect

庄 ¹寸 ₁扎 ¹厂 养 介 气 少

b-2. In characters containing an angled horizontal stroke under a dot, such as 空 and 户, the top corners are assigned the code number "3."

(c) Points to be remembered in obtaining corner codes:

c-1. For corners with two simple strokes or one simple and one compound stroke configuration, always use the leftmost or rightmost stroke configuration, regardless of height. E.g.:

症 非 帚 白 物 句 州

梁 治 巾 掉 拍 鸣 郑

c-2. When there are two compound strokes to choose from, always use the topmost compound stroke in the upper corners

and the bottom-most compound stroke in the lower corners.
E.g.:

$$\text{功} \quad \text{九} \quad \text{力} \quad \text{内} \quad \text{皮} \quad \text{也} \quad \text{成} \quad \text{军}$$

c-3. For a left-falling stroke starting from the middle of the character, as long as there is another stroke in the lower left corner, always use the other stroke to obtain the lower-left corner code. E.g.:

$$\text{衣} \quad \text{左} \quad \text{奎} \quad \text{友} \quad \text{右} \quad \text{寿} \quad \text{春} \quad \text{复}$$

But if the left-falling stroke starts on the left side of the character, then use it to obtain the lower-left corner code. E.g.:

$$\text{辟} \quad \text{尉} \quad \text{仓}$$

The following is a Chinese verse which may be used as a mnemonic device to help remember the Four Corner Coding System:

横一垂二三点捺；

Héng yī, chuí èr, sān diǎn nà;

Horizontal stroke 1, vertical stroke 2, 3 dot and right-falling stroke;

叉四插五方框六；

chā sì, chā wǔ, fāng kuāng liù;

Cross 4, insertion 5, square frame 6;

七角八八九是小；

qī jiǎo, bā bā, jiǔ shì xiǎo;

7 corner, 8 eight (八), 9 is small (小);

点下有横变零头。

diǎn xià yǒu héng biàn líng tóu.

Dot over horizontal stroke takes the lead.

The advantage of the four-corner code system is that it satisfies the transparency standard. After becoming proficient in its use, the student can look up characters very quickly. The drawback is that it fails to satisfy the simplicity standard; there are too many rules with too many exceptions. The beginning learner will find it a hard system to grasp.

5) Character Referencing by Hanyu Pinyin 拼音字母查字法

This method makes use of the Hanyu Pinyin alphabet, which is identical to the twenty-six letter English alphabet. Characters are ordered alphabetically, just as in an English dictionary. For instance, the order of the characters 拼 (pīn, put together), 音 (yīn, sound), 字 (zì, character), and 母 (mǔ, mother) is mǔ (母), pīn (拼), yīn (音), and zì (字). The order of 包 (bāo, bundle), 帮 (bāng, help), 北 (běi, north), and 班 (bān, class) is bān (班), bāng (帮), bāo (包), and běi (北).

In Pinyin alphabet ordering, letters that carry an additional symbol are placed after those that do not: thus ê is placed after e, and ü is placed after u. The digraphs zh, ch, sh, and ng are all arranged according to the order of their individual letters; thus we find under syllables beginning with z the ordering: zan, zeng, zhan, zhen, zheng, zhong, zhun, zhuo, zi, zong, zou, zu, zuan, zui, zun, zuo...

Characters composed of identical sounds are arranged in order according to tone: 1) first tone (high level), 2) second tone (rising), 3) third tone (low dipping), 4) fourth tone (falling), and 5) neutral tone. Thus: bā, bá, bǎ, bà, ba. Characters whose phonetic form and tone are both identical are arranged according to the form of their first stroke, in the following order: 1) horizontal stroke 一, 2) vertical stroke ｜, 3) left-falling stroke 丿, 4) dot 丶, and 5) turning stroke 乛乚. To use as an example characters with the pronunciation bā, their ordering according to first stroke is; 芭 (banana), 捌 (eight, on cheques, etc.), 八 (eight), 笆 (basketry), 粑 (cake), and 巴 (hope).

To arrange a table of whole words, one may first arrange the individual characters and then under each character separately arrange the multisyllabic words beginning with that character. Multisyllabic words with the same character are arranged according to the Pinyin spelling of the second character; those whose first and second characters are the same, according to the spelling of the third character, and so on. E.g.:

红　　hóng (red)
红榜　hóngbǎng (honor roll)
红茶　hóngchá (black tea)
红军　hóngjūn (the Red Army)
红旗　hóngqí (red flag)
红色　hóngsè (red)
红松　hóngsōng (Korean pine)

6.3 STANDARDIZATION OF CHINESE CHARACTER ORDERING

Standardization here refers mainly to the standardization of character referencing methods. This sort of standardization is extremely important for looking up characters in dictionaries, and also for the teaching of Chinese characters.

Each of the five types of character referencing methods introduced in the previous section faces the problem of standardization. Among the five, the method of referencing by radicals is the most common and has been in use for the longest time; it also presents the most problems for standardization. In the discussion below, we will focus on the problem of standardization as it relates to the radical method.

Three urgent problems confront the radicals method:

1) The Need for Consistency in Number and Kind of Radicals

One reason why the number and kind of radicals vary from dictionary to dictionary is that there are two principles by which radicals are determined: the principle of character construction and the principle of character referencing. Some lexicographers abide by the one principle and others by the other. Owing to the complexity of character structure, sometimes even systems that determine radicals on the basis of character form which apply the same principle of character referencing will still produce variant systems of radicals.

The three most representative systems of radicals in current use are the system of 214 radicals used by the Kāngxī Zìdiǎn, the system of 250 radicals used by the Cí Hǎi dictionary (revised edition), and the system of 189 radicals used by the Xīnhuá Zìdiǎn. Each of these systems embraces a different number and a different variety of radicals. Thus the same character may be classified under a certain radical in dictionary A and under another radical in dictionary B. This gives rise to confusion in looking up characters and makes studying characters more difficult.

(2) The Need for Standardization of Each Character's Radical

Even if the number and kind of radicals are consistent in

every dictionary, a common principle for determining which part of a character is the radical is still necessary to bring order to any system of radicals. There are many examples of the confusion caused by the lack of such a principle:

Should the character 麾 (huī, to command) be classified under 麻 (má, hemp) or under 毛 (máo, feather or fur)?

Should the character 盅 (zhōng, cup) be classified under 中 (zhōng, middle) or under 皿 (mǐn, dish)?

Should the character 鸿 (hóng, goose or swan) be classified under 氵 (shuǐ, water) or under 鸟 (niǎo, bird)?

Should the character 荆 (jīng, chaste tree) be classified under 艹 (cǎo, grass) or under 刂 (dāo, knife)?

Should the character 整 (zhěng, entire) be classified under 束 (shù, tie) or under 攵 (pū, hit lightly)?

Should the character 糶 (tiào, sell grain) be classified under 米 (mǐ, rice), under 屮 (chè, burgeoning grass), under 羽 (yǔ, feather), or under 隹 (zhuī, short-tailed bird)?

(3) The Need for Unity in Arranging Characters with the Same radical

Characters with the same radical are usually arranged in sequence according to number of strokes. Sometimes, however, there are many characters with the same number of strokes under one radical; if they are not arranged according to some rule, looking up characters will still be a great deal of trouble. To take an example from the Kāngxī Zìdiǎn: under the radical 木 (mù, wood), there are 128 characters with eight strokes (not counting the strokes in 木 itself), and 125 with nine strokes. If as many as 128 characters are listed in random order, looking up any particular one will take an immense amount of time. Clearly, a rule is needed by which to arrange these characters. Various dictionaries use various rules; standardization is called for.

In 1961, the Working Group to Rectify Character-Referencing Methods was jointly set up by the Ministry of Culture, the Ministry of Education, the Committee for the Reform of the Chinese Language and the Linguistics Research Institute in the Chinese Academy of Sciences. In 1964 this group put forward drafts for character referencing by radicals, by four-corner code, by stroke form, and by phonetic alphabet (Pinyin). In 1983. the Working Group to Unify Character Referencing by Radicals, sponsored by the Committee for the Reform of the Chinese Language and the Ministry of Culture, was jointly established by several organizations specializing in editing and publishing dictionaries. By consulting the radical systems used in the Kāngxī Zìdiǎn, the Cí Hǎi and the Xīnhuá Zìdiǎn, this group formulated a new system of unified radicals. The general content and the referencing method of this system are introduced below.

1) The table of unified radicals contains 201 radicals altogether, arranged according to number of strokes. Those radicals with the same number of strokes are arranged according to the form of their first stroke, in the following order: 1) horizontal stroke ⼀, 2) vertical stroke ｜, 3) left-falling stroke ノ, 4) dot 丶, and 5) turning stroke ㇇. (The table itself is appended at the end of this section.)

2) This table is applicable to both simplified characters and original-form complex characters.

3) Radicals are assigned on the basis of the form of characters, the point being to classify every character under one of the 201 standardized radicals if at all possible. The classifying radical is usually taken from the upper, lower, left, right or outside portion of a character. The middle portion and that occupying any of the four corners is the second choice. Any characters which cannot be assigned a radical on the basis of any of these may be assigned a single-stroke radical, of which there are five: 一、 丨 、 丿 、 丶 、 and 乙.

The method for referencing characters is as follows:

1) The usual position of the radical is in the upper, lower, left, right, or outside portion of a character.

Radical at the top:	宜	(yí, suitable)	radical:	宀′
	原	(yuán, primary)	radical:	厂
	置	(zhì, to put)	radical:	四
Radical at the bottom:	型	(xíng, mold)	radical:	土
	货	(huò, goods)	radical:	贝
	盎	(àng, an ancient vessel)	radical:	皿
Radical on the left:	词	(cí, word)	radical:	言
	研	(yán, pestle)	radical:	石
	躯	(qū, human body)	radical:	身
Radical on the right:	歌	(gē, song)	radical:	欠
	领	(lǐng, neck)	radical:	页
	馗	(kuí, thoroughfare)	radical:	首
Radical on the outside:	同	(tóng, same)	radical:	冂

巨	(jù, huge)	radical: 匚
固	(gù, solid)	radical: 囗

2) For those characters that have no radical in any of the five locations designated above, the radical is taken from the middle portion; for those without a radical in the middle, a radical is taken from one of the four corners, in the following order: upper left, lower left, upper right, and lower right.

Radical in the middle:	办	(bàn, to manage)	radical:	力
	爽	(shuǎng, clear)	radical:	大
	幽	(yōu, secluded)	radical:	山
	乘	(chéng, to ride)	radical:	禾
Radical in a corner:	疑	(yí, to doubt)	radical:	乚
	巯	(qiú, hydrosulfide)	radical:	工
	豫	(yù, pleased)	radical:	龴
	叛	(pàn, to betray)	radical:	又

3) For characters with several possible radicals, the correct radical is determined according to the following rules:

a) For characters that have radicals on both the top and the bottom, the top is used as the radical.

牢	(láo, prison)	radical:	宀, not	牛
冬	(dōng, winter)	radical:	夂, not	冫

b) For characters that have radicals on both the left and the right, the left is used as the radical.

相	(xiāng, mutual)	radical:	木, not	目
酒	(jiǔ, wine)	radical:	氵, not	酉

c) For characters that have radicals on both the inside and the outside, the outside is used as the radical.

闷	(mèn, stuffy)	radical:	门, not	心

句 (jù, sentence)　　radical: 勹, not 口

d) For characters that have both a single-stroke and a multi-stroke radical, the multi-stroke radical is used.

灭 (miè, extinguish) radical: 火, not 一

旧 (jiù, old)　　　　radical: 日, not 丨

e) For characters in which a possible radical of few strokes makes up part of another possible radical with more strokes, the radical with the most strokes is used.

章 (zhāng, chapter), 竟 (jìng, finish), 意 (yì, meaning) contain the radicals 丶, 亠, 立, and 音; 音 is used as the radical.

磨 (mó, rub), 糜 (mí, rotton), and 靡 (mí, waste) contain the radicals 丶, 广, and 麻; 麻 is used as the radical.

4) For characters that have no radicals in the top, bottom, left, right, outside, middle or in any of the four corners, the first stroke of the character is used as a single-stroke radical.

屯 (tún, store up)　　radical: 一

凸 (tū, protrude)　　radical: 丨

年 (nián, year)　　　radical: 丿

半 (bàn, half)　　　radical: 丶

也 (yě, also)　　　　radical: 乙(一)

The table of unified radicals is appended below.

THE 201 UNIFIED CHARACTER RADICALS (JUNE 1983)

Radical	Example

1 Stroke

1. 一　　丁
2. 丨　　半
3. 丿　　川
4. 丶　　之
5. 乙（一乁乚）亂

2 Strokes

6. 十　　克
7. 厂（厂）厅
8. 匚　　区
9. 卜（卜）下
　　刂＝刀　刑
10. 冂（冂）同
　　亻＝人　他
　　厂＝厂　后
11. 八（丷）分
12. 人（入亻）今
　　入＝人　余
　　勹＝刀　危
13. 勹　　勿
　　冂＝冂　周
14. 匕　　旨
15. 儿　　兜
16. 几（几）凡

17. 亠　　市
18. 冫　　冲
　　丷＝八　关
19. 冖　　冗
　　讠＝言　计
20. 凵　　凶
21. 卩（㔾）印
　　阝（左）＝阜　队
　　阝（右）＝邑　邦
22. 刀（勹刂）切
23. 力　　动
24. 厶　　台
25. 又　　双
26. 廴　　廷
　　㔾＝卩

3 Strokes

27. 干　　刊
28. 工　　巧
29. 土（士）地
　　艹＝艸　艺
30. 廾　　弊
31. 大　　夺
32. 尢（尢尣）尬
　　尢＝尢
　　扌＝手　打
33. 寸　　封

34. 戈　　式
　　⺌＝小　肖
35. 口　　吹
36. 囗　　国
37. 巾　　帆
38. 山　　岭
39. 彳　　行
40. 彡　　形
　　犭＝犬　狂
41. 夕　　外
42. 夂　　冬
　　饣＝食　饭
43. 丬（爿）妆
44. 广　　庆
　　忄＝心　忙
45. 门（門）问
　　氵＝水　江
46. 宀　　宁
　　辶＝　　边
47. 彐（彐彑）录
48. 尸　　尾
49. 己　　异
50. 弓　　引
51. 屮（屮）出
52. 女　　姑
53. 飞（飛）飞

257

54. 小（⺌）	尘	
55. 子	孔	
56. 马（馬）	驰	
纟 ＝糸	红	
彑 ＝彐	彘	
57. 幺	幼	
58. 巛	巢	

4 Strokes

59. 王（玉）	玩
60. 无（旡）	无
61. 韦韋	韧
耂 ＝老	孝
62. 木	村
63. 支	翅
64. 犬（犭）	献
65. 歹（歺）	殔
66. 车（車）	轨
67. 戈	战
68. 比	毙
旡 ＝无	既
69. 牙	鸦
70. 瓦	瓶
71. 止	肯
72. 攴（攵）	敲
73. 日（曰冃）	旭
冃 ＝月	背
74. 贝（貝）	财

75. 见（見）	览
76. 牛	物
77. 手（手扌）	挚
78. 毛	毡
79. 气	氛
夂 ＝攴	收
80. 长（長镸）	长
81. 片	版
82. 斤	斯
83. 爪（爫）	爬
84. 父	爸
尣 ＝尢	尴
爫 ＝爪	采
85. 月（⺼）	肝
86. 氏	昏
87. 欠	欧
88. 风（風）	飑
89. 殳	段
90. 文	斌
91. 方	旗
92. （火灬）	灯
93. 斗	斟
灬 ＝火	然
94. 户	启
礻 ∥示	礼
95. 心（忄小）	想
聿 ＝聿	肃

爿 ＝丬（壮）	
⺗ ＝心	恭
96. （母）	贯
97. 水（氵氺）	桨

5 Strokes

玉 ＝王	玺祭
98. 示（礻）	祭
99. 甘	某
100. 石	研
101. 龙（龍）	聋
歺 ＝歹	殔
102. 业	凿
103. 目	眷
104. 田	町
105. 四	罗
106. 皿	盂
钅 ＝金	钉
107. 生	甥
108. 矢	矩
109. 禾	私
110. 白	的
111. 瓜	瓢
112. 鸟（鳥）	鸠
113. 广	疾
114. 立	端
115. 穴	究
衤 ＝衣	衬

聿＝聿 （盡）	139.齐（齊） 剂	161.采 悉
116.疌(疌) 楚	140.衣(衤) 袋	162.谷 豁
117.皮 颇	141.羊(⺶⺷) 翔	163.豸 豹
米＝水 泰	142.米 粉	164.龟（龜）（鼀）
118.癶 登	143.聿(⺻聿) 肆	165.角 触
119.矛 矛	144.艮 垦	166.言(讠)（講）
母＝毋 毑	145.艸(艹) 花	167.辛 辣
6 Strokes	146.羽 翌	**8 Strokes**
120.耒 耕	147.糸(纟) 繁	168.青 静
121.耳 耶	**7 Strokes**	169.卓 乾
122.老(耂) 耋	148.麦(麥) 麸	170.雨 雪
123.臣 卧	149.走 赴	長＝长 （長）
124.西(覀西) 贾	150.赤 赭	171.齿(齒) 龄
125.而 耐	車＝车 （輪）	172.非 斐
126.页（頁） 顺	151.豆 豇	虎＝虍 彪
127.至 到	152.酉 酌	173.黾(黽) 鼋
128.虍（虎） 虏	153.辰 辱	174.隹 雏
129.虫 虾	154.豕 豭	175.阜(阝) 隅
130.肉 胬	長＝长 肆	176.金(钅) （铜）
131.缶 缺	155.卤(鹵) 鹾	177.鱼（魚） 鲤
132.舌 甜	貝＝贝 （货）	門＝门 （間）
133.竹(⺮) 笔	見＝见 （观）	178.隶 （隸）
134.臼 儿	156.里 野	**9 Strokes**
135.自 臭	157.足(⻊) 蹇	179.革 靴
136.血 衅	158.邑(阝) 鞀	頁＝页 （領）
137.舟 舰	159.身 躬	180.面 靦
138.色 艳	160.辵(辶) （巡）	181.韭 齑

182.骨	骼	191.高	膏	**13 Strokes**	
183.香	馥	**11 Strokes**		198.鼓	瞽
184.鬼	魂	192.黄	黉	黽黾	（鼋）
185.食	餐	麥=麦	（麸）	199.鼠	鼬
風=风	颺	鹵=卤	（鹹）	**14 Strokes**	
186.音	韵	鳥=鸟	（鷄）	200.鼻	鼾
187.首	尩	魚=鱼	（鯉）	齊=齐	（齋）
韋=韦（靱）		193.麻	靡	**15 Strokes**	
飛=飞（飜）		194.鹿	麋	齒=齿	（齡）
10 Strokes		**12 Strokes**		**16 Strokes**	
188.鬲	融			龍=龙	（龔）
189.髟	髦	195.鼎	鼐	**17 Strokes**	
馬=马	（骑）	196.黑	黝	201.龠	龢
190.鬥	（鬧）	197.黍	黏	龜=龟	（鼈）

Additional notes:

1) Radicals in parentheses represent several components (including the complex-styled components) that have merged into one radical, e.g.: 人（入亻）

2) Radicals connected by an equal sign represent two character components subsumed in one radical, e.g.: 入＝人, 犭＝犬, 饣＝食, 飛＝飞

3) Characters in parentheses in the right column represent complex forms or obsolete variant forms e.g.: （壯）, （講）, （盡）, （齃）

6.4 CHINESE CHARACTER DATA PROCESSING

Another important application of Chinese character ordering is in Chinese character data processing 汉字信息处理, also known as Chinese-language data processing. This includes the data processing used in telegraphy, computers, machine translation and other areas. The first problem that must be solved in Chinese-language data processing is how to input Chinese characters. Inputting has never been a problem with alphabetic writing systems; for the Chinese character system, however, inputting is a major obstacle that has not yet been totally overcome.

There are between seven and ten thousand commonly used Chinese characters. Consider the problem of how to adapt these to a computer or typewriter keyboard. If every character is assigned a different key (as in the so-called "large keyboard" of traditional Chinese typewriters), the keyboard will be extremely awkward to use. The commonly used international keyboard (the so-called "small keyboard") has only forty or fifty eys, which include the letters of the Latin alphabet, the Arabic numerals, punctuation marks, and various other symbols. The most realistic goal for Chinese-language data processing is to devise a system which can use this small keyboard to produce any of the nearly ten thousand common characters of Chinese.

Character inputting systems as they have developed over the past several decades of research and experimentation may be separated into two types: form code — character conversion systems and Pinyin — character conversion systems. In this section we will provide a simple introduction to each of these types of systems.

Form Code — Character Conversion Systems 形码—汉字
转换系统

These systems take the form of characters as their starting
point. They separate characters into basic component units,
assign codes 代码 to these units (using Latin letters or Arabic
numerals), input the codes, and let the computer convert the
codes back into characters. This method is usually called by
the simpler name of character coding 汉字编码. The main
problem of form code — character conversion systems is how to
choose and arrange in order the basic units of characters. Based
on the different sorts of units they use, form code — character
conversion systems can be roughly separated into the three types
below.

**1) Systems which take the characters themselves as basic
units**

These systems do not divide characters into component
units, but treat each character as its own basic unit. The most
typical example of this type is the Chinese telegraphic code
电报码. The telegraphic code uses the four-digit codes from
0001 to 9999 and can accommodate up to ten thousand characters, approximately the number of commonly used characters.
The code first orders characters according to radicals, and then
assigns every character a code between 0001 and 9999. For
example, the telegraphic codes for the four characters 母病速归
(mother ill return quickly) are:

3018 母   4016 病   6643 速   2981 归

The four digits 3018 have no logical relation to the character
母, nor do any other characters have logical relations to their

codes. This kind of utterly arbitrary coding is sometimes called "unreasonable coding" 无理编码; internationally, it may be perceived as a sort of secret code 密码.

An ordinary person using this code must use the telegraphic code conversion book to look up characters' codes one by one. Even telegraph operators with many years of experience can, through rote memorization, recall only a portion of the more frequently used characters. This type of code can be used only by specialists, and is not suitable for use by ordinary people in data processing. Because the telegraphic code has been in use for a long time, however, it will continue to be used until a better system comes along to replace it. On the other hand, its use will never extend beyond the field of telegraphy.

2) Systems which use character components as basic units

There are between four and five hundred components which combine to make up all the thousands of characters. Using components as basic units greatly reduces the number of basic units one must use in coding. Systems using components as basic units are the most numerous of all form code — character conversion systems in use at present. We will look at this type of system below, using as our example the "See Character Know Code" (见字识码 jiàn zì shí mǎ) system advanced by Zhī Bǐngyí. 支秉彝.

The "See Character Know Code" system separates characters into four components. The first letter of the Pinyin name of each component are joined to produce a four-letter series, which is used as the character's code. E.g.:

路——口 (Kou), 止 (Zhi), 夂 (Wen), 口 (Kou) ——KZWK

個——忄(Xin), 冂(Tong), 土(Tu), 口(Kou) ——XTTK
The component 冂 has no name, so the name, 同 tóng, of the character is used to stand for it. 同 is called the "related character" of 冂.

If a character has only three components, then in order to provide a fourth letter for the code, the last stroke of the character is taken as the fourth component. E.g.:

余——人(Ren), 于(Yu), 八(Ba), 丶(Dian) ——RYBD
虎——虍(Hu), 七(Qi), 几(Ji), 乙(Zhe) ——HQJZ

If a character has only two components, then the last stroke of the character is used as the third component and the entire character itself as the fourth component. E.g.:

吴——口(Kou), 天(Tian), 乀(Na), 吴(Wu) ——KTNW
天——二(Er), 人(Ren,) 乀(Na), 天(Tian) ——ERNT

In order to use the twenty-six Latin letters to the fullest and to decrease the number of duplicate codes 重码, certain component forms are given abbreviated names which must be memorized. For example, "A" represents the component 辶; "E" represents 日, 曰; "I" represents 衣, 衤; "O" represents 手, 扌; and "U" represents 水, 氵.

3) Systems which use strokes as basic units

The different kinds of strokes that make up Chinese characters do not exceed ten in number; thus, using strokes as basic units would seem an ideal method. However, most characters have about ten strokes, and some have more than twenty. If codes undertook to represent every stroke in a character, most codes would be of an unwieldy length. Furthermore, the stroke order system, as we have seen, fails to satisfy the transparency standard; this will affect the efficiency of the codes. Therefore it is usually necessary to adopt certain special methods in coding by strokes. To demonstrate this, we will use as an example the "Stroke Encoding Method" 笔形编码法 created by Lǐ Jīnkǎi 李金铠.

The Stroke Encoding Method separates stroke forms into eight kinds (two of which are compound strokes): 1) horizontal 一, ╱, 2) vertical ⏐, 3) left-falling ╱, 4) dot 、, ㇄, 5) left turning ㇀, ㇄, 6) right turning ㇄, 7) cross 十, ✕, and 8) square 口. Three strokes (the first three) at most are used to define every component and single-component character. The order and method of taking strokes is the same as that described above in Section 6.2, Number 3), "Character referencing by stroke form". Strokes are taken according to the principle: "first high, then low; first left, then right". Thus:

舟 (╱ ╱]) 335   光 (⏐ 、 ╱) 243   立 (、 一 、) 414
来 (十 十 十) 777   酉 (⏐ ╱ ㇄) 136

Compound characters are coded according to the written order of their components. Three components at most define every character. If a character has more than three components, then the first, second, and last components are used. As no more than three components define a character and no more than three strokes define a component, no character's code will exceed nine Arabic numerals in length. E.g.:

荣——艹, 冖, 木→ 77, 25, 734→7725734
树——木, 又, 寸→734, 54, 74→7345474
型——开, 刂, 土→177, 25, 71→1772571
缠——纟, 广, 里→661,413, 077→661413077

The originator of this system felt that the codes thus produced were still too long, and permitted further shortening by taking only the first stroke of the last component. E.g.:

鸿——氵，工，鸟→441，121，356→4411213
磨——广，木，石→413，734，130→4137341
戀——立，早，心→414，017，464→4140174

Pinyin—Character Conversion Systems　拼音汉字转换系统

To date, more than five hundred different systems of form code — character conver ion have been devised. New systems are still being brought forward. Sadly, not one of these systems is totally satisfactory. Because of the complexity of character structure, there is simply no ideal method for ordering characters, and so form code — character conversion systems are bound to encounter all sorts of unsurmountable difficulties. For instance, the concept of a "component" has never been rigidly defined; nor has a definite method for determining components been settled on. In application, this lack of definition inevitably leads to divergence and confusion, and greatly reduces the practical value of form code — character conversion systems. Moreover, when using a computer to draft documents or do creative writing, the necessity of analyzing characters into components adds an extra mental burden extremely disruptive to one's train of thought. This is particularly true for non-specialist users unfamiliar with the conversion systems. Therefore, form code — character conversion systems are difficult to popularize among the wider masses.

In the past few years, both in China and abroad, many researchers of Chinese-language data processing have gradually turned away from form code — character conversion systems and toward methods of using phonetics to input characters. They have brought forward all sorts or Pinyin—character conversion systems. "Pinyin is the Chinese phonetic alphabet. Anyone who understands modern Mandarin Chinese and Pinyin can use such systems with only a bit of training. There is no need to consider complicated character forms. Pinyin-character conversion systems may be divided into three types, according to their degree of development.

1) Pinyin plus meaning symbol

The large number of homophonous characters in Chinese presents a major problem for Pinyin-character conversion systems. For example, the different Chinese characters: 风，丰，疯，封，蜂，峰，锋，枫，烽，and 鄷 are all represented in speech by the syllable fēng. One method of differentiating homophones is to add symbols expressing various different meanings to the ends of syllables. These symbols are simply called meaning symbols 意符. A given system may use over a hundred symbols; these can be conveniently represented by one or two Latin letters each. E.g.:

风 feng (wind)   ◦ (no meaning symbol added)

丰 fengx (rich)   (x indicates an adjective)

疯 fengb (crazy)   (b indicates the radical 疒 [bìng, illness])

封 fengcn (seal)   (cn indicates the radical 寸 [cùn, a unit of length])

蜂 fengch (bee)   (ch indicates the radical 虫 [chóng, insect])

峰 fengsh (peak)   (sh indicates the radical 山 [shān, mountain])

锋 fengjn (edge of   (jn indicates the radical 金 [jīn, metal])
a sword)

烽　fengh (beacon)　(h indicates the radical 火 [huǒ, fire])

枫　fengm (maple)　(m indicates the radical 木 [mù, wood])

It may be seen that this method does not rely wholly on phonetics, but uses semantic elements as well; thus it cannot be considered a pure phonetic input system. This sort of system is usually called a sound-form code system 音形码. Sound-form code systems are really just a kind of form coding, despite their use of phonetic indicators. One drawback to this kind of coding system is that the meaning symbols must be memorized; this increases the amount of study necessary for mastery and the burden on the user.

2) Pinyin homophone selection

The Pinyin plus meaning symbol method, because of the defects described above, is not used by most Pinyin-character conversion systems. Most Pinyin systems at present use a simpler method called Pinyin homophone selection. With this method, when one wishes to input a character, one first inputs the Pinyin written form of its syllable (tones are marked with Arabic numerals, 1 through 5), and then selects the character one wants from among all its homophones. For example, when one types in feng[1] (the syllable feng in the first tone), all of the characters pronounced fēng appear on the screen (ideally in order of frequency of occurrence):

风1　封2　丰3　锋4　疯5　峰6　蜂7　枫8　烽9

If one wishes to use the character 丰, one then simply types in "3" to select it.

This kind of system is perhaps the simplest of all character input systems. It requires no special training to use, only a familiarity with Pinyin. It too has a drawback, however: since one must carry out homophone selection for almost every character (barring those few that have no homophones), overall speed and efficiency are necessarily low. For a long essay or any piece of writing containing many characters, this system is particularly slow and troublesome.

3) Pinyin word input

When one takes characters as the unit of input, troubles with homophones arise which are difficult to overcome. Some people have thought of avoiding these problems by using whole words rather than characters as the unit of input. Using words as the unit of input, i.e. inputing whole words at a time, greatly reduces the homophone problem. Still using fēng as an example, we have

微风	weifeng (breeze)
风吹草动	fengchuicaodong (the rustle of leaves in the wind)
丰富	fengfu (rich)
丰功伟绩	fenggongweiji (great achievements)
封闭	fengbi (seal off)
蜜蜂	mifeng (honeybee)
山峰	shanfeng (peak)
烽火	fenghuo (beacon fire)
枫叶	fengye (maple leaf)

None of these words and phrases have homophones, so the bottleneck of character selection is altogether avoided.

When inputting whole words in this manner, it is almost never necessary to add tone indicators. Tone indicators (usually

Arabic numerals) are generally necessary only for certain mono-syllabic words, as in the following example:

Huayu Jiaoxue Chubanshe wei⁴ guowai xuexi Hanyu Hanzi de renmen tigong hen duo shi²yong de cailiao. →华语教学出版社为国外学习汉语汉字的人们提供很多实用的材料。 (The Sinolingua Press provides a lot of practical materials for people overseas who study Chinese and Chinese characters.)

In this example, a tone indicator is added to 实用 (shíyòng, practical) to avoid confusion with its homophones 使用 (shǐyòng, use) and 试用 (shì yòng, try out). Also, for convenience long expressions such as "Huayu Jiaoxue Chubanshe" may be abbreviated to HJC, and may be preprogrammed in by the user as needed; abbreviations of this sort can increase speed and efficiency considerably.

Obviously all such Hanyu Pinyin systems rely on the technology of programming and computer memory. In addition, this particular system requires both that the input user (1) know standard Hanyu Pinyin spelling and (2) also know the correct divisions and groupings of Chinese monosyllables into whole words, according to the standard rules for the Hànyǔ Pīnyīn zhèngcífǎ 汉语拼音正词法, or Hanyu Pinyin orthography, established by the State Language Commission of the People's Republic of China in 1988.

Place names are best capitalized for clarity, as: Beijing →北京, Sichuan→四川. Characters used in personal names are generally selected from among homophones, as described in 2) above.

A relatively large number of monosyllabic words require

tone indicators in order to avoid the bottleneck of homophone selection. The user may, however, set up a system whereby the most commonly used monosyllabic words need not be so marked. This reduces the frequency of tone indicators and increases input speed. For example: wo 我 (I, me; the most frequenty used word of this pronunciation), wo¹ 窝 (nest; rarely used), and wo⁴ 握 (grip; rarely used).

Computers using the word input method have already been developed. This method avoids complicated character forms and decreases the disturbance to thought caused by character codes. The user can easily perform Chinese-language data processing such as the composition of scientific papers and the creation of literary works on the computer. This method is therefore well-received by users in China and abroad. The general consensus is that Pinyin word input is the main direction of development for Chinese-language data processing in the future.

7. THE WRITING OF CHINESE CHARACTERS

Students of Chinese often make the comment that it is an easy language to learn to speak, but difficult to learn to write — on account of the characters. Characters, they add, are easier to read than to write. Many students and even scholars who have learned to speak excellent Chinese still write characters very poorly; this is quite as unfortunate as a handsome person being forced to wear unattractive clothes.

In writing characters, there are three demands that must be satisfied: correctness, neatness, and attractiveness.

Correctness Characters must be written correctly. Wrong or superfluous strokes and the incorrect substitution of one character for another are especially to be avoided. This is the very least demand that can be made.

Neatness Characters correctly written may still be so carelessly or sloppily executed as to be unrecognizable. Such characters, instead of transmitting information, hinder its transmission. The Chinese writer Lǔ Xùn criticized sloppy writers in these words (recorded in Xiāo Hóng's *In Memory of Lu Xun* 回忆鲁迅先生): "They don't care if others waste enormous amounts of time trying to decipher their writing, since the time wasted is not their own. This is the worst possible attitude". Neatness, over and above correctness, is a fundamental requirement.

Attractiveness The two preceding demands are pragmatic ones, taking writing as means of communication. The demand of attractiveness goes one step farther, taking writing as an artistic creation — what is referred to as the art of Chinese calligraphy 书法.

The first and second demands are of course the most vital for the student to master; the third, however, should not be considered beyond reach. One cannot demand that all students of Chinese be masters of calligraphy, but one may certainly encourage them to write as attractively as possible.

The key in learning to write characters correctly, neatly and attractively is determination. With determination and a grasp of the correct method, conscientious practice will produce good writing skills. A man of the Eastern Hàn Dynasty named Zhāng Zhī 张芝 practiced writing characters daily. He washed his brush and inkstone in a pool behind his house, and after long practice the pool became as black as ink itself. Zhāng Zhī became a noted calligrapher, and the story of his diligence has been passed down through the centuries. Another famous calligrapher, Zhōng Yóu 钟繇 of the Wèi-Jìn period, when young would lie in bed before sleeping and practice brush strokes with his finger on the blanket. In time, his practice wore holes in the blanket. Such industriousness is worthy of emulation.

This chapter will treat with some of the basic concepts in the writing of characters.

7.1 PREPARATION

The following section should be perused before beginning to practice writing.

1) Writing Instruments

Writing tools may be divided into two types: brushes and hardtipped pens. (The second category includes pencils as well as ballpoints and fountain pens.) The brush is the traditional tool for writing characters and is preferred by serious calligraphers. Most students are more familiar with the pen than with the brush; accordingly, this chapter will focus on the brush and its use. In fact, apart from some differences in the holding of the brush as compared to the pen, the same basic principles for writing characters apply to both.

The Chinese writing brush has a history of over two thousand years. A good brush is an essential prerequisite to practicing writing. Traditionally, a good-quality brush possesses the four characteristics of roundness, evenness, a fine tip, and strength. "Roundness" refers to the handle of the brush but more particularly to the tip, which should be full and plump, tapering to the end of the tip. "Evenness" means that when the brush hairs are dampened and pinched flat at the tip, the ends of the hairs should lie in an even line. "Fine tip" indicates that when the hairs are squeezed together, they should come to a sharp point. "Strength" means that the hairs should be elastic, so that the brush tip readily regains its original shape after being spread out.

The student should be aware that there are many different

kinds of brushes. They are classified according to the qualities of the brush tip into stiff-haired, soft-haired, and medium (between the other two in stiffness) brushes. Medium is the most suitable for someone just learning to use a brush.

2) Posture

The normal writing position is a seated one; the standing position is reserved for writing very large characters. The following indications are key to cultivating good writing posture:

a) **Sit up straight.** One must not slouch or bend forward over the paper. There should be a hand's-breadth of space between one's chest and the edge of the table.

b) **Hold the head straight.** The head should rest straight and slightly inclined forward, so that the eyes rest about a foot above the paper.

c) **Keep the arms relaxed.** The shoulders should be relaxed and the arms should hang naturally, with the left hand resting on the paper and the right hand holding the brush.

d) **Keep the feet still.** The feet should rest flat on the floor, with the legs relaxed and the body stable.

3) Holding the Brush

The technique of gripping a writing brush deserves careful attention. An ordinary pen or pencil is held clasped between the thumb and the index and middle fingers, which curl about it naturally. The pen itself is angled at about 50-60 degrees from the paper. Things are a bit more complicated, however, with the brush. There are three main points to consider:

a) **Finger positioning** 指法. Here is a step-by-step exposition of how to position the fingers on the brush. First, pick up

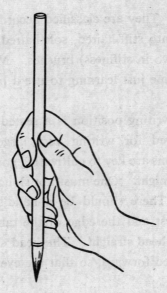

Fig. 14: How to
hold the brush.

the brush near the middle of the handle with the thumb and
index finger, holding it tip down between the last joints of these
fingers. Then let the middle finger lightly hook around the pen
handle below the other two fingers. Let the ring finger rest
below the middle finger, supporting the handle with the pad of
flesh beside the nail. The little finger should not touch the
handle; let it press against and support the ring finger from behind. The effect to strive for in the grip is "fingers solid, palm
relaxed". Only when the fingers' whole strength is concentrated
on the brush handle can one write freely and flexibly.

    b) **Wrist** 腕法. The Chinese stress "wrist flat, palm vertical" in writing. "Wrist flat" means that the wrist should rest parallel to the paper, while "palm vertical" indicates that the palm should be obliquely perpendicular to the paper. When these indications are observed, the brush will naturally position itself perpendicular to the paper. The wrist must be relaxed, never tense or stiff. A relaxed wrist allows unhindered motion.

The relative position of the wrist and palm are determined by the size of the characters one is writing. When writing small characters (around 1 cm. tall), the wrist may rest against the desktop, letting the fingers do most of the work. This is called "pillowed wrist" 枕腕 writing. When writing medium-sized characters (around 3 cm. tall) or large characters (around 6 cm. tall), the wrist should be raised from the paper (but still relaxed), and the fingers and wrist should work together to move the brush. This is called "raised wrist" 提腕 writing. Characters larger than this (taller than 10 cm.) are best written standing up, with the hand and arm well above the desk. This is called "suspended wrist" 悬腕 writing. Remember to keep the shoulder and elbow relaxed; otherwise, the tension will cause the brush hand to tremble.

c) **Brush position** 笔位. This refers to the spot where the hand grasps the brush handle. If the hand is high on the handle (far away from the tip), one has a wider and freer range of motion, but at the cost of stability. If the hand is placed nearer the brush head, stability is increased while the range and freedom of movement are restricted. Except for when one is writing very small characters, it is best to hold the brush at the middle of the handle or slightly higher.

7.2 STROKES AND MOVEMENT OF THE BRUSH

Yùn bǐ 运笔 (movement of the brush), or yòng bǐ 用笔 (use of the brush), is the name given to the various methods of using the brush in writing. Because the brush tip is pliant, there are more ways to use it than there are to use a hard-tipped pen, and thus more techniques to learn. Once these techniques are mastered, they can be used to produce all kinds of brush strokes. These brush strokes in turn unite to form all the different characters.

The process of using the brush is divided into three phases: opening, moving, and closing. Each phase has its own associated methods of brush movement. (Note that the discussion of writing below is limited to the techniques for regular style calligraphy.)

a) Opening 起笔

This refers to the first contact of brush to paper at the beginning of a stroke. There are two basic methods of opening:

Exposed-point 露锋 ("forward" method). In this method, the place where the stroke begins is left exposed; the brush moves continuously forward. This produces a vigorous, flowing visual effect. (See Fig. 15-a.)

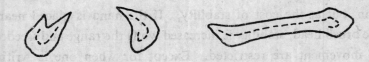

Fig. 15-a: Exposed-point opening.

Hidden-point 藏锋 ("backward" method). Here the place where the stroke begins is covered over by the subsequent movement of the brush as it turns back on its tracks. No sharp points are left exposed. The visual effect produced is sedate and fully rounded. (See Fig. 15-b.)

Fig. 15-b: Hidden-point opening.

b) Moving   行笔

This refers to the movement of the brush on the paper in the part of the stroke between opening and closing. An example is seen in the stroke — in Fig. 15; everything between the opening at far left and the closing at far right is moving. In general, and especially when writing in regular style script, the brush tip rests square on the paper during moving. Occasionally the side of the tip may be used, but it is not suitable in most cases.

There are two techniques associated with the process of moving: these are lifting and pressing.

Lifting 提（笔）is employed to decrease the width of the stroke. The effect is achieved by allowing the fingers and wrist to raise the brush up away from the paper while it is still moving. Pressing 按（笔）(also known as pausing 顿〔笔〕) is used to increase the width of the stroke, and it is achieved by the opposite motion: while the brush continues to move across the paper, the fingers and wrist press it down onto the paper.

Lifting and pressing are often used within the same stroke. Usually one first lifts up and then presses down on the brush. (See Fig. 16 for examples of this method's application.)

There are two ways of changing direction in the course of moving: curving and cornering.

Curving 转（锋）: in this method, the brush tip gradually shifts direction without a noticeable pause, forming an arc-shaped stroke. The curving stroke is said to "make circles". (See Fig. 16-a.)

Fig. 16-a: "Round" curving.

Cornering 折（锋）: in this method, the brush point is first lifted up and then pressed down, pausing in its forward motion at the turning point. Then it follows the direction of the second half of the stroke when it begins to move again. The place where the brush pauses forms the vertex of an angle; the cornering stroke is said to "make squares". (See Fig. 16-b.)

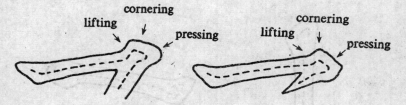

Fig. 16-b: "Square" cornering.

c) Closing 收笔

This refers to the conclusion of a stroke. The same two methods of exposed-point and hidden-point apply to closing as to opening, though they are called by different names here:

Trailing-off 送出 (exposed-point): at the end of the stroke, the brush is gradually lifted away from the paper, allowing the stroke to trail off thinner and thinner into nothing.

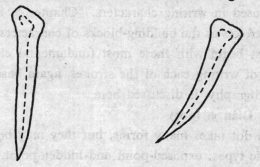

Fig. 17-a: Trailing-off closing.

Turned-back 回锋 (hidden-point): as the stroke ends, the brush is first lifted up and then pressed down, turning the stroke back on itself to close.

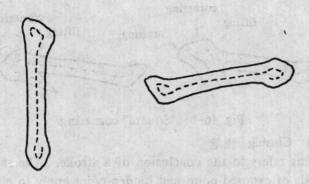

Fig. 17–b: Turned-back closing.

Once these methods of brush movements are grasped, it is easy to understand the proper way of writing the individual strokes used in writing characters. Chapter 3, Section 1 discussed strokes as the building-blocks of characters. In writing, one must begin with these most fundamental elements. The method of writing each of the strokes, again based on regular style calligraphy, is discussed here.

a) **Diǎn** 点 (dot)

The dot takes many forms, but they may be divided into two basic types: exposed-point and hidden-point. The former is more common in regular style script. The exposed-point dot is written with the exposed opening and either the trailing-off or the turned-back closing. The hidden-point dot is written with the hidden opening and the turned-back closing.

Dots may come singly (as in 言，文，主，下), in pairs (as in 斗，小，只，火), by threes (as in 江，河，心), or by fours (as in 求，雨，然，燕).

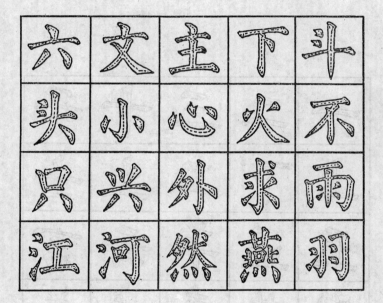

b) **Héng** 横 (horizontal stroke)

The horizontal stroke is divided into two types, long and short. The opening of the stroke may be either hidden-point or exposed-point; the closing is usually turned-back. Generally speaking, the two extremities of the horizontal stroke are thick, while the middle is somewhat thinner; the middle should not be too thin, though, to avoid a wasp-waisted appearance.

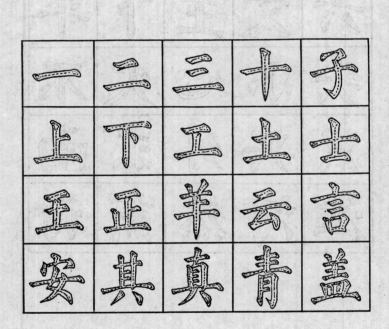

c) **Shù** 竖 (vertical stroke)

There are many ways of writing this stroke, but the two most important types are "hanging needle" 悬针 and "dewdrop" 垂露. The hanging-needle stroke trails off at the closing. The movement of the brush should be accomplished slowly and carefully, to form a closure like a needle's point (as the vertical stroke in the first nine characters in the illustration below). The dewdrop stroke, in contrast, ends with the turned-back closing. The lower extremity of the stroke is thus somewhat rounded, like a drop of dew hanging on the stroke (as the vertical stroke in the last eleven characters in the illustration below).

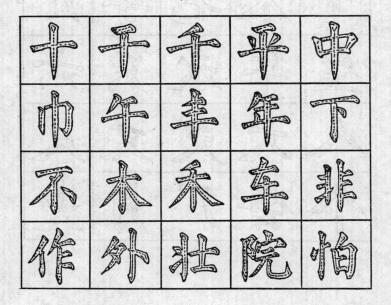

d) Piě 撇 (left-falling stroke)

This stroke comes in all different lengths and angles, but these are only variations on the basic method. The stroke is always begun with a hidden-point opening, and the closing is a trailing-off to the lower left. A short piě may be written with a quicker movement of the brush, using the side of the tip; a long piě should be written more slowly, with the tip squarely over the stroke.

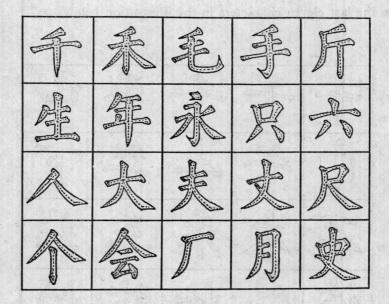

e) **Nà** 捺 (right-falling stroke)

There are two basic forms of this stroke, flat nà and slanted nà. Flat nà (as in the last row of five characters below) is generally written with a hidden-point opening, while slanted nà (as in the first fifteen characters below) is usually written with an exposed-point opening. The closing of nà is somewhat complicated: when the brush reaches the bottom of the stroke, the fingers and wrist should press down hard on the brush, causing the brush hairs to spread flat and widening the stroke. Then the brush is drawn off to the right, slowly trailing off to close. The upper part of the stroke should be nearly a straight line, while the bottom should angle away to the right at approximately 120 degrees.

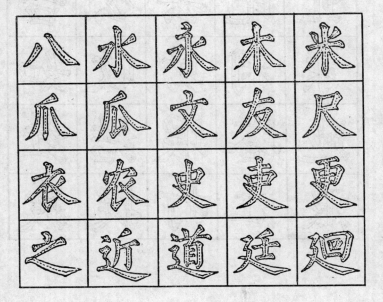

f) **Tiǎo** 挑 (rising stroke)

This stroke, like piě, comes in many forms, long and short, flat and slanted. The basic method is to open with a hidden point, then to press down and lift up to allow the brush tip to change direction, and finally to draw the brush upwards to the right to close. A short tiǎo (as in 北, 比, 浪) may be written with a quicker brush movement, while a long tiǎo (as in 台 and 云) should be written more slowly.

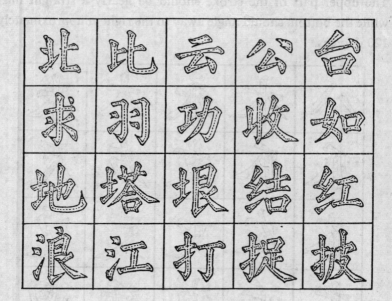

g) **Gōu** 钩 (hook)

There are over ten varieties of this stroke, such as "standing hook" (as in 丁，寸，月), "sleeping hook" (as in 心，思，必), "flat hook" (as in 元，九，也), and "slanted hook" (as in 成，我，代). All these different kinds are formed in the same way when it comes to the hooked part of the stroke: when the brush reaches the turning point of the hook, it is first lifted and then pressed down again, causing the tip to point in the opposite direction from that the brush itself will follow to finish the stroke; then the brush is drawn along and slowly lifted to trail off at the closing.

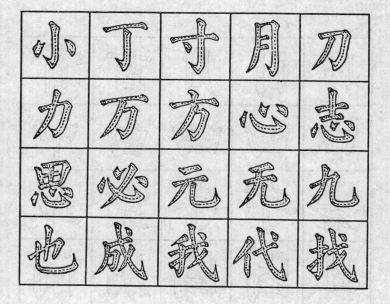

h) **Zhé** 折 (cornering stroke)

There are several types of cornering strokes, among them the héng corner (as in 日，月，且，国), the shù corner (as in 山，区，亡，击), and the piě corner (as in 乡，幼，玄，好). The héng corner is begun in the same way as a héng stroke, the shù corner as a shù stroke, and so on. When the brush reaches the turning point, it is first lifted and then pressed in order to change the direction in which the tip points; then it follows the direction of the second half of the stroke. If the brush is allowed to pause at the corner and pressure is applied, the outer edge of the corner will be square; if the brush does not pause, or if less pressure is applied, a rounded edge will result.

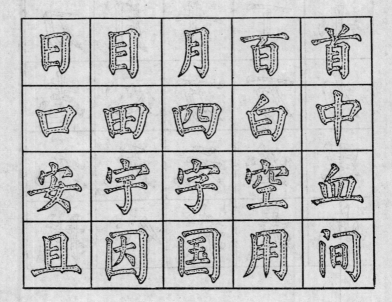

7.3 STROKE ORDER AND WRITING

After one has learned how to form the various strokes, the next step is to learn the order in which they combine to form all the characters. Stroke order is an extremely important part of writing characters. In written English or French, for example, letters in a word follow each other more or less according to sound, and their order can be seen by merely looking at the word written out. The strokes of a Chinese character, on the other hand, are all piled together; it is impossible to tell which stroke comes after which just by looking at the character. There are certain rules of stroke order, however, an understanding of which will help one to write correctly.

Rule	Example	Stroke Order
1) First left, then right	到	至 到
	谢	讠 谢 谢
	川	丿 川 川
2) First top, then bottom	思	田 思
	意	立 音 意
	三	一 二 三
3) First outside, then inside	用	冂 用
	问	门 问
	风	几 风

| | 司 | 丆 | 司 |
| | 居 | 尸 | 居 |

4) First center, then sides	小	丨	小
	水	亅氺	水
	亦	亣亦	亦
	业	丿丨业	业

5) "Let him come in, then close the door."	回	冂 回	回
	目	冂月	目
	国	冂国	国

6) First horizontal, then vertical	十	一	十
	干	二	干
	井	二	井
	丰	三	丰

7) First left-falling, then right-falling	人	丿	人
	尺	尸	尺
	父	丷	父
	史	丷	史

8) First horizontal, then left-falling	厂 左 夫 丈	一 ナ 丯 一ナ	厂 左 夫 丈
9) First the main body, then thread it together	中 串 韦 册	口 吕 弓 刪	中 串 韦 册
10) First the main body, then the dot	犬 发 戈 我	大 发 戈 扐	犬 发 戈 我

The following three points are of vital importance to understanding the rules of stroke order:

a) The rules may appear to be complicated and excessively numerous, but the essence of stroke order can actually be summed up quite simply in the form of the first two rules: "First left, then right; first top, then bottom". The other eight rules, and their exceptions, can all be understood with reference to the spirit of the first two.

For example, not all "enclosed" characters follow the rule (number 3 above) of "first outside, then inside"; but the exceptions always follow the spirit of the first two rules. The characters 凶: ㄨ凶，函: 承函，画: 冂画，建: 聿建，速: 束速，and others like them are all "first top, then bottom" characters. The characters 赶: 走赶，毯: 毛毯，and others like them all go by the "first left, then right" rule.

The exceptions to "first horizontal, then vertical" are also formed according to the first two rules. The bottom horizontal stroke in characters like 王，土 and 工 must be written last of all (as 王: 一干王), because only in this way does the stroke order accord with "first top, then bottom". The stroke order of 占 is vertical before horizontal rather than the expected opposite because the other stroke order would violate the principle of "first left, then right".

Consider the case of characters that bear a dot. Rule 10 above states that the dot should be added last, but this only applies when the dot is in the right-hand part of the character. If the dot is squarely above (as in 主，文，and 户) or to the left (as in 斗，为，and 头), it must be written first, in accordance with the two basic principles.

Thus there is no need to go to the length of memorizing the stroke order rules. It is more useful to have an active understanding of the spirit of the first two principles: "first left, then right", and "first top, then bottom".

b) Rules of stroke order are seldom applied singly; more often they are applied recursively, one on top of another, to build up a character. One will usually apply a whole series of rules in writing a single character. To write the twelve-stroke character 堡, for example, the following sequence of rules comes into play through which we can tell that all the rules would come down to the two basic principles:

First 保, then 土 —— first top, then bottom
First 亻, then 呆 —— first left, then right
First 丿, then 丨 —— first top, then bottom
First 口, then 呆 —— first top, then bottom
First 丨, then ㄱ —— first left, then right
First 冂, then 一 —— first top, then bottom
First 十, then 八 —— first center, then sides
    (first top, then bottom)
First 一, then 丨 —— first horizontal, then vertical
    (first top, then bottom)
First 丿, then 乀 —— first left-falling, then right-falling
    (first left, then right)
First 十, then 一 —— first top, then bottom
First 一, then 丨 —— first horizontal, then vertical
    (first top, then bottom)

c) Because stroke order rules are most often applied recursively, disagreements about which rule to apply sometimes arise. Contradictions arise even between the two basic principles. For example, there are two ways of writing the simple character 成. Some people write it 一厂斤成成, on the basis of "first top, then bottom"; others write it 丿厂斤成成, on the basis of "first left, then right". Such contradictions are, unfortunately, unavoidable in practice.

Characters take many forms, and some of them are built up in very peculiar ways. It can be difficult to tell what the stroke order of such characters ought to be. For reference purposes, some of the commonest of these idiosyncratic characters are written out below (number of strokes is given in parentheses).

也：乛 乜 也 （3）　　北：丨 十 扌 才 北 （5）

万：一 丁 万 （3）　　母：乚 乚 母 母 母 （5）

及：丿 乃 及 （3）　　州：丿 州 州 州 （6）

长：丿 一 长 长 （4）　　我：扌 我 我 我 （7）

火：丶 丷 少 火 （4）　　非：丨 刂 刲 非 （8）

区：一 区 区 （4）　　垂：千 禾 垂 （8）

必：丶 心 心 必 （5）　　兜：白 皍 兜 兜 （11）

世：一 廿 世 世 （5）　　鼎：日 鼎 鼎 鼎 鼎 （12）

凹：丨 卩 凹 冂 凹 （5）

凸：丨 凵 凸 凸 凸 （5）

7.4 STRUCTURE AND COMPOSITION

Armed with the knowledge of how to form strokes and an understanding of the rules of stroke order, the student is now ready to begin using this knowledge to build characters. It is essential when writing characters to consider the relative proportions of the individual components and strokes of which they are formed. The components must be well balanced to assure an aesthetically pleasing end product. Thus the next subject of study must be the form and structure of characters. This concept is known as jiétǐ 结体 in Chinese calligraphy; in this discussion the word "structure" 结构 is used to represent the idea.

In Chapter 3, "The Shapes of Chinese Characters", characters were divided into four types according to their structure: unitary, left-right, top-bottom, and enclosed. In this section, structure will be considered as it applies to writing, with the emphasis on the size, length and height of each component, and its situation and proportion in relation to the rest of the character; the goal here is to achieve an understanding of how to write characters that are aesthetically pleasing as well as correct. The theory of jiéti in calligraphy is a highly developed one; what follows here is only a rough outline of the concepts involved.

1) Unitary Structure 单一结构. Characters with this structure are made up of a single component and are usually composed of relatively simple strokes. The most common four types are described below:

a) **Square** 方形: this type should be written straight and square, with distinct angles.

王　正　主　本　亚

b) **Tall** 长形: these should be taller than they are broad, with the strokes evenly spaced.

目　月　自　身　耳

c) **Broad** 扁形: these should be broader than they are tall.

白　田　四　回　曲

d) **Slanted** 斜形: these characters are dominated by oblique strokes, but they should appear "straight" as a whole.

力　勿　乃　母　戈

Strokes should be evenly spaced and the character as a whole well-centered.

   2)   **Left-right (including left-centre-right) Structure** 左右结构. The two (or three) sections of these characters must be coordinated in size, height, and breadth.   There are many varieties of left-right characters; twelve common kinds are outlined below.

   a)   **Evenly split** 平分: the left and right halves occupy equal amounts of space.   The top and bottom must be well balanced too.

秋　静　辅　版　鼓

   b)   **Double** 并行: the two halves are essentially the same, but for the sake of variation the right half should be allowed to dominate the left.

竹　林　羽　朋　所

   c)   **Back to back** 相背: the two halves face away from each other.   They should match much like mirror images and should not be spaced too far apart.

北　兆　非　张　孔

   d)   **Face to face** 相向: the two halves face in towards each other.   The right half should be slightly larger than the left;

好　舒　朗　约　政

298

the two should match evenly and not jab into each other.

e) **Left-dominant** 让左: the left side forms the main body of the character, while the right acts as a complement. The left should squarely set and dominate the total space, but the right must not be skimped over either.

都　教　彩　勃　歌

f) **Right-dominant** 让右: the left complements the right, which forms the main body of the character. The right should be rather larger than the left and set squarely.

晴　绩　球　校　院

g) **Flat top** 上平: the left side is smaller than the right; it should be written somewhat higher than centre so that the two halves are level across the top.

明　端　辉　增　师

h) **Flat bottom** 下平: the right half is smaller than the left, and should be written low down enough that the two halves are level across the bottom.

叙　叔　红　初　勤

i) **In the middle** 居中：here again one half is smaller than the other, but it should sit at centre height, tending toward neither the top nor the bottom of the character.

如 知 和 叶 仁

j) **Even thirds** 三分：left, centre, and right should be equal in size. The three should stand close together and match evenly.

谢 嫩 柳 锄 脚

k) **Left side simple** 左简：the left section is less complicated than the centre and right, and should take up less space. The three parts should not bump into each other.

做 湖 啦 渐 概

l) **Narrow centre** 中窄：the centre section is much narrower than the others, taking up about one-fifth of the total width while left and right each occupy two-fifths. The outside components, left and right, should be well balanced.

班 衍 附 辨 袄

3) **Top-bottom (including top-middle-bottom) Structure** 上下结构. With characters of this construction, as with left-right characters, the key is in coordination of the relative size,

300

height, and breadth of the components. The more important types of top-bottom characters are outlined below:

a) **"Roofed-in"** 天覆: these are topped by components such as 冖, 宀, 穴, 八, 夂, and 耂. The "roof" should extend over the whole of the parts beneath it.

冠　宣　空　冬　春

b) **"Floored-in"** 地載: these are underlaid by components such as 皿, 土, 山, 心 and 亚. The "floor" should be broad enough to support the rest of the character above it.

盖　至　豆　忘　望

c) **Evenly split** 两段: the top and bottom halves occupy equal amounts of space. The strokes should be evenly distanced and must not jab into each other.

留　禁　监　粪　蛮

d) **Double** 重叠: the top and bottom are essentially identical. To avoid exact repetition, the bottom half should be somewhat larger; the corresponding strokes in each half should be varied slightly.

昌　圭　炎　哥　多

e) **Wide top** 上宽: the top half is broader than the bottom. For balance, the bottom should be emphasized by spacing the top widely and the bottom compactly.

普 香 否 番 雷

f) **Wide bottom** 下宽: the bottom is broader than the top. Here the top should be compact and the bottom more spread out, as before for balance.

界 岸 吴 晃 泉

g) **Elaborate top** 上繁: here there are more strokes in the top half than in the bottom. In order to keep the whole from becoming top-heavy, the strokes in the top half should be relatively small and close together, while the bottom half should be written more broadly.

整 督 集 壁 柴

h) **Elaborate bottom** 下繁: here the bottom half has more strokes than the top. The top should be written compactly with emphasis, and the bottom with a lighter touch.

最 置 嵌 翁 露

i) **Thirds** 三段: the three sections, top, middle, and bot-

意 曼 素 累 霄

302

tom, should be in good proportion, positioned compactly together and balanced on the centre of the character.

4) Enclosed structure 包围结构. These characters have two components, the enclosing and the enclosed. Understanding the relative position of the two parts is the key to writing a good character here, and the best assurance of an ugly character is to fail to pay attention to this question. There are many types of enclosed characters, each with its own method of writing. Some of the most common types are outlined here:

a) **Four sides** 四面包: the enclosing frame should be straight and symmetrical. The enclosed portion should be centered, and large enough to fill the enclosure.

因　团　国　图　圆

b) **Top and sides** 上三包: here the character has an enclosing line on every side except the bottom. The left and right edges should be roughly symmetrical; the enclosed portion should stand more or less in the centre, but tending toward the top.

同　周　网　凤　间

c) Bottom and sides 下三包: the left and right enclosing strokes should not extend higher than halfway up the character. The enclosed portion should be centered, but tending toward the bottom of the character.

函　幽　凶　画　幽

d) Top, left and bottom 左三包: as a rule, the top enclosing stroke should be a bit shorter than the bottom one. The enclosed portion should be centred slightly to the left of true centre.

区　巨　医　匠　匪

e) Top and left 左上包: the upper left encloses the lower right part of the character. The left-falling stroke of the enclosure should be nearly vertical. The enclosed portion should hug the upper left corner, so as to keep the character from becoming too spread out.

原　度　病　居　扇

f) Bottom and left 左下包: the bottom left encloses the upper right. The bottom part of the enclosure, a flat right-falling stroke, should be long

进　还　道　通　建

304

enough to balance the enclosed portion. The latter should stand straight and not wander away from the enclosing strokes.

g) **Extending hook** 伸钩 包: here again, the lower left encloses the upper right. The hook itself should be flat and broad enough to take in the whole of the enclosed portion, which in turn should hug in close to the lower left.

旭　勉　毯　尴　抛

h) **Top and right** 右上包: the upper right encloses the lower left. The hook of the right side should be visibly angled; the enclosed portion should nestle inside it toward the top.

司　句　匀　可　氧

In addition to the structure of characters and the methods of writing them outlined above, there still remains the question of the overall placement of characters and lines of writing relative to each other on the page. This falls under the heading of composition 布局. Composition is quite as important as structure, for a whole sheet of well-written characters will look bad if they are unflatteringly laid out on the page.

Three main aspects of composition are outlined below:

1) The size of all the characters in a given piece of writing should be approximately equal. Accordingly, one must make an effort to squash down excessively tall characters (such as 霄, 篡, and 鼻) making them shorter and to make unusually broad ones (such as 轍, 衢, and 掰) thinner, to pack the strokes close together in characters like 鸞 and 纛 and to spread the mout in charac ters like 人 and 儿. Ideally, every character should be able to fit into the same size frame.

2) Each line of characters should be flat and straight on the page. When writing in horizontal lines, the characters should all sit at the same level, and must not leap up from the the line or droop down below it. Equally, when writing vertically one must avoid characters ranging off to the right or left of the line. The line itself should run quite straight across or down the page.

3) Characters should be spaced the same distance apart, and each line of characters should be separated from its neighbors by a set distance. For the sake of clarity in reading, the space between lines should be somewhat larger than that between the characters in each line. In regular style script, each line should contain the same number of characters. In the xíngshū (running) style, by contrast, the number of characters per line may vary; this is because some variation in the size of the individual characters is permitted. In either style, however, the individual lines must be clearly separated.

It should be noted that these three requirements are outlined primarily with the regular style in mind. These are only the most basic demands of composition, but once mastered they will go a long way in improving one's writing.

APPENDIX: TRACING AND COPYING

The preceding sections of this chapter have outlined the fundamentals of writing characters. For the student who already has a firm grasp of these basics and wishes to pursue the art of Chinese calligraphy seriously, the best course is to work by copying from the works of masters.

Calligraphy in China has a long and distinguished history. Each dynasty has produced many noted calligraphers. Limiting the discussion to practitioners of regular and running style script, among the most famous masters are Zhōng Yóu 钟繇, (151-230), Wáng Xīzhī 王羲之, (321-379), and Wáng Xiànzhī 王献之, (344-386) of the Wèi-Jìn period; Yú Shìnán 虞世南, (558-638), Ouyáng Xún 欧阳询, (557-641), Chǔ Suìliáng 褚遂良, (596-658), Yán Zhēnqīng 颜真卿, (709-785), and Liǔ Gōngquán 柳公权, (778-865) of the Táng Dynasty; Sū Shì 苏轼, (1037-1101), Huáng Tíngjiān 黄庭坚, (1045-1105), Mǐ Fú, 米芾 (1051-1107), and Cài Xiāng 蔡襄, (1012-1067) of the Sòng Dynasty; Zhào Mèngfǔ 赵孟頫, (1254-1322) of the Yuán Dynasty; and Wén Zhēngmíng 文徵明, (1470-1559) and Dǒng Qíchāng 董其昌, (1555-1636) of the Míng Dynasty. Copying their works is a way of learning from the great masters of the past.

In copying, it is best to begin with regular style script, going on to running style only after achieving fluency in the first style. (The cǎoshū or cursive style is best left alone by anyone who does not yet have a strong foundation in calligraphy.) What

307

follows is an outline of the three phases of copying (note that these phases are not to be rigorously partitioned; they should overlap naturally):

1) Studying the Model 读帖

This phase consists of carefully studying a reproduction of of a specimen of the calligrapher's writing, analyzing the artist's use of the brush in forming the different strokes, the structure of the different sorts of characters, and the overall composition of the entire piece. Thoroughly studying the model and mentally copying it over, "inputs" it into one's head before brush ever touches paper. This step is good mental preparation for the next step of copying, and also improves one's ability to understand and appreciate calligraphy.

2) Tracing 摹帖

Tracing is a good way to grasp the structure of characters in a piece of writing. The method consists of placing a sheet of paper directly on top of the model and "tracing" it with brush and ink as exactly as possible. In order to prevent damage to the model, it is best to use semi-transparent paper of a sort which will not allow the ink to bleed through.

Tracing should be practiced thoroughly before proceeding to the next step.

3) Copying 临帖

As opposed to tracing, where the model lies under the paper, in copying it sits out in front of the writer and serves as a visual guide, as before, to be copied as accurately as possible. Copying is most effective when performed in conjunction with the two previous steps.

308

In practice, copying is best divided into stages. Each stage should concentrate on different aspect of writing, such as brush movement, character structure, and so on. Only when these aspects are mastered individually should the final stage of copying the model in its entirety be undertaken.

A useful method for determining the relative positions of the strokes in characters on the model is to use paper marked out with one of the sorts of frames illustrated below. A transparent sheet of this sort is laid over the model so that each frame houses a character, and then a sheet of paper similarly marked is used for copying. This is an exceedingly helpful device in copying.

For the student's reference and examination, some of the finest examples of regular and running style calligraphy and their artists are listed here:

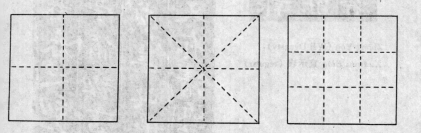

Fig. 18: Four-square frame
Diagonal-marked frame
Nine-square frame

Zhōng Yóu (Wèi Dynasty):
Xuānshì Biǎo 宣示表 (regular)

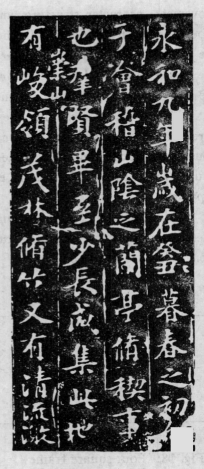

Wáng Xīzhī (Jìn Dynasty):
Lán Tíng Xù 兰亭序 (regular)

天下為心者必致

王苟君臣同符斯

之志千載一是也

Wáng Xīzhī (Jìn Dynasty):
Yuè Yì Lùn 乐毅论 (regular)

流芳越長吟以慕

靈雜還命疇嘯侶

珠氏拾翠羽從南

Wáng Xiànzhī (Jìn Dynasty):
Luò Shén Fù 洛神赋 (regular)

可以經緯闡其圖諧

有人馬法師俗姓陳

陳世傅纓晉

爰祖

Yú Shìnán (Táng Dynasty):
Pò Xié Lùn 破邪论 (regular)

鏡澈用之日新

之無渇道隨時

泰慶與泉流我

Ōuyáng Xún (Táng Dynasty):
Jiǔ Chéng Gōng Lǐ Quán Míng

九成宫醴泉铭 (regular)

Chǔ Suìliáng（Táng Dynasty）:
Shèng Jiào Xù 圣教序（regular）

Yán Zhēnqīng（Táng Dynasty）:
Duō Bǎo Tǎ Gǎn Yìng Bēi
多宝塔感应碑（regular）

Yán Zhēnqīng（Táng Dynasty）:
Qín Lǐ Bēi 勤礼碑（regular）

Liǔ Gōngquán（Táng Dynasty）:
Xuán Mì Tǎ Bēi 玄秘塔碑（regular）

Liǔ Gōngquán（Táng Dynasty）
Jīn Gāng Jīng 金刚经（regula

Sū Shì（Sòng Dynasty）:
Fēng Lè Tíng Jì 丰乐亭记（regular）

Sū Shì（Sòng Dynasty）：*Hán Shí Shī* 寒食诗（running）

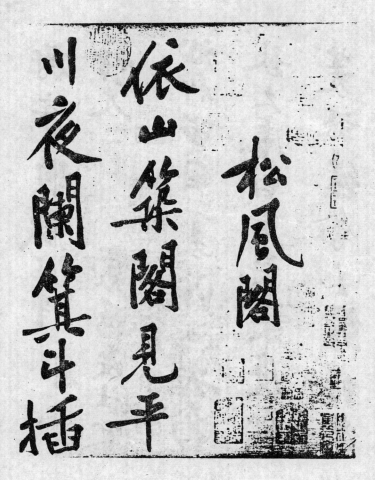

松風閣

依山築閣見平
川夜闌簷斗插

Huáng Tíngjiān (Sòng Dynasty): *Sōng Fēng Gé Shī* 松风阁诗 (running)

Mǐ Fú (Sòng Dynasty): *Tiáo Xī Shī* 苕溪诗 (running)

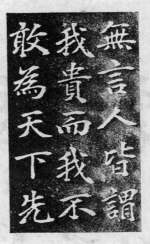

Zhào Mèngfǔ (Yuán Dynasty):
Dào Jiào Bēi 道教碑 (regular)

Zhào Mèngfǔ (Yuán Dynasty):
Xián Xié Gōng Zhuàn 闲邪公传 (regular)

赤壁賦

壬戌之秋七月既望

蘇子與客泛舟遊於

赤壁之下清風徐來

Wén Zhēngmíng（Míng Dynasty）：*Chì Bì Fù* 赤壁賦（running）

禹張湯文章則
司馬遷相如滑
洪業亦講論六

Dǒng Qíchāng (Míng Dynasty): *Chuán Zàn* 传赞 (regular)

8. DICTIONARIES AND REFERENCE WORKS

Good dictionaries and reference works are indispensable in learning Chinese characters. In Chapter 2 we discussed the large number of Chinese characters. Usually one can only learn a small portion of these, i.e., those characters in common use. Thus when we read or write, we are bound to come across characters that we don't recognize or ones that we don't know how to write, and then we have to consult a dictionary or refer to a reference book. Sometimes we may recognize a character, but that does not necessarily mean that we know it completely, because there are many polyphonetic characters, as well as characters with multiple meanings. In such cases we have to turn to dictionaries for help. Even if we do know the form, pronunciation, and meaning of a character, we may still be uncertain about the meaning and usage of the compound word in which the character is being used. Again we have to refer to a dictionary. One simply cannot learn Chinese characters well without dictionaries and reference works. Whenever you encounter a problem, be sure to consult a good dictionary or refer to a good reference book. Even if you don't have a specific problem, it is always interesting and informative to turn over a few pages of a dictionary as a pastime. As the Chinese saying goes, 开卷有益 (kāi juàn yǒu yì, To open a book will always do you good).

In this chapter we will discuss the problem of choosing and using dictionaries and reference books. First and foremost, we will discuss the classification of dictionaries so that the reader can get a general idea of the nature and uses of the different sorts of dictionaries. Then we will show the reader how to use these dictionaries — how to consult them and how to get a satisfactory answer from the entry (either a "character" or a "word"). Finally we will introduce twenty major dictionaries and reference works of both classical and modern Chinese, all published in the People's Republic of China, from which the reader can choose those most suitable for his or her own use. (Unless otherwise noted, all works are primarily printed in modern "simplified" Chinese characters.)

8.1 CLASSIFICATION OF CHINESE DICTIONARIES

The classification of dictionaries properly belongs to the study of lexicography. Here we will confine ourselves to some basic concepts concerning Chinese dictionaries from a pragmatic point of view.

1) Character Dictionaries and Word Dictionaries

Many people confuse the terms 字 (zì, character) and 词 (cí, word), which are in fact two entirely different concepts. A character 字 is the basic symbol of the Chinese written language. A character may represent an independent spoken word (e.g., 书 represents the independent spoken word pro-

311

nounced shū, meaning "book"), or it may represent a bound morpheme (e.g., 典 represents the bound morpheme diǎn, as in 字典 zìdiǎn, character dictionary.). A word 词 is the smallest independent unit of the language. A word may happen to consist of one independent character (e.g. 书 book), or of two characters (e.g. 字典 character dictionary), or three characters (e.g. 字典学 lexicography), etc. One should always keep this distinction in mind, particularly in understanding the two basic types of Chinese dictionaries.

A **character dictionary** 字典 (zìdiǎn) is a dictionary with characters as its main entries, which defines the standardized forms, standard pronunciations, and correct meanings of characters. Since most words in present-day spoken Chinese are polysyllabic compounds, however, it is not enough to make clear the form, pronunciation, and meaning of a character only. This is why modern Chinese character dictionaries often also include polysyllabic words in which the individual characters occur, with additional explanations of the meanings and usage of these words.

A **word dictionary** 词典 (cídiǎn) is a dictionary with words as its main entries, which defines the pronunciation, meaning, and usage of the words. But as we have just noted, words in modern Chinese are represented by one or more characters. Thus the entries in a word dictionary are also arranged according to the first character in the word. Words which begin with the main entry character are listed after the main entry character as sub-entries, usually with their pronunciation, definitions, and sometimes usage.

In ancient Chinese, most words were monosyllablic, represented by one character only, so in ancient China there were only "character dictionaries" and no "word dictionaries". (Or we could also say that in ancient times character dictionaries were dictionaries of words.) "Word dictionaries" only came into being in modern times after the majority of words in Chinese became polysyllabic. Though we now have both "character dictionaries" and "word dictionaries", the distinction between the two is not a strict one. We might put it this way: a "character dictionary" defines characters as its main object, although it may also include some polysyllabic words as well. A "word dictionary" defines words as its main object, although it may also include some characters which cannot make independent words alone. Since there is now no strict distinction between these two types of dictionaries, both are often referred to as 辞书 (císhū, dictionaries).

2) Dictionaries of Classical Chinese and Dictionaries of Modern Chinese

Chinese dictionaries may first be sub-classified into dictionaries of classical Chinese and dictionaries of modern Chinese. This classification is made not on the basis of the time at which the compilers lived, nor when the work originally appeared, but rather on the basis of the content and purpose of the dictionary.

Dictionaries of classical Chinese 古代辞书 include characters and words of classical literary Chinese, to assist in reading Chinese classics. They may give the pronunciation of characters at a given time in the past, define the meaning in classical Chinese, and give examples from classical works. They may also show the earlier forms of the characters (for example, seal style character forms) and explain the etymology and construction of each character from a characterological point of view. The Shuō Wén Jiě Zì and Kāngxī Zìdiǎn are two examples of dictionaries of classical Chinese.

Dictionaries of modern Chinese 现代辞书, on the other hand, mainly include characters and words from modern Chinese, to help in reading works written in modern Chinese. These dictionaries usually indicate the standard pronunciation of characters and words in contemporary Putonghua, define their meanings in modern Chinese, and give examples from works written in modern times or from modern spoken Chinese. Since modern Chinese may be said to have developed from classical Chinese, a large number of classical words and phrases have been retained in modern Chinese, particularly in the written style. As these classical words and phrases are still in current use, they must also be regarded as part of modern Chinese; hence their inclusion in modern Chinese dictionaries. But ancient words and phrases which are archaic or in rare use are not included. Dictionaries of modern Chinese do not, as a rule, give the ancient forms of characters, nor explain the etymology or construction of each character, but rather give only the standardized forms, standard pronunciation, and exact meaning of characters, words, and phrases in modern Chinese. The Xīnhuá Zìdiǎn and Xiàndài Hànyǔ Cídiǎn are two good examples of dictionaries of modern Chinese.

The distinction between these two types of dictionaries is not absolute, however. There are some dictionaries which include both classical and modern characters, words, and phrases. Dictionaries such as these are difficult to classify exactly. It is probably best to classify them according to their main tendencies. Thus dictionaries such as the Zhōnghuá Dà Zìdiǎn 中华大字典, Zhōngwén Dà Zìdiǎn 中文大字典, Hànyǔ Dà Zìdiǎn 汉语大字典, Hànyǔ Dà Cídiǎn 汉语大词典, and Cí Yuán 辞源 are probably best classified as classical Chinese dictionaries, while such comprehensive dicitonaries as the Hànyǔ Cídiǎn 汉语辞典 and Cí Hǎi 辞海 may be classified as dictionaries of modern Chinese. These works will be examined in detail in sections 8.3 and 8.4 below.

3) General Purpose Dictionaries and Dictionaries for Special Purposes

All of the dictionaries mentioned so far have been general purpose dictionaries 通用辞书. For example, modern Chinese dictionaries such as the Xīnhuá Zìdiǎn and the Xiàndài Hànyǔ Cídiǎn contain characters and words which are in general use in modern Chinese. On the other hand, dictionaries for special purposes 专用辞书 include words of a particular kind or words used in a particular sphere. There are many such dictionaries for special purposes. Some examples are:

Dictionaries of Chinese "idioms" or set phrases 成语词典: This type of dictionary collects Chéngyǔ 成语, which are set phrases from literary Chinese usually four or more characters long which are used as fixed expressions in modern Chinese, explaining their meanings and use, and sometimes giving their origins as well. One example is the Hànyǔ Chéngyǔ Cídiǎn 汉语成语词典 (*A Dictionary of Chinese Set Phrases*).

Dictionaries of Chinese proverbs 谚语词典: Such a dictionary as the Hànyǔ Yànyǔ Cídiǎn 汉语谚语词典 collects modern Chinese proverbs, explaining their meaning and use, and sometimes giving their origin, if known.

Dictionaries of Xiēhòuyǔ 歇后语词典: Xiēhòuyǔ 歇后语, or "enigmatic folk similes", are popular two-part metaphorical expressions, sometimes involving a play on words in their second part (or "resolution"), which are often opaque in meaning, even to native speakers of Chinese. Recently, a few dictionaries of xiēhòuyǔ, for example, the Xiēhòuyǔ Xiǎo Cídiǎn 歇后语小词典 (*Small Dictionary of Enigmatic Folk Similes*), have collected and explained some of the more popular of these expressions.

Dialect dictionaries 方言词典: Most general purpose dictionaries of modern Chinese contain only words in Putonghua (modern standard "Mandarin" Chinese), although they may occasionally also include a few words from other "dialects" which have come into general use in Putonghua as well. There are also specialized dictionaries which contain words and expressions found only in one "dialect" of one of the Han Chinese languages, with equivalents and explanations given in standard putonghua. Some examples are the Běijīng Fāngyán Cídiǎn 北京方言词典 (*Beijing Dialect Dictionary*), the Jiǎnmíng Wú Fāngyán Cídiǎn 简明吴方言词典 (*Concise Wu Dialect Dictionary*), the Guǎngzhōuhuà Fāngyán Cídiǎn 广州话方言词典 (*Dialect Dictionary of Spoken Cantonese*), and the Pǔtōnghuà-Mǐnnán Fāngyán Cídiǎn 普通话闽南方言词典 (*Mandarin-Amoy Dialect Dictionary*).

Dictionaries of loanwords 外来语词典: This type of dic-

316

tionary especially lists and explains words borrowed from non-Han Chinese languages into contemporary Chinese. One example is the Xiàndài Hànyǔ Wàiláicí Cídiǎn 现代汉语外来词词典 or "Contemporary Chinese Dictionary of Loanwords".

In addition, there are dictionaries of place names 地名词典, of book titles 书名词典, biographical dictionaries 人名词典, all of which may be regarded as reference works or dictionaries for special purposes.

The dictionaries introduced in sections 8.3 and 8.4 below are almost all general purpose dictionaries, with a few exceptions such as the *Dictionary of Chinese Set Phrases* mentioned above.

8.2 HOW TO USE MODERN CHINESE DICTIONARIES

You cannot get the greatest benefit from a good dictionary unless you know how to make good use of it. As we have seen, there are various kinds of Chinese dictionaries, yet most of them share something in common. In what follows, we shall discuss only dictionaries of modern Chinese. For the use of dictionaries of classical Chinese, some specialized knowledge is required which is beyond the scope of this book.

1) Locating 检索

Locating means finding the character or word required in a dictionary. The first thing you should do when you get a new dictionary is to familarize yourself with the indexing system(s) employed in that dictionary. This is the most efficient way to locate the information you want as quickly as possible.

The various indexing systems for Chinese characters were

discussed in detail in Chapter 6. (See above.) Usually every dictionary explains the indexing system for Chinese characters which it employs at the outset. This explanation should be studied very carefully. In this chapter, we will limit ourselves to discussing some special problems which may arise in locating characters in a dictionary.

Modern Chinese dictionaries published in the People's Republic generally adopt at least two indexing systems. The Xīnhuá Zìdiǎn and the Xiàndài Hànyǔ Cídiǎn both have their entries organized alphabetically in Hanyu Pinyin (the standard Chinese phonetic alphabet), with a radical index as an appendix. Other dictionaries, such as Cí Hǎi 辞海 have their entries organized according to the system of radicals, with an alphabetically ordered Hanyu Pinyin index as an appendix. The advantages of having more than one indexing system are obvious; some people are more familiar with one type of system than another, and sometimes when it is difficult to locate a character or word by one system, you can try another system instead.

Indexing systems for Chinese characters usually combine more than one way of ordering. For example, if the characters in a dictionary have as their overall ordering alphabetization according to Hanyu Pinyin, there is still the problem of subordering those different characters within the same group which are all spelled alike in Hanyu Pinyin. Nowadays many dictionaries arrange such characters with the same Hanyu Pinyin spelling (which of course includes grouping by tone) into subgroups based on shared phonetic components, in order to make it easier to find the desired character. For example:

huì; 慧彗嘒槥篲，会绘桧烩荟，惠谪憓潓蕙，缋襀阓，哕秽秽，晦海…

When using a radical index, problems sometimes arise because a few characters have rather peculiar forms and it is not always easy to tell which radical group they belong to, as for instance, with characters such as 爻, 或, and 兽. If one is not sure of their pronunciation, then the Hanyu Pinyin index may be of no help. For such cases, some dictionaries, such as the Xīnhuá Zìdiǎn, have a special list of "hard to classify" characters, or characters with "obscure radicals", arranged according to the total number of strokes in the character. Other dictionaries have a third listing of characters by some other system, such as the total stroke order listing in the Cí Hǎi dictionary, or the so-called "four-corner" system listing given in the Xiàndài Hànyǔ Cídiǎn. (See 6.2.4).

Learners of Chinese should familiarize themselves with these different indexing systems for characters. Then if you cannot locate a character by means of one system, try another in the same dictionary, and if you still cannot locate the character in that dictionary, then you may wish to try yet another dictionary as well.

2) Phonetic Notation 注音

As was explained in Chapter 4 (see 4.1) above, lacking a precise alphabetic notation, the older Chinese dictionaries were forced to adopt the methods of giving a homophonic character 直音 (zhíyīn) or conveying the sounds of the initial consonant and final rhyme of a character by giving two other characters

反切 (fǎnqiè). Beginning in the 1930's, some dictionaries began to use Mandarin Phonetic Symbols 注音字母 (Zhùyīn Zìmǔ) for syllabary notation (see 4.1) which are still used in Taiwan province, as well as use 国语罗马字 (Guóyǔ Luómǎzì, "G.R." alphabetic system), which today is mostly seen only in a few language textbooks. (Students wishing to use these older reference books will also have to master at least some of these older systems later on in their studies, but for general purposes they are not necessary.) Nowadays, modern Chinese dictionaries simply note the pronunciation in Hanyu Pinyin so that anyone familiar with this standard phonetic alphabet can easily pronounce characters and words accurately.

Special attention must be paid to the multiple listings due to polyphony and polysemy. The character 贾, for example, is pronounced jiǎ when used as a surname, and as gǔ in the sense of "merchant". Thus in alphabetically ordered listings, it is listed twice, often with a cross-listing 另见... (lìngjiàn..., see also...) in both entries. Again, the character 参 has three different pronuncations, cān (join, enter, consult), cēn (uneven), and shēn (ginseng), usually listed in three different places in alphabetically ordered dictionaries, with similar cross-references.

Note also that the pronunciation of an isolated character is not always the same as its pronunciation when it occurs in a word or phrase. The most common instance of this phenomenon is in the case of syllables assuming the so-called "neutral tone" 轻声 (qīngshēng), as in the case of the character 生, which is pronounced as shēng in the first tone when read alone, but which loses its tone and changes to the "neutral tone" when it occurs in the compound word 先生, pronouced xiānsheng, meaning "mister" or "teacher". Such cases of neutral tone are clearly noted by an absence of a tone mark in modern Chinese dictionaries which employ Hanyu Pinyin notation, and readers should pay careful attention to such tone markings. A second common example of a change in pronunciation is the change in a character's tone in some set phrases. Thus, for example, while the character 油 (oil, fat, grease) is normally pronounced yóu in the second, rising tone, but when it occurs as a post-adjectival modifier after the word 绿 (lǜ, green) in the phrase 绿油油 (lǜyōuyōu, a sleek, dark, pleasing green), its pronunciation changes to high-level first tone, and this should be noted in modern general purpose dictionaries employing Hanyu Pinyin phonetic notation (usually under the 绿 [lǜ, green] entry).

The most commonly encountered case of changes in tonal pronunciation, however, are not usually noted in general purpose dictionaries. These are the cases of normal tone change (or tone sandhi) which affect tones in certain phonetic environments. Thus, for example, when the low, third-tone word 五 (wǔ, five) occurs before another third tone syllable as in the expression 五谷 (wǔgǔ, five grains, food crops), almost all dictionaries will note the pronunciation as just given — wǔgǔ — with two successive third tones marked, leaving it to the reader's general knowledge of Chinese pronunciation and tone sandhi to make the necessary mandatory tone shifts (in this case from low, third tone, to rising, second tone before another low, third tone) in actual pronunciation.

3) Explanation of the Meaning 释义

Obviously the most important function of a dictionary, particularly for foreign language learners, is its explanation of meanings. The meanings of the individual subentries for (polysyllabic) "words" are fairly easy to identify. But in the primary entries for the head character, one must be careful to distinguish between the different (clusters of) meanings represented by one character. Thus, for example, under the one reading of cān given for the character 参 discussed in the previous section the Xiàndài Hànyǔ Cídiǎn lists four core sub-meanings equivalent to ① "join, enter"; ② "consult"; ③ "call to pay ones respect to"; ④ "impeach".

In such cases, one must decide on the appropriate meaning for a character by virtue of the context in which it occurs. For example, in the popular novel 红楼梦 (Hónglóu Mèng, *A Dream of Red Mansions*,) there occurs the following sentence:

岂不闻古人说的 "大丈夫相时而动"。

Qǐ bù wén gǔrén shuō de "Dàzhàngfū xiàng shí ér dòng"?

(Have you not heard the ancients' saying: "Great men don't take action until they see the [right] time"?)

If you are not sure of the correct pronunciation and meaning of the character 相 in this passage, and consult the Xīnhuá Zìdiǎn, you will find more than one pronunciation as well as several meanings listed as follows:

    xiāng (1) mutual; from both parties

             (2) to see

    xiàng (1) appearance, mien

            (2) observe; examine

> (3) to assist; assistant; in ancient times, an official
> of the highest level

In the given context, we can see that 相 in the expression 相时而
动 here must mean "observe", pronounced xiàng, in order to
give the appropriate meaning of "not taking action until one
has *observed* the [right] time".

When consulting a dictionary, be sure to persist and get
the maximum amount of information so as to enrich your understanding of Chinese. Suppose, for example, that in order
to understand the meaning of the set phrase 同舟共济 (tóng
zhōu gòng jì) you consult the Xiàndài Hànyǔ Cídiǎn. On
page 1153, near the end of the entries listed alphabetically under
the head character 同 tóng, we find this phrase, with the explanation: 同舟共济: "a metaphor for uniting in a common effort,
jointly pulling through difficulties". . You still, however, may
not feel completely clear about the meaning of the last character
in this phrase. If you persist, and look up the character 济
(jì) itself, you will find that it means to "ford or cross a river".
In this way the full imagery of the idiom becomes clear, and —
incidentally — we also learn why the character 济 has a "water"
radical.

Sometimes we cannot always find the word or expression
we want directly, so we have to look up the individual characters
which compose the word or expression one by one. Suppose,
for example, we wish to know the meaning of the literary word
苍穹, and we look under the character 苍 (cāng) in a certain
dictionary. We find that the character 苍 itself is glossed as
"bluish-green in color, or blue, or green", but that the word

323

苍穹 (cāngqióng) itself is not listed under the entry for 苍. What to do? If we consult the entry for 穹 (qióng) alone, we find it glossed as "vault or arched roof, also used to refer to the sky, the heavens". So by putting these two entries together, we can come to the conclusion that 苍穹 must refer to "blue skies" or "sky"

Many times example sentences are given after the explanations in dictionary entries. Such example sentences can help us to gain a deeper understanding of the meaning of the word in question, as well as its usage. Take, for example, the word 口风 kǒufēng which is glossed as "one's meaning as revealed in one's speech". If this explanation leaves one at a bit of a loss, the example sentence which follows helps clarify not only the meaning, but the usage of this expression as well: 你先探探他的口风，看他是不是愿意去。 "Sound him out first and see if he wants to go." Particularly the meaning and usage of structural function words such as prepositions, conjunctions, and particles are best shown through such example sentences. Thus in consulting dictionaries equal attention should be paid to these example sentences as well as to the meaning glosses.

4) Appendices 附录

Most modern Chinese dictionaries have some appendices at the back which can be very useful for reference. Often the following appendices are given: A Brief Chronology of the Chinese Dynasties, Units of Weights and Measures, A List of the Chinese National Minorities, Proper Names of Foreign Places and Persons with their Corresponding Chinese Translations, A Table of the Chemical Elements, Chinese Punctuation Usage,

the Scheme for the Chinese Phonetic Alphabet (Hanyu Pinyin),
etc.

8.3 A BRIEF INTRODUCTION TO DICTIONARIES OF MODERN CHINESE

1) The Xīnhuá Zìdiǎn 新华字典 (*Xinhua Dictionary*) was
the first new dictionary published by the state press after the
founding of the People's Republic of China in 1949. It is also
the most widely used Chinese dictionary today. First published
in 1953 by the People's Education Publishing House, it was
republished in 1957 by the Commercial Press and has been
revised three times, in 1971, 1976, and 1980.

The Xīnhuá Zìdiǎn gives the standardized forms for modern
(simplified) characters. Taking characters as its main focus,
this dictionary contains about 11,000 characters (including
variant forms and the original complex forms) as well as 3,500
polysyllabic words, phrases, and chéngyǔ idioms. The majority
of characters included are those in current use, plus a few characters from ancient books, dialects, and professional jargon. This
is an intermediate level dictionary useful for reading contemporary books, newspapers, and magazines.

The Xīnhuá Zìdiǎn has its characters arranged alphabetically
in Hanyu Pinyin and comes in two different editions, one with
a radical index, and the other with a four-corner code index,
so that users may choose the edition with the indexing system
with which they are most familiar.

The pronunciation of characters in the Xīnhuá Zìdiǎn is

noted in Hanyu Pinyin as well as in the older Zhùyīn Zìmǔ. Characters with more than one pronunciation have their various readings numbered using Chinese numerals ⊖, ⊜, ⊜, etc., with the most common pronunciation given first. For example, the character 参, discussed above, has its variant pronunciations noted as ⊖ cān, ⊜ shēn, ⊜ cēn. In the meaning glosses which follow, these differences in pronunciation are also noted. To give another example, 地道 is read dìdào when it means "an underground tunnel", but is read as dìdao when it means "genuine product of a famous place", as in 四川地道药材, "genuine Sichuan medicine". This dictionary is thus particularly useful for determining the standard pronunciation of Chinese characters and words.

In explaining the meaning of polysemous characters, the primary submeanings are indicated by white Arabic numberals in dark circles, like ❶, ❷, ❸, etc. Each of these entries may again be sub-divided by ordinary Arabic numberals: 1, 2, 3, etc. The explanations are simple and concise, and arranged in a clear-cut order for ease of use. Besides literal meanings, this dictionary also indicates extended meanings by the notation 引 (yǐn), figurative meanings by 喻 (yù), and transferred meanings by 转 (zhuǎn). The notation 连 (lián) indicates that the character under discussion may be joined with another character to form a disyllabic word similar in meaning to the original character. For example, 朋 (péng, friend) plus 友 (yǒu, friend) gives 朋友 (péngyǒu, friend). The notation 叠 (dié) indicates that the character in question can be repeated to create a reduplicative construction with a meaning similar to that of the single character. For example 爸（叠）indicates that the single character bà, "pa" or "dad", can be reduplicated to give 爸爸 (bàba), meaning "papa" or "daddy".

Under each character entry, polysyllabic words are indicated in two ways: 1) Polysyllabic words given in square brackets [ ] directly following the main single character heading indicate that the meaning of the polysyllabic word is closely related to the meaning of the single character. Thus, for example, immediately after defining the character 酬 (chóu) as "to thank with a gift", there follows [酬酢] chóuzuò "mutual treatment", and [应酬] yìngchóu, subglossed as (1) "same as 酬酢", (2) "to deal with perfunctorily". 2) Polysyllabic words listed separately in angular brackets « » as independent word entries beneath the single character glosses indicate that the meaning of the polysyllabic word is not related or not closely related to the original root meaning(s) of the single character under which the word is listed. For example, see the following sample entry (translated into English):

跋 bá　❶ to cross the mountains.　❷ an "afterword" appended to the end of an essay or book, usually evaluating its content.

《跋扈》 báhù arrogant and domineering.

2) The Tóngyīn Zìdiǎn 同音字典 (A Dictionary of Homophones) was compiled by the China Dictionary Editorial Board and published by the Commercial Press in 1956. This is a medium-sized dictionary for intermediate level readers which includes 10,500 characters and 30,000 words. In this dictionary can be found characters and words which appear in most general

reading matter, including that written in basic literary Chinese (wényánwén).

As the title of this work indicates, in this dictionary homophones are grouped together. As the pronunciation of the characters is noted in the Zhùyīn Zìmǔ, so the characters are also ordered according to that system. Thus users of this dictionary would best be familiar with this system. For readers who are not familiar with the Zhùyīn Zìmǔ, however, there is also a stroke order index given as an appendix. In this index, the characters are arranged by total order of strokes, and subcategorized into seven subgroups each sharing the intitial stroke shapes of ﹅ (dot), — (horizontal stroke), ｜ (vertical stroke), ノ (downward southwesterly stroke), ﹨ (downward southeasterly stroke), ⌐ (leftward angular stroke), or ⌊ (rightward angular stroke), in that order.

This dictionary has two additional special characteristics. First, besides listing characters in common use, it also lists quite a few rarely used characters as well as giving explanations of the archaic meanings of some characters. Second, under most of the head characters are also listed words beginning with that character, the number of such words varying from one or two to over a hundred, including words, phrases, chéngyǔ "idioms", as well as some words and expressions from classical Chinese, some scientific terms, proper names of places, etc., with explanations for many of the more difficult words and expressions.

3) The **Hànzì Zhèngzì Xiǎo Zìhuì** 汉字正字小字汇 (*An Orthorgaphical Glossary of Chinese Characters*) was first published by the Language Reform Publishing House in 1973. This

small-sized dictionary is different from other general purpose dictionaries in that it is an orthographical dictionary which aims to give standard pronunciations and standardized written forms for Chinese characters, so the meaning explanations are not very detailed.

This glossary contains about 4,000 commonly used single characters, while rarely used characters are not included. The characters are arranged in alphabetical order according to Hanyu Pinyin. Homophones are arranged by grouping together those which share the same phonetic components. There is also an index of characters by number of strokes.

The forms of the characters given follow the "List of Chinese Character Forms for General Printing" 印刷通用汉字字形表 as the standard, with the original complex forms of simplified characters, variant character forms, and older printed forms of characters given in brackets. The analysis of the structure of the character forms is also stressed, with annotations on peculiarities of certain forms. For example, the character 庆 (qìng, celebrate) is noted to be different in form from the character 厌 (yàn, detest) in that its form consists of the radical 广 (guǎng, vast) above and a simple 大 (dà, big) below. The number and order of strokes are supplied for characters considered difficult to write. For example, the character 长 (cháng, long) is shown to have four strokes written in the order 丿, 一, 七, 长.

Characters are annotated with their standard pronunciations. The different pronunciation of polyphonic characters are indicated separately by Arabic numbers (1), (2), . . . In addition, characters easily mispronounced are especially indicated; for example, "胼 is read pián instead of 并 (bìng)." Special pronunciations for characters are also indicated in parentheses. For example, the character 铅, normally pronounced qiān when it means the metal "lead", is annotated thus: "铅 qiān (read as yán when used in the name of Yánshān County 铅山县 in Jiangxi Province.)"

This small glossary can be very useful to beginning learners of Chinese in learning to pronounce and write the forms of Chinese characters correctly.

4) The **Xiàndài Hànyǔ Cídiǎn** 现代汉语词典 (*A Dictionary of Modern Chinese Words*), compiled by the Dictionary Editorial Office of the Linguistics Research Institute of the Chinese Academy of Social Sciences, was first published in 1965 in a trial edition by the Commercial Press, and then in an official edition in 1978.

This medium-sized dictionary includes words and expressions in Putonghua for readers above the intermediate level. It contains about 56,000 entries, including characters, words, phrases, and chéngyǔ idioms. In addition to common words and expressions in standard Putonghua, it also includes some words from dialects and literary Chinese in common use, as well as some scientific and technical terms.

This dictionary is intended to help popularize Putonghua and assist in the standardization of the Chinese language. Its editors intend it to become a standardizing reference work with unique features of arrangement, annotation of pronunciation, and explanations of meanings.

The single head characters in this dictionary are arranged

alphabetically in Hanyu Pinyin. Polyphonous characters have separate listings for each different reading, with cross referencing between them; e.g., 另见… ("See also…"). Under each single head character are listed those polysyllabic words which begin with that head character in that pronunciation. Those polysyllabic words are also spelled out in Hanyu Pinyin and arranged alphabetically, which makes for ease in consulting the dictionary.

Words of the same form but with different meanings are listed as separate entries under the head character. Here are two examples in translation:

帮¹ bāng (1) help; (2) formerly meant to be employed for labour, as in: 帮短工 (bāng duǎngōng, help out on a part-time basis).

帮² bāng (1) the sides of a hollow object, as in: 鞋帮儿 (xiébāngr, sides of shoes); 船帮 (chuánbāng, sides of a boat). (2) outer leaves.

帮³ bāng (1) gang, band, clique (mostly indicating a group organized for a political or economic purpose), as in: 马帮 (mǎbāng, a horse caravan), 匪帮 (fěibāng, a gang of bandits). (2) a measure word for people, meaning a group of, as in: 他带来了一帮小孩儿 (Tā dài lái le yībāng xiǎoháir, He brought along a group of children). (3) a secret society, as in: 青帮 (Qīng Bāng, the Green Gang), 洪帮 (Hóng Bāng, the Hong Triad Society).

虎口¹ hǔkǒu a metaphor for dangerous places, as in: 虎口余生 (hǔkǒu yú shēng, escape from the jaws of a tiger).

虎口² hǔkǒu　part of the hand between thumb and fore-
　　　finger.

The editors have tried to make the explanations to meanings
as exact, scientific, and comprehensive as possible. The explanations of structural or grammatical function words is especially detailed, giving not only the part of speech, but making
fine distinctions in the different grammatical functions of the
same function word, along with sufficient examples to show these
various usages.

The Xiàndài Hànyǔ Cídiǎn is the most comprehensive Chinese dictionary in popular use today.

5) The **Sìjiǎo Hàomǎ Xīn Cídiǎn** 四角号码新词典 (*New
Four-Corner Code Dictionary*) was first published by the Commercial Press in 1950, and two revised editions were published
in 1962 and 1978.

This is a general purpose intermediate level dictionary which
includes 9,000 characters (including monosyllabic words) and
15,000 polysyllabic words. Words were chosen for inclusion
on the basis of their occurence in language and literature, with
some encyclopaedic terms also included. This work primarily
contains words in current use, but a few classical words and
meanings are also included. The explanations of meanings are
clear, concise and easy to understand. Emphasis is laid on the
clear-cut explanation of present day meanings with no consideration of etymology. Take for example two chéngyǔ idioms listed
under the character 探 (tàn, explore). The first 探骊得珠 (tàn
lí dé zhū) is simply glossed as "writing an essay which captures
the main point". There is no explanation of the literal meaning

of the four characters (literally: to seek a black horse to obtain a pearl), which alludes to a story from the classical philosopher Zhuāngzǐ about getting pearls from a sacred horse who lives under the sea. Again, the second chéngyǔ idiom listed under 探 is 探囊取物 (tàn náng qǔ wù), which is simply glossed as "a matter easily handled". There is no explanation of the rare and complex character 囊 (náng), nor of the literal meaning "(as easy as) taking something out of one's pocket".

Characters in this dictionary are arranged according to the four-corner indexing system (see 6.2 (4) above). This is in fact the only dictionary using this system published since the founding of the People's Republic of China in 1949. For those not familiar with this system a table of characters arranged by radicals and a Hanyu Pinyin index are appended at the back.

The pronunciation of individual characters is noted in Hànyǔ Pīnyīn, and in the Zhùyīn Zìmǔ, as well as by the older method of giving a homophonous character(zhíyīn; see Chapter 4). For example, the entry for the character 扉 reads as follows in translation:

扉 (fēi ㄈㄟ 非) half of a pair of double doors; (e.g.) 柴扉 (cháifēi a door made of sticks).

6) The **Hànyǔ Cídiǎn** 汉语词典 (*Dictionary of the Chinese Language*), a medium-sized dictionary compiled by the China Dictionary Editorial Board and published by the Commercial Press in 1957, is an abridged version of the 1947 国语词典 (Guóyǔ Cídiǎn; *Dictionary of the National Language*). It includes 60,000 entries, including characters, polysyllabic words, phrases,

and chéngyǔ idioms. The pronunciation of characters and words are noted in the Zhùyīn Zìmǔ and the homophone method (zhíyīn) is also employed for single characters. For example, the notation for the character 衿 (the belt of a garment) is ㄐㄧㄣ 金. Word entries are sequenced according to the order of the Zhùyīn Zìmǔ, e.g. ㄅㄆㄇㄈ…, etc.

As far as the inclusion of words and the explanation of meanings are concerned, this dictionary is characterized by the following features:

a) More characters and words from classical Chinese are included than in other medium-sized dictionaries, e.g. 瞜 (lōu, see), 恧缩 (nù suō, ashamed and frightened), etc.

b) Many spoken words and expressions from the Beijing local dialect are included, e.g. 城门脸儿 (chéngmén liǎnr, a place near the city gate); 满没听提 (mǎn méi tīng tí, not pay any attention to), etc.

c) Clear and concise explanations are given in basic literary Chinese (wényánwén), e.g. 欢势 (huān shì) is glossed as 活泼欢跃貌 (so happy as to be jumping up and down); 蟹厄 (xiè è) is glossed as 谓蟹行田中为禾稼之害 (like crabs skurrying through the fields doing damage to the crops).

This dictionary may be used as a complement to the Xiàndài Hànyǔ Cídiǎn, introduced above. For example, under the entry for the character 近 (jìn, close) in the Hànyǔ Cídiǎn are listed such words as 近况 (jìnkuàng, recent developments), 近情 (jìnqíng, recent situation), 近支 (jìnzhī, close branches), 近畿 (jìnjī; outskirts of the capital), 近悦远来 (jìn yuè yuǎn lái, pleasing those near such that others also come from afar),

334

which are not included in the Xiàndài Hànyǔ Cídiǎn. But the latter work includes some specialized terms such as 近海 (jìnhǎi, coastal waters), 近似值 (jìnsìzhí, approximate value), 近似商 (jìnsìshāng, approximate quotient), and 近体诗 (jìntǐshī, Táng Dynasty modern style poetry", which are not included in the Hànyǔ Cídiǎn, so the two dictionaries may be said to complement each other.

7) The **Hànyǔ Pīnyīn Cíhuì** 汉语拼音词汇 (*Chinese Pinyin Glossary*) was compiled by the Glossary Group of the Committee for the Reform of the Chinese Language and published in a revised, enlarged edition by the Language Reform Publishing House in 1963.

This small book is a glossary of words in Putonghua given in Hanyu Pinyin transcription which includes about 59,100 words and expressions. As its aim is to define the standard written forms of Chinese words in Hanyu Pinyin as well as the standard pronunciation of words in Putonghua, it does not give glosses or explanations of meaning.

The word entries are written in Hanyu Pinyin transcription with the corresponding Chinese characters following for reference. The entries are arranged in alphabetical order and thus are convenient to use for those who are familiar with the Hanyu Pinyin system.

Words spelled in the same way are grouped together, with an asterisk (*) indicating words spelled the same way which differ only in tone, and a double asterisk (**) indicating words with exactly the same tones. These features make this work a comparatively comprehensive reference book on homophones in Putonghua.

8) The **Cí Hǎi** 辞海 (*Sea of Words*) is a revision of the old 1948 edition of Cí Hǎi as revised by the Cí Hǎi Editorial Committee and published by the Shanghai Lexicographic Publishing House in 1979. A supplement was published in 1982.

This new edition of Cí Hǎi is a comprehensive reference work of a philological and encylopaedic nature. The dictionary (including the supplement) glosses 14,872 character entries and contains 108,000 polysyllabic word subentries, including chéng-yǔ idioms, literary allusions, historical figures, important literary works, historical events, names of places of both present and ancient times, names of organizations and specialized terminology from various fields of learning. This comprehensive work is a kind of "desk-top encyclopaedia" and can satisfy the needs of readers above the intermediate level when they encounter difficult problems in reading and writing Chinese.

The head characters in this dictionary are arranged according to a radical indexing system, with all of the characters belonging to the same radical group arranged according to the remaining number of strokes. Characters with the same number of strokes are then arranged according to the first stroke of the characters, in the order — 丨 丿 乀 →. In addition, the dictionary has a "Table of Characters Arranged in Order of Total Number of Strokes" and an "Index of Chinese Characters According to Hanyu Pinyin Transcription".

The Cí Hǎi dictionary lays emphasis on comprehensive knowledge. It gives both detailed explanations of the specialized terminology of various fields and at the same time simple, straightforward explanations of the meanings of common words.

336

In this respect it is different from the Xiàndài Hànyǔ Cídiǎn and other dictionaries of a philological nature. This dictionary also carries more than a dozen appendices which are of great use to users for reference purposes.

9) **The Xiàndài Hànyǔ Bābǎi Cí** 现代汉语八百词 (*Eight Hundred Words of Modern Chinese*) was published by the Commercial Press in 1980 under the chief-editorship of the eminent linguist Lǚ Shūxiāng 吕叔湘. Taking as its primary focus the usage of function words in modern Chinese, this grammatical reference work includes over 800 such words and expressions as its main entries, with some additional notional words of difficult or special usage also included.

The entries in this work have the following features:

a) The part of speech is indicated for every word entry. Words which may be used as more than one part of speech have separate sub-entries for each such usage.

b) Clear simple explanations of the various meanings of each word are given, with ample examples to show the different uses of each word, its collocations, its grammatical function in a sentence, etc.

c) For some entries, there is an additional "comparison" notation, in which words or usages often confused are contrasted and distinguished.

Let us examine the following entry in translation as an example:

以及 yǐjí
[conjunction] Expresses conjoining: can conjoin nouns, verbs, prepositional phrases, clauses; mostly used in written style.

a) The things conjoined are not equal; the things mentioned before yǐjí are stressed; e.g.

拖拉机、收割机以及各种小农具

(tractors, harvesters, *as well as* various small agricultural implements)

本店经销电视机、收音机、录音机，以及各种零件

(This store sells televisions, radios, tape recorders, *as well as* various miscellaneous items.)

b) The elements conjoined are sequenced chronologically; e.g.

老陈、小李以及另一位同志在会上先后作了发言

(Old Chen, Little Li and then one other comrade made some speeches at the meeting.)

问题是如何产生的，以及最后该如何解决，都需要调查研究

([The questions of] how the problem arose *as well as* how it ought to be finally settled, both have to be investigated.)

至于分不分组，以及如何分组，全由你们自己去考虑

(As to whether or not to divide into groups and (if so) how to divide into groups, you will have to decide that by yourselves.)

c) The things conjoined can be divided into two kinds; e. g.

鸡、鸭、鱼、肉、蛋，以及糖果、糕点等商品应有尽有。

(They have chicken, duck, fish, pork, eggs as well as candy, cakes, and all the other things that a store ought to have.)

钢铁、煤炭、石油，以及纺织、造纸等工业部门都有很大发展。

(There has been great development in the iron and steel,

coal, and petroleum industries, as well as in textiles, paper-making, etc.)

(Compare:) 以及 (yǐjí) vs. 及 (jí) vs. 和 (hé)

   (1) 及 (jí) can only conjoin nominal elements.

   (2) There can be a pause before 以及 (yǐjí) but not before 及 (jí).

   (3) 及 (jí) can be followed by 其 (qí, its). 以及 (yǐjí) may be followed by 其他 (qítā, other).

   (4) When either 以及 (yǐjí) or 及 (jí) are used to conjoin, the thing(s) mentioned before the conjunction is/are stressed, while the thing(s) given after the conjunction is/are secondary.

   (5) 以及 (yǐjí) can conjoin clauses, while 及 (jí) and 和 (hé) cannot.

This book has an "Essentials of Chinese Grammar" section as an introduction, and a "Table of Nouns with Their Corresponding Measure Words" as an appendix, both of which are useful for reference.

   10) The **Hànyǔ Chéngyǔ Cídiǎn** 汉语成语词典 (*Dictionary of Chinese Set Phrases*) was compiled by the Chinese Language Department of Gānsù Normal University and published by the Shanghai Educational Publishing House in 1978. It includes 5,500 chéngyǔ (成语), which are proverb-like set expressions usually from literary Chinese and mostly four or more characters long. The term chéngyǔ is often misleadingly translated as "idiom(s)" in English. The entries are arranged alphabetically in Hanyu Pinyin and a radical index to the first characters of each chéngyǔ is given in an appendix at the back of the work.

This dictionary is characterized by the following features:

(1) It contains a large number of chéngyǔ, including both those in common use as well as others more rarely seen.

(2) Before explaining the entire meaning of each chéngyǔ, the dictionary first explains the meaning of the characters and words which make up that chéngyǔ.

(3) For most chéngyǔ the origin is given, i.e. where the chéngyǔ first appeared. In addition examples are given to show the use of each chéngyǔ.

(4) Characters or words which are easily mispronounced, miswritten, or misunderstood are explained and distinguished.

Here is a sample entry in translation:

[唯唯诺诺] wěi wěi nuò nuò. 唯唯: modest response; 诺诺: stuttering in reply, submissive. Describes a submissive response by one who does not dare to express a contrary opinion. [From:] 韩非子 [the philosopher Hán Fēizǐ's work entitled] 八奸 (Bā Jiān):"未命而唯唯，未使而诺诺，先意承旨；观貌察色，以先主心者也。"
("Yes-yesing before the order had been given and fawning assent before being told what to do, those who try to anticipate the emperor's every wish, would hang on his very word and change in expression.")

Note: 唯 does not have its usual pronunciation of wéi.

As these set phrases are so commonly encountered in Chinese writing and speech, the Hànyǔ Chéngyǔ Cídiǎn is also a valuable basic reference work.

8.4 A BRIEF INTRODUCTION TO DICTIONARIES OF CLASSICAL CHINESE

1) The **Shuō Wén Jiě Zì** 说文解字 (*An Analysis and Explanation of Characters*) was compiled by Xǔ Shèn in the Eastern Hàn Dynasty, and was completed after twenty-two years of work in 121 A.D. It was the first Chinese character dictionary and the first work of characterology in Chinese history, and is still in wide use today.

The Shuō Wén Jiě Zì classifies and explains 9,353 characters from pre-Hàn Dynasty times, as well as giving 1,163 variant character forms. The head characters for each entry are written in the small seal character style. All of the characters in this work are arranged under 540 semantic radicals. This is in fact the first dictionary to adopt the semantic radical indexing system.

For the annotation of pronunciation, the Shuō Wén Jiě Zì adopts the method of giving a homophonous character 直音 (zhí yīn), using such phrases as 从X声 (following the sound of character X) or 读若 X (reads like character X) or 读与 X 同 (reads the same as character X).

Usually only the original meaning is given in explaining characters, as for example 亡，逃也 (wáng means "flee)" or 作，起也 (zuò means "begin"). But occasionally the entries contain additional information, as for example:

"狼，似犬，锐头、白颊、高前、广后"
("Wolf, like a dog, pointed face, white whiskers, high forehead, wider at the back of the head")

"贝，海介虫也……。古者货贝而宝龟。周而有泉，至秦废贝行钱"

(Cowrie, a sea animal with a shell, ... the ancients used them as small currency, and tortoise shells as large currency. In the Zhōu Dynasty, it was called "currency", but the Qín abandoned using cowrie shells as money.)

One of the most significant contributions that this dictionary made to characterology is that it advanced the theory of the "Six Types" 六书 (Liù Shū) of characters, based on a model of six basic types of character formation, and using this model, attempted a systematic analysis of all Chinese characters (see Chapter 1, Section 2.). Under this system, picto-phonetic characters 形声字 are indicated in this dictionary by the notation 从 X, Y 声 (from X, sounds like Y), e.g. the character 江 (river, now pronounced jiāng) was then noted as 从水，工声 (from [the semantic radical] water, sounds like the word 工 [gōng, which it did then sound like, and still does in Cantonese and other southern Chinese dialects today]). Again, the picto-phonetic character 俭 (jiǎn, frugal) is noted as 从人，金声 (from [the semantic radical] people, and pronounced like 金 [jiǎn, which it still resembles today]).

Associative compounds 会意字 are noted 从X，从Y (from X and from Y) or simply 从 X, Y (from X and Y), as for example, the character 初 (chū, beginning, first) is annotated as 从刀从衣 (from knife and clothing) and the character 解 (jiě, divide) is noted as 从刀判牛角 (from a knife 刀 dividing a cow's horn 牛角)."

Pictographic characters 象形字 are noted as 象X 之形

342

(resembling the form of X) or simply 象形 (resembling the form); for example, the entry for 鹿 (lù, deer) reads 兽也。象头角四足之形 (an animal. Looks like its horned, four-footed form.), and the entry for the character 竹 (zhú, bamboo) reads 冬生草也。象形。下垂者，箁箬也。 (a plant which grows in winter. Looks like it. Has hanging leaves. *Indocalamus tessellatus*.)

As for indicative (or "self-explanatory") characters, except for a very small number like 上 (shàng, above) and 下 (xià, below) which are simply labelled "indicative" 指事 (zhǐshì) without any additional explanation, the remainder of this type are explained in the same manner as used for pictographic or associative characters that we have just seen. For example, here are the entries for the characters 刃 (rèn, knife edge) and 旦 (dàn, daylight):

刃，刀坚也。象刀有刃之形。

(rèn is knife edge. Looks like a knife with an edge [i.e. the dot points towards the sharp edge of the knife character 刀]).

旦，明也。从日见一上。一，地也。

(dàn is daylight. From "sun" 日 appearing over the horizon 一. Here [the horizontal stroke] 一 represents the earth 地.)

(The other two types of characters given in Shuō Wén Jiě Zì are "borrowed" characters 假借字, characters borrowed purely for their sound value to represent a homophonous word, long before Xǔ Shèn's time, and "notative characters" 转注字, a category whose exact meaning is still not entirely clear to scholars.)

The Shuō Wén Jiě Zì is different from modern Chinese dictionaries both in nature and function. Modern Chinese dictionaries aim to explain the meaning and usage of characters and/or words, while the Shuō Wén Jiě Zì aims to analyze the forms of characters and trace the origins of the formation of the characters.

2) The Zì Huì 字汇 (*Character Glossary*) was compiled by Méi Yīngzuò 梅膺祚 in 1615 during the Ming Dynasty. Next to the Shuō Wén Jiě Zì just mentioned, the Zì Huì has had the greatest influence on the compilation of Chinese dictionaries.

This dictionary includes 33,179 characters, including characters from ancient Chinese classics as well as colloquial characters then in common use. To express the pronunciation of each character, the Zì Huì employs the initial consonant — final rhyme method 反切 (fǎnqiè) followed by the homophonous character 直音 (zhíyīn) method. Usually only the basic literal sense of each character is given, but the explanations are simple, straightforward, and useful.

The Zì Huì dictionary simplifed the 540 semantic radicals of the Shuō Wén Jiě Zì down to 214 radicals. All characters classified under the same radicals were then arranged according to the total number of strokes remaining after those of the radical are subtracted. This much simpler indexing system of organizing and indexing Chinese characters was a great improvement over the previous system based on the principle of character formation, and made it much more convenient to locate characters. This type of radical indexing system, which originated in the Zì Huì dictionary, is still employed in Chinese dictionaries today.

344

The appendix of the Zì Huì dictionary was also rich and creative in its content. For example, in this appendix Méi Yīngzuò proposed the principle that the forms of characters then in current use should be adopted as the standard forms rather than continuing to take the ancient forms as standard. The appendix also explains the order of strokes in writing characters and distinguishes between different characters having similar forms, such as 盲 and 肓, or 巳, 巴, and 己. The appendix also contains a list of characters difficult to locate according to the radical indexing system, in which those characters are listed simply in order of their total number of strokes. All of these innovations have exerted an important influence on the compilation of Chinese dictionaries since that time.

3) The **Kāngxī Zìdiǎn 康熙字典** (*Kangxi Dictionary*) was compiled by Zhāng Yùshū 张玉书, Chén Tíngjìng 陈廷敬, and twenty-eight other scholars by order of the Emperor Kāngxī and came off the press in 1716 in the Qing Dynasty. As this reference work was an official government publication, it has had a great influence and been widely used over the intervening years.

The Kāngxī Zìdiǎn includes 47,035 characters, including all types of characters from classical writing as well as rarely used characters, and was the biggest Chinese dictionary of its time. For noting pronunciation, it adopts the fǎnqiè and zhíyīn methods and it explains the basic meanings of the characters. It also includes variant pronunciations (expressed through fǎnqiè) as well as variant explanations of meaning, based on different earlier dictionaries, as well as citing examples of the first instance of the characters' appearance. Thus this work is of great use in reading the classics, in understanding the original meanings of characters, and tracing the origins of characters, and still has great scholary value today.

The Kāngxī Zìdiǎn adopts the radical indexing system of the Zì Huì dictionary, dividing the characters under 214 semantic radicals, and then ordering those characters in each radical group according to their number or strokes. As in the Zì Huì, the Kāngxī Zìdiǎn also provides a table of difficult to locate characters, and also distinguishes among characters with similar forms.

But the Kāngxī Zìdiǎn does have its shortcomings. Unfortunately the source materials were chosen indiscriminantly and there appears to have been no unified principle for editing the work. In addition, the compilation was done in a hurry, without careful proof-reading, so that there are many mistakes. Later a scholar named Wáng Yǐnzhī 王引之 wrote a "Textual Criticism of the Kāngxī Zìdiǎn", listing 2,588 mistakes which is now reprinted at the back of the dictionary for reference.

4) The **Zhōng Huá Dà Zì diǎn** 中华大字典 (*Zhonghua Unabridged Dictionary*) was published by the Zhonghua Book Company in 1915 under the chief editorship of Lù Fèikuí 陆费逵 and Ouyáng Pǔcún 欧阳溥存. This dictionary includes over 48,000 characters, slightly more than the Kāngxī Zìdiǎn, on which it is based. It also differs in that it includes characters for words in modern spoken Chinese and some dialects, as well as some new characters from modern science and technology, such as 氩 (yà, argon), 氪 (kè, krypton), etc.

346

For pronunciation, the Zhōnghuá Dà Zìdiǎn also employs the fǎnqiè initial consonant-final rhyme method, basing its pronunciation on that of Middle Chinese as noted in the medieval work 集韻 (Jí Yùn, Collected Rhymes), followed by the zhíyīn homphone notation. In its explanation of meanings, this work improves upon its predecessor in that in addition to literal meanings, it also gives extended meanings, transferred meanings, and borrowed meanings. Thus its explanations are much more detailed than those of the Kāngxī Zìdiǎn, and also sources are indicated for the examples given so that readers may verify them if necessary.

The Zhōnghuá Dà Zìdiǎn also adopts the 214 radical indexing system, with a slight rearrangement in the order of the radicals. For example, this dictionary groups the radicals 手，毛，心，and 爪 together because they are connected in meaning, and groups 八，入，儿，and 几 together because they are similar in form. This rearrangement makes this dictionary easier to consult.

Although the Zhōnghuá Dà Zìdiǎn is a great improvement over the Kāngxī Zìdiǎn and corrects its mistakes, it does still contain many errors and ommissions itself.

5) The **Cí Yuán** 辞源 (*Source of Words*) is a comprehensive dictionary which includes both ancient and modern words and expressions with an emphasis on words and expressions from classical Chinese writings and on documenting the origins of words with quotations. It was begun in 1908 and the first volume was published by the Commercial Press in 1915 under the chief editorship of Lù Erkuí 陆尔奎 and others, with its

first update in 1931. The dictionary continued to be expanded and enlarged until 1949. It was completely revised and reprinted in 1979, making it an excellent dictionary of classical Chinese for readers above the intermediate level in reading classical Chinese writings.

The Cí Yuán dictionary now includes over 10,000 character entries and more than 100,000 words and expressions, including polysyllabic words, chéngyǔ idioms, quotations from the classics, names of persons and places, book titles, names of important historical events and specialized terminology from various fields of study. The 1979 revised edition employs Hanyu Pinyin, the Zhùyīn Zìmǔ and the fǎnqiè system for the notation of pronunciation. In its explanations, the Cí Yuán gives first the literal meaning, followed by any extended meanings, borrowed meanings, etc. The examples in the entries are arranged in chronological order according to the dates of the sources from which examples are taken, with the year, author, book title, essay title, and volume numbers of all sources being fully cited.

The Cí Yuán employs the 214 radical indexing system, with characters arranged in the text as they are ordered in the index. In addition, a four-corner code index is given in an appendix at the back of the work.

6) The **Zhōngwén Dà Zìdiǎn** 中文大字典 (*A Complete Chinese Dictionary*), compiled by a special editorial committee in Taiwan, had its first edition published in 1973 by the Chinese Cultural Institute Press there, with a revised edition in 1976. Based on the Kāngxī Zìdiǎn, this work contains about

50,000 character entries, and approximately 370,000 words and expresssions, including chéngyǔ idioms, technical terms, mottoes, names of persons and places, official titles, imperial reign titles, book titles, plant and animal names, decrees and regulations. The inclusion of words is quite comprehensive, and the work is rich in quotations from a variety of sources.

This dictionary pays special attention to the origins and evolution of Chinese characters. The various forms and pronunciations of characters are arranged in chronological order so that the reader can see their development over time. In the explanations of the characters, the literal meaning is given first, followed by any extended or borrowed senses. The sources and book titles from which examples are taken are all clearly indicated.

For the notation of pronunciation, the Zhōngwén Dà Zìdiǎn employs fǎnqiè, the Zhùyīn Zìmǔ, as well as the old Guóyǔ Luómǎzì (G.R.) system. This dictionary employs the 214 radical indexing system adopted from the Kāngxī Zìdiǎn under which characters belonging to the same radical category are grouped together by number of strokes, and characters with the same number of strokes are subdivided into four subgroups depending on whether their intitial stroke is a dot, a horizontal, vertical, or a diagonal one. In addition, a four-corner code index and a total stroke index are provided in the dictionary.

7) The **Hànyǔ Dà Zìdiǎn** 汉语大字典 (*Great Chinese Character Dictionary*), compiled by a special editorial committee and jointly published by the Sichuan and Hubei Lexicographic Publishing Houses, had its first volume published in 1986.

The Hànyǔ Dà Zìdiǎn includes about 56,000 character entries, making it the largest of all the Chinese dictionaries published to date. Its aim is to explain the forms, pronunciations, and meanings of Chinese characters. For the character forms, it adopts the regular script form as the main form for each entry, followed by representative oracle bone inscription style, ancient bronze inscription style, small seal style, and official script style forms in order to show the evolution of the forms of the characters since ancient times. For the notation of pronunciation, the present day standard pronunciation is noted in Hanyu Pinyin. For the Middle Chinese pronunication, fǎnqiè is given, and for the Ancient Chinese pronunciation, only the ancient rhyme category 韵 (yùn) is indicated. As for the explanation of meanings, this dictionary not only includes the common meanings of common characters, but also uncommon meanings for those characters, as well as the meanings for rarely used characters. In addition, it also explains the meanings of characters as they represent morphemes in modern polysyllabic words.

The characters in the Hànyǔ Dà Zìdiǎn are classified and arranged under 200 radicals, in a manner similar to that of the Hànyǔ Dà Cídiǎn (to be discussed below under No. 8). The radicals are arranged in order of the number of strokes, and radicals with the same number of strokes are arranged in the order ⼀ ⼁ ⼃ 丶 ⼄ . Within these groups, characters belonging to the same radical group are arranged in this same way.

8) The **Hànyǔ Dà Cídiǎn** 汉语大辞典 (*Great Chinese Word Dictionary*) compiled by the Hànyǔ Dà Cídiǎn Editorial

Committee and Editorial Office, had its first volume published in 1986.

This large, historical dictionary includes approximately 370,000 words and expressions, including single characters, polysyllabic words, chéngyǔ idioms, classical allusions, proverbs, colloquial sayings, and specialized terms from various fields of learning. For common Chinese words and expressions, which are the principal focus of this work, it provides a comprehensive explanation of these words and expressions from a historical point of view so as to show changes in meaning over time. It includes only those characters that appear in classical writings, and excludes rarely used and obsolete characters. In this respect, its principles for inclusion differ from that of the Hànyǔ Dà Zìdiǎn discussed in the previous section.

The Hànyǔ Dà Cídiǎn takes as its standard those forms of the characters listed in the "List of Chinese Character Forms for General Printing". Since this is a dictionary of a historical nature, it includes both the modern simplified forms and their original complex forms. For the notation of present day pronunciation, Hanyu Pinyin is used, and for ancient pronunciation, the fǎnqiè method is employed. The explanation of meaning is made as comprehensive, exact, and concise as possible. Examples cited provide the dates, authors, book or essay titles, and the relevant volume, chapter or section numbers, all of which are arranged in chronological order. For common words and expressions in current use, however, only uncited examples are given.

The characters in the Hànyǔ Dà Cídiǎn are arranged in

order of the 200 radicals, in the same manner as in the Hànyǔ Dà Zìdiǎn discussed in No. 7 above. There are two additional indices for the characters given as appendices: a Hanyu Pinyin index and a Total Stroke Count Index.

9) The **Gǔ Hànyǔ Chángyòngzì Zìdiǎn** 古汉语常用字字典 (*Dictionary of Common Characters in Classical Chinese*) was compiled by a special editorial group and was published by the Commercial Press in 1979.

This dictionary was compiled to assist ordinary Chinese readers to read works written in classical Chinese. It includes 3,700 character entries in the dictionary proper, with an additional 2,600 characters listed in a "Table of Difficult Characters", which gives only pronunciations and explanations of meaning, but no examples.

The characters in this work are arranged alphabetically according to Hanyu Pinyin. A radical index is also provided, which classifies the characters under 189 radicals. For the notation of pronunciation, the dictionary gives both Hanyu Pinyin and the Zhùyīn Zìmǔ. The common meanings for characters in ancient Chinese are given, while rarely encountered ancient meanings and meanings in modern Chinese are not given. The basic literal meanings are followed by extended borrowed meanings which are ordered according to their closeness to the basic meaning. Special mention is made of changes in meaning over time as well as of synonyms and near-synonyms and any fine shades of difference in their meanings. As far as possible, typical examples are cited, the more difficult ones being annotated and explained. In addition to single characters, this dictionary also includes more than 2,000 disyllabic words, most of which are listed as entries under the first of the two characters, but a very few of which are listed under the second character. For example, the expression 九垓 (jiǔ gāi), meaning "nine states, whole country" is listed under the character 垓.

This is a concise and practical dictionary, very easy to understand, which can be especially useful to the beginning student of classical Chinese, as well as to average readers.

10) The **Liánmián Zìdiǎn** 联绵字典 (*A Dictionary of Liánmián Words*), was compiled by Fú Dìngyī 符定一 and was published by the Commercial Press in 1943.

This work is a dictionary of classical Chinese, primarily containing disyllabic words, especially so-called liánmiáncí 联绵词, i.e. Chinese words consisting of two characters, often alliterated or rhymed, such as 仿佛 (fǎngfú, seem; alike), 伶俐 (línglì, clever), 逍遥 (xiāoyáo, free and unfettered), etc. It also includes reiterated words such as 皎皎 (jiǎojiǎo, clear and bright), 津津 (jīnjīn, take delight in), etc., and other closely related disyllabic words such as 妯娌 (zhóuli, sisters-in-law), 交待 (jiāodài, make clear; confess), 何以 (héyǐ, how), etc.

Words in this dictionary are arranged according to the first character of the expression in the order of the 214 radicals under the Kāngxī Zìdiǎn indexing system, with characters belonging to the same radicals then arranged by number of strokes. It also adopts the fǎnqiè system for the notation of pronunciation. The explanations of meaning are as detailed as possible, with ample examples arranged in chronological order. The examples quoted are cited so as to preserve the complete meaning and indicate the source in detail. This work also makes detailed explanations of interchangeable characters, vulgar or popular forms of characters, variant forms of characters, and common errors in texts.

The Liánmián Zìdiǎn is an important reference work for reading and annotating Chinese classical writings.

Dictionaries of classical Chinese are useful when we read works written in classical or literary Chinese, or want to learn about the evolution of the Chinese language or Chinese characters over time. Even when we read works written in modern Chinese, we may occasionally come across words or expressions from classical Chinese as well. In such cases, we may do well to consult a dictionary of modern Chinese such as the Xiàndài Hànyǔ Cídiǎn first, before turning to these more specialized works.

APPENDICES

1. A CHRONOLOGY OF CHINESE DYNASTIES

Xià　夏　(2140 B.C. — 1711 B.C.)

Shāng　商　(1711 B.C. — 1066 B.C.)

Zhōu　周　(1066 B.C. — 256 B.C.)

　　Xī Zhōu　西周　(1066 B.C. — 771 B.C.)

　　Dōng Zhōu　东周　(770 B.C. — 256 B.C.)

Qín　秦　(221 B.C. — 206 B.C.)

Hàn　汉　(206 B.C. — A.D. 220)

　　Xī Hàn　西汉　(206 B.C. — A.D. 25)

　　Dōng Hàn　东汉　(25 — 220)

Sān Guó　三国　(220—280)

　　Wèi　魏　(220—265)

　　Shǔ Hàn　蜀汉　(221—263)

　　Wú　吴　(222—280)

Jìn　晋　(265—420)

　　Xī Jìn　西晋　(265—317)

　　Dōng Jìn　东晋　(317—420)

Nán-Běi Cháo　南北朝　(420—589)　*Liu Cháo*

　　Nán Cháo　南朝：Sòng　宋　(420—479)

　　　　　　　　　　Qí　齐　(479—502)

　　　　　　　　　　Liáng　梁　(502—557)

		Chén	陈	(557—589)
Běi Cháo	北朝:	Běi Wèi	北魏	(386—534)
		Dōng Wèi	东魏	(534—550)
		Běi Qí	北齐	(550—577)
		Xī Wèi	西魏	(535—556)
		Běi Zhōu	北周	(557—581)

Suí 隋 (581—618)

Táng 唐 (618—907)

Wǔ Dài 五代 (907—960)

Hòu Liáng	后梁	(907—923)
Hòu Táng	后唐	(923—936)
Hǒu Jìn	后晋	(936—947)
Hòu Hàn	后汉	(947—950)
Hòu Zhōu	后周	(951—960)

Sòng 宋 (960—1279)

Běi Sòng	北宋	(960—1127)
Nán Sòng	南宋	(1127—1279)

Liáo 辽 (907—1125)

Jīn 金 (1115—1234)

Yuán 元 (1206—1368)

Míng 明 (1368—1644)

Qīng 清 (1616—1911)

Zhōnghuá Mínguó 中华民国 (1912—1949)

简化字总表 （1986 年新版）

第一表

不作简化偏旁用的简化字

本表共收简化字 350 个，按读音的拼音字母顺序排列。本表的简化字都不得作简化偏旁使用。

A	标〔標〕	忏〔懺〕	辞〔辭〕	电〔電〕
	表〔錶〕	偿〔償〕	聪〔聰〕	冬〔鼕〕
碍〔礙〕	别〔彆〕	厂〔廠〕	丛〔叢〕	斗〔鬥〕
肮〔骯〕	卜〔蔔〕	彻〔徹〕	**D**	独〔獨〕
袄〔襖〕	补〔補〕	尘〔塵〕		吨〔噸〕
B	**C**	衬〔襯〕	担〔擔〕	夺〔奪〕
		称〔稱〕	胆〔膽〕	堕〔墮〕
坝〔壩〕	才〔纔〕	惩〔懲〕	导〔導〕	**E**
板〔闆〕	蚕〔蠶〕①	迟〔遲〕	灯〔燈〕	
办〔辦〕	灿〔燦〕	冲〔衝〕	邓〔鄧〕	儿〔兒〕
帮〔幫〕	层〔層〕	丑〔醜〕	敌〔敵〕	
宝〔寶〕	挦〔攙〕	出〔齣〕	籴〔糴〕	**F**
报〔報〕	谗〔讒〕	础〔礎〕	递〔遞〕	
币〔幣〕	馋〔饞〕	处〔處〕	点〔點〕	矾〔礬〕
毙〔斃〕	缠〔纏〕②	触〔觸〕	淀〔澱〕	范〔範〕

---

① 蚕：上从天，不从天。　　② 缠：右从㕓，不从厘。

飞〔飛〕	购〔購〕	坏〔壞〕②	茧〔繭〕	据〔據〕
坟〔墳〕	谷〔穀〕	欢〔歡〕	拣〔揀〕	惧〔懼〕
奋〔奮〕	顾〔顧〕	环〔環〕	硷〔鹼〕	卷〔捲〕
粪〔糞〕	刮〔颳〕	还〔還〕	舰〔艦〕	
凤〔鳳〕	关〔關〕	回〔迴〕	姜〔薑〕	**K**
肤〔膚〕	观〔觀〕	伙〔夥〕③	浆〔漿〕④	开〔開〕
妇〔婦〕	柜〔櫃〕	获〔獲〕	桨〔槳〕	克〔剋〕
复〔復〕		〔穫〕	奖〔獎〕	垦〔墾〕
〔複〕	**H**		讲〔講〕	恳〔懇〕
	汉〔漢〕	**J**	酱〔醬〕	夸〔誇〕
G	号〔號〕	击〔擊〕	胶〔膠〕	块〔塊〕
	合〔閤〕	鸡〔鷄〕	阶〔階〕	亏〔虧〕
盖〔蓋〕	轰〔轟〕	积〔積〕	疖〔癤〕	困〔睏〕
干〔乾〕①	后〔後〕	极〔極〕	洁〔潔〕	
〔幹〕	胡〔鬍〕	际〔際〕	借〔藉〕⑤	**L**
赶〔趕〕	壶〔壺〕	继〔繼〕	仅〔僅〕	腊〔臘〕
个〔個〕	沪〔滬〕	家〔傢〕	惊〔驚〕	蜡〔蠟〕
巩〔鞏〕	护〔護〕	价〔價〕	竞〔競〕	兰〔蘭〕
沟〔溝〕	划〔劃〕	艰〔艱〕	旧〔舊〕	拦〔攔〕
构〔構〕	怀〔懷〕	歼〔殲〕	剧〔劇〕	栏〔欄〕

① 乾坤、乾隆的乾读qián（前），不简化。　② 不作坏。坏是砖坯的坯，读 pī〔批〕，坏坯二字不可互混。　③ 作多解的夥不简化。　④ 浆、桨、奖、酱：右上角从夕，不从夕或⺈。　⑤ 藉口、凭藉的藉简化作借，慰藉、狼藉等的藉仍用藉。

烂〔爛〕	岭〔嶺〕④	亩〔畝〕	千〔韆〕	认〔認〕
累〔纍〕	庐〔廬〕	**N**	牵〔牽〕	
垒〔壘〕	芦〔蘆〕	恼〔惱〕	纤〔纖〕	**S**
类〔類〕①	炉〔爐〕	脑〔腦〕	〔縴〕⑦	洒〔灑〕
里〔裏〕	陆〔陸〕	拟〔擬〕	窍〔竅〕	伞〔傘〕
礼〔禮〕	驴〔驢〕	酿〔釀〕	窃〔竊〕	丧〔喪〕
隶〔隸〕	乱〔亂〕	疟〔瘧〕	寝〔寢〕	扫〔掃〕
帘〔簾〕		**P**	庆〔慶〕⑧	涩〔澀〕
联〔聯〕	**M**	盘〔盤〕	琼〔瓊〕	晒〔曬〕
怜〔憐〕	么〔麼〕⑤	辟〔闢〕	秋〔鞦〕	伤〔傷〕
炼〔煉〕	霉〔黴〕	苹〔蘋〕	曲〔麯〕	舍〔捨〕
练〔練〕	蒙〔矇〕	凭〔憑〕	权〔權〕	沈〔瀋〕
粮〔糧〕	〔濛〕	扑〔撲〕	劝〔勸〕	声〔聲〕
疗〔療〕	〔懞〕	仆〔僕〕⑥	确〔確〕	胜〔勝〕
辽〔遼〕	梦〔夢〕	朴〔樸〕		湿〔濕〕
了〔瞭〕②	面〔麵〕	**Q**	**R**	实〔實〕
猎〔獵〕	庙〔廟〕	启〔啟〕	让〔讓〕	适〔適〕⑨
临〔臨〕③	灭〔滅〕	签〔籤〕	扰〔擾〕	势〔勢〕
邻〔鄰〕	蔑〔衊〕		热〔熱〕	兽〔獸〕

---

① 类：下从大，不从犬。　② 瞭：读 liǎo（了解）时，仍简作了，读 liào〔瞭望〕时作瞭，不简作了。　③ 临：左从一短竖一长竖，不从刂。　④ 岭：不作岺，免与岑混。　⑤ 读 me 轻声。读 yāo〔夭〕的么应作幺（么本字）。吆应作吆。麼读 mó（摩）时不简化，如幺麼小丑。　⑥ 前仆后继的仆读 pū（扑）。　⑦ 纤维的纤读 xiān（先）。　⑧ 庆：从大，不从犬。　⑨ 古人南宫适、洪适的适（古字罕用）读 kuò（括）。此适字本作适，为了避免混淆，可恢复本字适。

书〔書〕	体〔體〕	雾〔霧〕	亵〔褻〕	医〔醫〕
术〔術〕①	粜〔糶〕		衅〔釁〕	亿〔億〕
树〔樹〕	铁〔鐵〕	**X**	兴〔興〕	忆〔憶〕
帅〔帥〕	听〔聽〕		须〔鬚〕	应〔應〕
松〔鬆〕	厅〔廳〕②	牺〔犧〕	悬〔懸〕	痈〔癰〕
苏〔蘇〕	头〔頭〕	习〔習〕	选〔選〕	拥〔擁〕
〔囌〕	图〔圖〕	系〔係〕	旋〔鏇〕	佣〔傭〕
虽〔雖〕	涂〔塗〕	〔繫〕④		踊〔踴〕
随〔隨〕	团〔團〕	戏〔戲〕	**Y**	忧〔憂〕
	〔糰〕	虾〔蝦〕		优〔優〕
T	椭〔橢〕	吓〔嚇〕⑤	压〔壓〕⑦	邮〔郵〕
		咸〔鹹〕	盐〔鹽〕	余〔餘〕⑨
台〔臺〕	**W**	显〔顯〕	阳〔陽〕	御〔禦〕
〔檯〕		宪〔憲〕	养〔養〕	吁〔籲〕⑩
〔颱〕	洼〔窪〕	县〔縣〕⑥	痒〔癢〕	郁〔鬱〕
态〔態〕	袜〔襪〕③	响〔響〕	样〔樣〕	誉〔譽〕
坛〔壇〕	网〔網〕	向〔嚮〕	钥〔鑰〕	渊〔淵〕
〔罎〕	卫〔衛〕	协〔協〕	药〔藥〕	园〔園〕
叹〔嘆〕	稳〔穩〕	胁〔脅〕	爷〔爺〕	远〔遠〕
誊〔謄〕	务〔務〕		叶〔葉〕⑧	

---

① 中药苍术、白术的术读 zhú（竹）。　② 厅：从厂，不从广。
③ 袜：从末，不从未。　④系带子的系读 jì（计）。　⑤ 恐吓的吓
读 hè（赫）。　⑥ 县：七笔。上从且。　⑦ 压：六笔。土的右旁
有一点。　⑧ 叶韵的叶读 xié（协）。　⑨ 在余和馀意义可能混淆
时，仍用馀。如文言句"馀年无多"。　⑩ 喘吁吁，长吁短叹的吁
读 xū（虚）。

愿〔願〕	凿〔鑿〕	征〔徵〕②	肿〔腫〕	妆〔妝〕
跃〔躍〕	枣〔棗〕	症〔癥〕	种〔種〕	装〔裝〕
运〔運〕	灶〔竈〕	证〔證〕	众〔衆〕	壮〔壯〕
酝〔醞〕	斋〔齋〕	只〔隻〕	昼〔晝〕	状〔狀〕
Z	毡〔氈〕	〔祇〕	朱〔硃〕	准〔準〕
杂〔雜〕	战〔戰〕	致〔緻〕	烛〔燭〕	浊〔濁〕
赃〔臓〕	赵〔趙〕	制〔製〕	筑〔築〕	总〔總〕
脏〔臟〕	折〔摺〕①	钟〔鐘〕	庄〔莊〕③	钻〔鑽〕
〔髒〕	这〔這〕	〔鍾〕	桩〔樁〕	

第 二 表

可作简化偏旁用的简化字和简化偏旁

本表共收简化字 132 个和简化偏旁 14 个。简化字按读音的拼音字母顺序排列，简化偏旁按笔数排列。

A	备〔備〕	**C**	尝〔嘗〕⑤	窜〔竄〕
	贝〔貝〕		车〔車〕	
爱〔愛〕	笔〔筆〕	参〔參〕	齿〔齒〕	**D**
B	毕〔畢〕	仓〔倉〕	虫〔蟲〕	达〔達〕
	边〔邊〕	产〔產〕	刍〔芻〕	带〔帶〕
罢〔罷〕	宾〔賓〕	长〔長〕④	从〔從〕	单〔單〕

① 在折和摺意义可能混淆时，摺仍用摺。　② 宫商角徵羽的徵读 zhǐ（止），不简化。　③ 庄：六笔。土的右旁无点。　④ 长：四笔。笔顺是：丿一匕长。　⑤ 尝：不是赏的简化字。赏的简化字是赏（见第三表）。

	G	夹〔夾〕	乐〔樂〕	罗〔羅〕
当〔當〕		戈〔戔〕	离〔離〕	
〔噹〕	冈〔岡〕	监〔監〕	历〔歷〕	**M**
党〔黨〕	广〔廣〕	见〔見〕	〔曆〕	
东〔東〕	归〔歸〕	荐〔薦〕	丽〔麗〕④	马〔馬〕⑤
动〔動〕	龟〔龜〕	将〔將〕②	两〔兩〕	买〔買〕
断〔斷〕	国〔國〕	节〔節〕	灵〔靈〕	卖〔賣〕⑥
对〔對〕	过〔過〕	尽〔盡〕	刘〔劉〕	麦〔麥〕
队〔隊〕		〔儘〕	龙〔龍〕	门〔門〕
	H	进〔進〕	娄〔婁〕	黾〔黽〕⑦
E	华〔華〕	举〔舉〕	卢〔盧〕	
尔〔爾〕	画〔畫〕		虏〔虜〕	**N**
	汇〔匯〕	**K**	卤〔鹵〕	
F	〔彙〕	壳〔殼〕③	〔滷〕	难〔難〕
发〔發〕	会〔會〕		录〔錄〕	鸟〔鳥〕⑧
〔髮〕		**L**	虑〔慮〕	聂〔聶〕
丰〔豐〕①	**J**		仑〔侖〕	宁〔寧〕⑨
风〔風〕	几〔幾〕	来〔來〕		农〔農〕

---

① 四川省酆都县已改丰都县。姓酆的酆不简化作邦。　② 将：右上角从夕，不从夕或⺊。　③ 壳：几上没有一小横。　④ 丽：七笔。上边一横，不作两小横。　⑤ 马：三笔。笔顺是：乛马马。上部向左稍斜，左上角开口，末笔作左偏旁时改作平挑。　⑥卖：从十从买，上不从士或土。　⑦黾：从口从电。　⑧ 鸟：五笔。⑨ 作门屏之间解的宁（古字罕用）读 zhù（柱）。为避免此宁字与宁的简化字混淆，原读 zhù 的宁作㝉。

Q	圣〔聖〕	为〔爲〕	业〔業〕	**简化偏旁**
齐〔齊〕	师〔師〕	韦〔韋〕	页〔頁〕	讠〔言〕⑨
岂〔豈〕	时〔時〕	乌〔烏〕④	义〔義〕⑧	饣〔食〕⑩
气〔氣〕	寿〔壽〕	无〔無〕⑤	艺〔藝〕	𠃓〔昜〕⑪
迁〔遷〕	属〔屬〕	**X**	阴〔陰〕	纟〔糸〕
佥〔僉〕	双〔雙〕	献〔獻〕	隐〔隱〕	収〔取〕
乔〔喬〕	肃〔肅〕②	乡〔鄉〕	犹〔猶〕	艹〔茻〕
亲〔親〕	岁〔歲〕	写〔寫〕⑥	鱼〔魚〕	临〔臨〕
穷〔窮〕	孙〔孫〕	寻〔尋〕	与〔與〕	只〔戠〕
区〔區〕①	**T**	**Y**	云〔雲〕	钅〔金〕⑫
S	条〔條〕③	亚〔亞〕	**Z**	𭕄〔巽〕
啬〔嗇〕	**W**	严〔嚴〕	郑〔鄭〕	睪〔睪〕⑬
杀〔殺〕	万〔萬〕	厌〔厭〕	执〔執〕	亦〔䜌〕
审〔審〕		尧〔堯〕⑦	质〔質〕	呙〔咼〕
			专〔專〕	

---

① 区：不作区。　② 肃：中间一竖下面的两边从八，下半中间不从米。　③ 条：上从夂，三笔，不从夊。　④ 乌：四笔。　⑤ 无：四笔。上从二，不可误作旡。　⑥ 写：上从一，不从宀。　⑦ 尧：六笔。右上角无点，不可误作尧。　⑧ 义：从乂（读yì）加点，不可误作又（读chā）。　⑨ 讠：二笔。不作讠。　⑩ 饣：三笔。中一横折作一，不作、或点。　⑪ 昜：三笔。　⑫ 钅：第二笔是一短横，中两横，竖折不出头。　⑬ 睾丸的睾读 gāo（高），不简化。

第 三 表

应用第二表所列简化字和简化偏旁得出来的简化字

本表共收简化字 1,753 个（不包含重见的字。例如"缆"分见"纟、忛、见"三部，只算一字），以第二表中的简化字和简化偏旁作部首，按第二表的顺序排列。同一部首中的简化字，按笔数排列。

爱	呗〔唄〕	测〔測〕	贺〔賀〕	债〔債〕
嗳〔嗳〕	员〔員〕	浈〔湞〕	陨〔隕〕	赁〔賃〕
媛〔嫒〕	财〔財〕	恻〔惻〕	涢〔溳〕	渍〔漬〕
叇〔靆〕	狈〔狽〕	贰〔貳〕	资〔資〕	惯〔慣〕
瑗〔瑷〕	责〔責〕	贲〔賁〕	祯〔禎〕	琐〔瑣〕
暖〔曖〕	厕〔厠〕	赍〔賫〕	贾〔賈〕	赉〔賚〕
罢	贤〔賢〕	费〔費〕	损〔損〕	匮〔匱〕
摆〔擺〕	账〔賬〕	郧〔鄖〕	赘〔贅〕	掼〔摜〕
〔襬〕	贩〔販〕	勋〔勛〕	埙〔塤〕	殒〔殞〕
罴〔羆〕	贬〔貶〕	帧〔幀〕	桢〔楨〕	勚〔勩〕
糯〔糯〕	败〔敗〕	贴〔貼〕	唝〔嗊〕	赈〔賑〕
备	贮〔貯〕	贶〔貺〕	唢〔嗩〕	婴〔嬰〕
惫〔憊〕	贪〔貪〕	贻〔貽〕	赅〔賅〕	喷〔噴〕
贝	贫〔貧〕	贱〔賤〕	圆〔圓〕	赊〔賒〕
贞〔貞〕	侦〔偵〕	贵〔貴〕	贼〔賊〕	帻〔幘〕
则〔則〕	侧〔側〕	钡〔鋇〕	贿〔賄〕	偾〔僨〕
负〔負〕	货〔貨〕	贷〔貸〕	赆〔贐〕	铡〔鍘〕
贡〔貢〕	贯〔貫〕	赁〔賀〕	赂〔賂〕	绩〔績〕

溃〔潰〕	殒〔殞〕	赝〔贋〕	踌〔躊〕	糁〔糝〕
溅〔濺〕	瞆〔瞶〕	赟〔贇〕	**边**	**仓**
赓〔賡〕	腻〔膩〕	赠〔贈〕	笾〔籩〕	伧〔傖〕
愦〔憒〕	赛〔賽〕	鹦〔鸚〕	**宾**	创〔創〕
愤〔憤〕	禃〔禛〕	獭〔獺〕	傧〔儐〕	沧〔滄〕
黉〔黌〕	赘〔贅〕	赞〔贊〕	滨〔濱〕	怆〔愴〕
赍〔齎〕	撄〔攖〕	赢〔贏〕	摈〔擯〕	苍〔蒼〕
蒇〔蕆〕	槚〔檟〕	赡〔贍〕	嫔〔嬪〕	抢〔搶〕
赌〔賭〕	嘤〔嚶〕	癫〔癲〕	缤〔繽〕	呛〔嗆〕
赔〔賠〕	赚〔賺〕	攒〔攢〕	殡〔殯〕	炝〔熗〕
赎〔贖〕	赙〔賻〕	颖〔穎〕	槟〔檳〕	玱〔瑲〕
遗〔遺〕	罂〔罌〕	缵〔纘〕	膑〔臏〕	枪〔槍〕
赋〔賦〕	锧〔鑕〕	瓒〔瓚〕	镔〔鑌〕	戗〔戧〕
喷〔噴〕	篑〔簣〕	臜〔臢〕	髌〔髕〕	疮〔瘡〕
赌〔賭〕	锄〔鋤〕	赣〔贛〕	鬓〔鬢〕	鸧〔鶬〕
赎〔贖〕	缨〔纓〕	趱〔趲〕	**参**	舱〔艙〕
赏〔賞〕①	璎〔瓔〕	躜〔躦〕	渗〔滲〕	跄〔蹌〕
赐〔賜〕	聩〔聵〕	戆〔戇〕	惨〔慘〕	**产**
赒〔賙〕	樱〔櫻〕	**笔**	掺〔摻〕	浐〔滻〕
锁〔鎖〕	赜〔賾〕	滗〔潷〕	骖〔驂〕	萨〔薩〕
馈〔饋〕	箦〔簀〕	**毕**	毵〔毶〕	铲〔鏟〕
赖〔賴〕	濑〔瀨〕	荜〔蓽〕	瘆〔瘆〕	**长**
赪〔赬〕	瘿〔癭〕	哔〔嗶〕	碜〔磣〕	伥〔倀〕
碛〔磧〕	懒〔懶〕	筚〔篳〕	穇〔穇〕	怅〔悵〕

① 赏：不可误作尝。尝是嘗的简化字（见第二表）。

帐〔帳〕　软〔軟〕　渐〔漸〕　输〔輸〕　**虫**

张〔張〕　浑〔渾〕　惭〔慚〕　毂〔轂〕　蛊〔蠱〕

枨〔棖〕　恽〔惲〕　皲〔皸〕　辔〔轡〕　**刍**

账〔賬〕　砗〔硨〕　琏〔璉〕　辖〔轄〕　诌〔謅〕

胀〔脹〕　轶〔軼〕　辅〔輔〕　辕〔轅〕　㑇〔㑇〕

涨〔漲〕　轲〔軻〕　辄〔輒〕　辗〔輾〕　邹〔鄒〕

　　　　轱〔軲〕　辆〔輛〕　舆〔輿〕　惄〔惙〕

　尝　轷〔軤〕　堑〔塹〕　辘〔轆〕　驺〔騶〕

鎇〔鱛〕　轻〔輕〕　啭〔囀〕　撵〔攆〕　绉〔縐〕

　　　　轳〔轤〕　崭〔嶄〕　鲢〔鰱〕　皱〔皺〕

　车　轴〔軸〕　裤〔褲〕　辙〔轍〕　趋〔趨〕

轧〔軋〕　挥〔揮〕　裢〔褳〕　錾〔鏨〕　雏〔雛〕

军〔軍〕　荤〔葷〕　鏊〔鏊〕　辚〔轔〕

轨〔軌〕　轹〔轢〕　辋〔輞〕　　　　**从**

厍〔厙〕　轸〔軫〕　辍〔輟〕　**齿**

阵〔陣〕　轺〔軺〕　辊〔輥〕　龇〔齜〕　苁〔蓯〕

库〔庫〕　涟〔漣〕　椠〔槧〕　啮〔嚙〕　纵〔縱〕

连〔連〕　珲〔琿〕　辎〔輜〕　龆〔齠〕　枞〔樅〕

轩〔軒〕　载〔載〕　暂〔暫〕　龅〔齙〕　怂〔慫〕

诨〔諢〕　莲〔蓮〕　辉〔輝〕　龃〔齟〕　耸〔聳〕

轫〔軔〕　较〔較〕　辈〔輩〕　龄〔齡〕　**窜**

轭〔軛〕　轼〔軾〕　链〔鏈〕　龇〔齜〕　撺〔攛〕

瓯〔甌〕　轾〔輊〕　翚〔翬〕　龈〔齦〕　镩〔鑹〕

转〔轉〕　辂〔輅〕　辏〔輳〕　龉〔齬〕　蹿〔躥〕

轮〔輪〕　轿〔轎〕　辐〔輻〕　龊〔齪〕　**达**

斩〔斬〕　晕〔暈〕　辑〔輯〕　龌〔齷〕　达〔達〕

　　　　　　　　　　　　　　龋〔齲〕　闼〔闥〕

　　　　　　　　　　　　　　龌〔齷〕　挞〔撻〕

366

哒〔噠〕
鞑〔韃〕

带

滞〔滯〕

单

郸〔鄲〕
惮〔憚〕
阐〔闡〕
掸〔撣〕
弹〔彈〕
婵〔嬋〕
禅〔禪〕
殚〔殫〕
瘅〔癉〕
蝉〔蟬〕
箪〔簞〕
蕲〔蘄〕
辗〔輾〕

当

挡〔擋〕
档〔檔〕
裆〔襠〕
铛〔鐺〕

党

谠〔讜〕
傥〔儻〕

锐〔鑠〕

东

冻〔凍〕
陈〔陳〕
崇〔崬〕
栋〔棟〕
胨〔腖〕
鸫〔鶇〕

动

恸〔慟〕

断

簖〔籪〕

对

怼〔懟〕

队

坠〔墜〕

尔

迩〔邇〕
弥〔彌〕
〔瀰〕
祢〔禰〕
玺〔璽〕
猕〔獼〕

发

泼〔潑〕
废〔廢〕

拨〔撥〕
钹〔鈸〕

丰

沣〔灃〕
艳〔艷〕
滟〔灩〕

风

讽〔諷〕
沨〔渢〕
岚〔嵐〕
枫〔楓〕
疯〔瘋〕
飒〔颯〕
砜〔碸〕
飓〔颶〕
飔〔颸〕
飕〔颼〕
飖〔颻〕
飘〔飄〕
飙〔飆〕

冈

刚〔剛〕
扢〔摃〕
岗〔崗〕
纲〔綱〕
㭎〔棡〕

钢〔鋼〕

广

邝〔鄺〕
圹〔壙〕
扩〔擴〕
犷〔獷〕
纩〔纊〕
旷〔曠〕
矿〔礦〕

归

岿〔巋〕

龟

阄〔鬮〕

国

掴〔摑〕
帼〔幗〕
腘〔膕〕
蝈〔蟈〕

过

挝〔撾〕

华

哗〔嘩〕
骅〔驊〕
烨〔燁〕
桦〔樺〕
晔〔曄〕

铧〔鏵〕

画

婳〔嫿〕

汇

扝〔摀〕

会

刽〔劊〕
郐〔鄶〕
侩〔儈〕
浍〔澮〕
荟〔薈〕
哙〔噲〕
狯〔獪〕
绘〔繪〕
烩〔燴〕
桧〔檜〕
脍〔膾〕
鲙〔鱠〕

几

讥〔譏〕
叽〔嘰〕
饥〔饑〕
机〔機〕
玑〔璣〕
矶〔磯〕
虮〔蟣〕

灵

棂〔櫺〕

刘

浏〔瀏〕

龙

陇〔隴〕
泷〔瀧〕
宠〔寵〕
庞〔龐〕
垄〔壟〕
拢〔攏〕
茏〔蘢〕
咙〔嚨〕
珑〔瓏〕
栊〔櫳〕
龚〔龔〕
昽〔曨〕
胧〔朧〕
砻〔礱〕
袭〔襲〕
聋〔聾〕
龚〔龔〕
龛〔龕〕
笼〔籠〕
詟〔讋〕

娄

偻〔僂〕
溇〔漊〕
蒌〔蔞〕
搂〔摟〕
嵝〔嶁〕
喽〔嘍〕
缕〔縷〕
屡〔屢〕
数〔數〕
楼〔樓〕
瘘〔瘻〕
褛〔褸〕
窭〔窶〕
瞜〔瞜〕
镂〔鏤〕
屦〔屨〕
蝼〔螻〕
篓〔簍〕
耧〔耬〕
薮〔藪〕
擞〔擻〕
髅〔髏〕

卢

泸〔瀘〕
垆〔壚〕

栌〔櫨〕
轳〔轤〕
胪〔臚〕
鸬〔鸕〕
颅〔顱〕
舻〔艫〕
鲈〔鱸〕

虏

掳〔擄〕

卤

硵〔鹵〕

录

箓〔籙〕

虑

滤〔濾〕
摅〔攄〕

仑

论〔論〕
伦〔倫〕
沦〔淪〕
抡〔掄〕
囵〔圇〕
纶〔綸〕
轮〔輪〕
瘪〔癟〕

罗

萝〔蘿〕

啰〔囉〕
逻〔邏〕
猡〔玀〕
椤〔欏〕
锣〔鑼〕
箩〔籮〕

马

冯〔馮〕
驭〔馭〕
闯〔闖〕
吗〔嗎〕
犸〔獁〕
驮〔馱〕
驰〔馳〕
驯〔馴〕
妈〔媽〕
玛〔瑪〕
驱〔驅〕
驳〔駁〕
码〔碼〕
驼〔駝〕
驻〔駐〕
驵〔駔〕
驾〔駕〕
驿〔驛〕

驷〔駟〕
驶〔駛〕
驹〔駒〕
驺〔騶〕
驸〔駙〕
驻〔駙〕
驽〔駑〕
骂〔罵〕
蚂〔螞〕
笃〔篤〕
骇〔駭〕
骈〔駢〕
骁〔驍〕
骄〔驕〕
骅〔驊〕
骆〔駱〕
骊〔驪〕
骋〔騁〕
验〔驗〕
骏〔駿〕
骎〔駸〕
骑〔騎〕
骐〔騏〕
骒〔騍〕
雏〔雛〕
骖〔驂〕

骟〔騸〕	续〔續〕	闰〔閏〕	阉〔閹〕①	锏〔鐧〕
骘〔騭〕	横〔橫〕	闲〔閑〕	闽〔閩〕	阙〔闕〕
骛〔騖〕	觌〔覿〕	间〔間〕	娴〔嫻〕	阖〔闔〕
骚〔騷〕	赎〔贖〕	闹〔鬧〕①	阋〔鬩〕	阗〔闐〕
骞〔騫〕	犊〔犢〕	闸〔閘〕	阈〔閾〕	椢〔櫃〕
骜〔驁〕	牍〔牘〕	钔〔鍆〕	阉〔閹〕	简〔簡〕
蓦〔驀〕	窦〔竇〕	阂〔閡〕	阍〔閽〕	谰〔讕〕
腾〔騰〕	黩〔黷〕	闺〔閨〕	阎〔閻〕	阑〔闌〕
骝〔騮〕	麦	闻〔聞〕	阏〔閼〕	蔺〔藺〕
骗〔騙〕	唛〔嘜〕	闼〔闥〕	阅〔閲〕①	澜〔瀾〕
骠〔驃〕	麸〔麩〕	闽〔閩〕	阐〔闡〕	斓〔斕〕
骢〔驄〕	门	闾〔閭〕	阁〔閤〕	嘞〔囒〕
骡〔騾〕	闩〔閂〕	阃〔閫〕	焖〔燜〕	镧〔鑭〕
羁〔羈〕	闪〔閃〕	阄〔鬮〕	阑〔闌〕	蹒〔蹣〕
骤〔驟〕	们〔們〕	阁〔閣〕	裥〔襇〕	龟
骥〔驥〕	闭〔閉〕	阀〔閥〕	阔〔闊〕	渑〔澠〕
骧〔驤〕	闯〔闖〕	润〔潤〕	痫〔癇〕	绳〔繩〕
买	问〔問〕	涧〔澗〕	鹇〔鷴〕	鼋〔黿〕
荬〔蕒〕	扪〔捫〕	悯〔憫〕	阕〔闋〕	蝇〔蠅〕
卖	闱〔闈〕	阆〔閬〕	阒〔闃〕	鼍〔鼉〕
读〔讀〕	闵〔閔〕	阅〔閱〕	搁〔擱〕	难
渎〔瀆〕	闷〔悶〕	阐〔闡〕	锏〔鐧〕	傩〔儺〕

---

① 鬥字头的字，一般也写作門字头，如鬧、鬮、鬩写作閙、閾、閲。因此，这些鬥字头的字可简化作门字头。但鬥争的鬥应简作斗（见第一表）。

				农
滩〔灘〕	鸲〔鴝〕	鹑〔鶉〕	鹦〔鸚〕	侬〔儂〕
摊〔攤〕	鸰〔鴒〕	鹕〔鶘〕	鹜〔鶩〕	浓〔濃〕
瘫〔癱〕	鸳〔鴛〕	鹊〔鵲〕	鹚〔鷀〕	哝〔噥〕
鸟	鸵〔鴕〕	鹋〔鶓〕	鹧〔鷓〕	脓〔膿〕
凫〔鳧〕	袅〔裊〕	鹌〔鵪〕	鹨〔鷚〕	**齐**
鸠〔鳩〕	鸱〔鴟〕	鹏〔鵬〕	鹞〔鷂〕	剂〔劑〕
岛〔島〕	鸶〔鷥〕	鹆〔鵒〕	鹰〔鷹〕	侪〔儕〕
茑〔蔦〕	鸾〔鸞〕	鹅〔鵝〕	鹦〔鸚〕	济〔濟〕
鸢〔鳶〕	鸸〔鴯〕	鹄〔鵠〕	鹭〔鷺〕	荠〔薺〕
鸣〔鳴〕	鸿〔鴻〕	鹋〔鶓〕	鹬〔鷸〕	挤〔擠〕
枭〔梟〕	鸷〔鷙〕	鹕〔鶘〕	鹤〔鶴〕	脐〔臍〕
鸩〔鴆〕	鸹〔鴰〕	鹇〔鷳〕	**聂**	蛴〔蠐〕
鸦〔鴉〕	鸽〔鴿〕	鹒〔鶊〕	慑〔懾〕	跻〔躋〕
鸰〔鴒〕	鸺〔鵂〕	鹗〔鶚〕	滠〔灄〕	霁〔霽〕
鸥〔鷗〕	鸻〔鴴〕	鹓〔鵷〕	摄〔攝〕	鲚〔鱭〕
鸧〔鶬〕	鸽〔鴿〕	鹘〔鶻〕	嗫〔囁〕	齑〔齏〕
鸨〔鴇〕	鹄〔鵠〕	鸷〔鷙〕	镊〔鑷〕	**岂**
鸮〔鴞〕	鸼〔鵃〕	鹚〔鷀〕	颞〔顳〕	剀〔剴〕
莺〔鶯〕	鸲〔鴝〕	鹈〔鵜〕	蹑〔躡〕	凯〔凱〕
鸪〔鴣〕	鹈〔鵜〕	鹎〔鵯〕	**宁**	恺〔愷〕
捣〔搗〕	鸾〔鸞〕	鹛〔鶥〕	泞〔濘〕	闿〔闓〕
鸫〔鶇〕	鹏〔鵬〕	鹏〔鵬〕	拧〔擰〕	垲〔塏〕
鸬〔鸕〕	鹃〔鵑〕	鸥〔鷗〕	咛〔嚀〕	桤〔榿〕
鸭〔鴨〕	鹁〔鵓〕	鹙〔鶖〕	狞〔獰〕	觊〔覬〕
鸯〔鴦〕	鹋〔鶓〕	鹜〔鶩〕	柠〔檸〕	硙〔磑〕
鸱〔鴟〕	鹅〔鵝〕	鹦〔鸚〕	聍〔聹〕	

371

皑〔皚〕
铠〔鎧〕

气

忾〔愾〕
饩〔餼〕

迁

跹〔躚〕

金

剑〔劍〕
俭〔儉〕
险〔險〕
捡〔撿〕
猃〔獫〕
验〔驗〕
检〔檢〕
殓〔殮〕
敛〔斂〕
脸〔臉〕
裣〔襝〕
睑〔瞼〕
签〔簽〕
潋〔瀲〕
蔹〔蘞〕

乔

侨〔僑〕
挢〔撟〕

荞〔蕎〕
峤〔嶠〕
骄〔驕〕
娇〔嬌〕
桥〔橋〕
轿〔轎〕
硚〔礄〕
矫〔矯〕
鞒〔鞽〕

亲

榇〔櫬〕

穷

䓖〔藭〕

区

讴〔謳〕
伛〔傴〕
沤〔漚〕
怄〔慪〕
抠〔摳〕
奁〔奩〕
呕〔嘔〕
岖〔嶇〕
妪〔嫗〕
驱〔驅〕
枢〔樞〕
瓯〔甌〕

欧〔歐〕
殴〔毆〕
鸥〔鷗〕
眍〔瞘〕
躯〔軀〕

啬

蔷〔薔〕
墙〔墻〕
嫱〔嬙〕
樯〔檣〕
穑〔穡〕

杀

铩〔鎩〕

审

谉〔讅〕
婶〔嬸〕

圣

柽〔檉〕
蛏〔蟶〕

师

浉〔溮〕
狮〔獅〕
蛳〔螄〕
筛〔篩〕

时

埘〔塒〕

莳〔蒔〕
鲥〔鰣〕

寿

俦〔儔〕
涛〔濤〕
祷〔禱〕
焘〔燾〕
畴〔疇〕
铸〔鑄〕
筹〔籌〕
踌〔躊〕

属

嘱〔囑〕
瞩〔矚〕

双

扨〔攙〕

肃

萧〔蕭〕
啸〔嘯〕
潇〔瀟〕
箫〔簫〕
蟏〔蠨〕

岁

刿〔劌〕
哕〔噦〕
秽〔穢〕

孙

荪〔蓀〕
狲〔猻〕
逊〔遜〕

条

涤〔滌〕
绦〔縧〕
鲦〔鰷〕

万

厉〔厲〕
迈〔邁〕
励〔勵〕
疠〔癘〕
虿〔蠆〕
趸〔躉〕
砺〔礪〕
粝〔糲〕
蛎〔蠣〕

为

伪〔偽〕
沩〔溈〕
妫〔媯〕

韦

讳〔諱〕
伟〔偉〕
闱〔闈〕

违〔違〕	妩〔嫵〕	**厌**	**业**	颊〔頰〕
苇〔葦〕	**献**	恹〔懨〕	邺〔鄴〕	颉〔頡〕
韧〔韌〕	谳〔讞〕	厣〔厴〕	**页**	颍〔潁〕
帏〔幃〕	**乡**	餍〔饜〕	顶〔頂〕	颌〔頜〕
围〔圍〕	芗〔薌〕	魇〔魘〕	顷〔頃〕	颐〔頤〕
纬〔緯〕	飨〔饗〕	黡〔黶〕	项〔項〕	濒〔瀕〕
炜〔煒〕	**写**	**尧**	顸〔頇〕	颐〔頤〕
袆〔褘〕	泻〔瀉〕	侥〔僥〕	顺〔順〕	蓣〔蕷〕
玮〔瑋〕	**寻**	浇〔澆〕	须〔須〕	频〔頻〕
韨〔韍〕	浔〔潯〕	挠〔撓〕	颃〔頏〕	颓〔頹〕
涠〔潿〕	荨〔蕁〕	荛〔蕘〕	烦〔煩〕	颔〔頷〕
韩〔韓〕	挦〔撏〕	峣〔嶢〕	顼〔頊〕	颖〔穎〕
韫〔韞〕	鲟〔鱘〕	哓〔嘵〕	顽〔頑〕	颗〔顆〕
韬〔韜〕	**亚**	娆〔嬈〕	顿〔頓〕	额〔額〕
乌	垩〔堊〕	骁〔驍〕	颀〔頎〕	颜〔顏〕
邬〔鄔〕	垭〔埡〕	绕〔繞〕	颂〔頌〕	撷〔擷〕
坞〔塢〕	挜〔掗〕	饶〔饒〕	颁〔頒〕	题〔題〕
呜〔嗚〕	哑〔啞〕	烧〔燒〕	倾〔傾〕	颙〔顒〕
钨〔鎢〕	娅〔婭〕	桡〔橈〕	预〔預〕	颛〔顓〕
无	恶〔惡〕	晓〔曉〕	庼〔廎〕	缬〔纈〕
怃〔憮〕	〔噁〕	硗〔磽〕	硕〔碩〕	濒〔瀕〕
庑〔廡〕	氩〔氬〕	铙〔鐃〕	颅〔顱〕	颠〔顛〕
抚〔撫〕	壶〔壺〕	翘〔翹〕	领〔領〕	巅〔巔〕
芜〔蕪〕	**严**	蛲〔蟯〕	颈〔頸〕	颢〔顥〕
呒〔嘸〕	俨〔儼〕	跷〔蹺〕	颇〔頗〕	颣〔纇〕
	酽〔釅〕		颏〔頦〕	嚣〔囂〕

颢〔顥〕　鲨〔鯊〕　噜〔嚕〕　鲯〔鰭〕　鳖〔鱉〕
颠〔顛〕　鲒〔鮖〕　鲤〔鱷〕　鲹〔鰺〕　鳗〔鰻〕
巅〔巔〕　鲆〔鮃〕　鲠〔鯁〕　鳊〔鯿〕　鳝〔鱔〕
颥〔顬〕　鲅〔鮁〕　鲢〔鰱〕　鲽〔鰈〕　鳟〔鱒〕
癫〔癲〕　鲅〔鮁〕　鲫〔鯽〕　鲲〔鯤〕　鳞〔鱗〕
灏〔灝〕　鲈〔鱸〕　鲥〔鰣〕　鳃〔鰓〕　鳜〔鱖〕
颦〔顰〕　鲇〔鮎〕　鲩〔鯇〕　鳄〔鱷〕　鳣〔鱣〕
颧〔顴〕　鲊〔鮓〕　鲣〔鰹〕　镥〔鐒〕　鳢〔鱧〕

义　　鲋〔鮒〕　鲤〔鯉〕　鳅〔鰍〕　　　**与**

议〔議〕　稣〔穌〕　鲦〔鰷〕　鳆〔鰒〕　屿〔嶼〕
仪〔儀〕　鲋〔鮒〕　鲧〔鯀〕　鳇〔鰉〕　欤〔歟〕
蚁〔蟻〕　鲍〔鮑〕　橹〔櫓〕　鳌〔鰲〕　　　**云**

艺　　鲐〔鮐〕　氇〔氌〕　鳎〔鰨〕　芸〔蕓〕
呓〔囈〕　鲞〔鯗〕　鲸〔鯨〕　鳒〔鰜〕　昙〔曇〕

阴　　鲞〔鯗〕　鲭〔鯖〕　鳒〔鰜〕　叇〔靆〕
荫〔蔭〕　鲚〔鱭〕　鲮〔鯪〕　鳍〔鰭〕　叆〔靉〕
隐〔隱〕　鲛〔鮫〕　鲰〔鯫〕　鳎〔鰨〕　　　**郑**

瘾〔癮〕　鲜〔鮮〕　鲲〔鯤〕　鳏〔鰥〕　掷〔擲〕

犹　　鲑〔鮭〕　缁〔緇〕　鲳〔鯧〕　踯〔躑〕
犹〔猶〕　鲒〔鮚〕　鲳〔鯧〕　癣〔癬〕　　　**执**

鱼　　鲔〔鮪〕　鲱〔鯡〕　鳖〔鱉〕　垫〔墊〕
刿〔劌〕　鲟〔鱘〕　鲵〔鯢〕　鳙〔鱅〕　挚〔摯〕
渔〔漁〕　鲖〔鮦〕　鲷〔鯛〕　鳌〔鰲〕　贽〔贄〕
鲂〔魴〕　鲖〔鮦〕　鲶〔鯰〕　鳕〔鱈〕　鸷〔鷙〕
鱿〔魷〕　鲙〔鱠〕　薛〔薛〕　鳔〔鰾〕　蛰〔蟄〕
鲁〔魯〕　鲨〔鯊〕　鳍〔鰭〕　鳎〔鰦〕　絷〔縶〕

374

质	讳〔諱〕	诈〔詐〕	诮〔誚〕	课〔課〕
锧〔鑕〕	讵〔詎〕	诊〔診〕	说〔說〕	诽〔誹〕
踬〔躓〕	讴〔謳〕	诒〔詒〕	诚〔誠〕	诿〔諉〕
专	诀〔訣〕	译〔譯〕	诬〔誣〕	谁〔誰〕
传〔傳〕	讷〔訥〕	该〔該〕	语〔語〕	谀〔諛〕
抟〔摶〕	设〔設〕	详〔詳〕	诵〔誦〕	调〔調〕
转〔轉〕	讽〔諷〕	诧〔詫〕	罚〔罰〕	谄〔諂〕
胂〔膞〕	讹〔訛〕	诓〔誆〕	误〔誤〕	谂〔諗〕
砖〔磚〕	诉〔訢〕	诖〔詿〕	诰〔誥〕	谛〔諦〕
啭〔囀〕	许〔許〕	诘〔詰〕	诳〔誑〕	谮〔譖〕
讠	论〔論〕	诙〔詼〕	诱〔誘〕	谜〔謎〕
计〔計〕	讼〔訟〕	试〔試〕	诲〔誨〕	谚〔諺〕
订〔訂〕	讻〔訩〕	诗〔詩〕	诶〔誒〕	谝〔諞〕
讣〔訃〕	诂〔詁〕	诩〔詡〕	狱〔獄〕	谘〔諮〕
讥〔譏〕	词〔詞〕	诤〔諍〕	谊〔誼〕	谌〔諶〕
议〔議〕	评〔評〕	诠〔詮〕	谅〔諒〕	谎〔謊〕
讨〔討〕	诏〔詔〕	诛〔誅〕	谈〔談〕	谋〔謀〕
讧〔訌〕	词〔詞〕	诔〔誄〕	谆〔諄〕	谍〔諜〕
讦〔訐〕	译〔譯〕	诉〔訴〕	谝〔譜〕	谐〔諧〕
记〔記〕	诎〔詘〕	诣〔詣〕	译〔譯〕	谏〔諫〕
讯〔訊〕	诃〔訶〕	话〔話〕	请〔請〕	谞〔諝〕
讪〔訕〕	诅〔詛〕	诡〔詭〕	诺〔諾〕	谲〔譎〕
训〔訓〕	识〔識〕	询〔詢〕	诸〔諸〕	谒〔謁〕
讫〔訖〕	诌〔謅〕	诚〔誠〕	读〔讀〕	谔〔諤〕
访〔訪〕	诋〔詆〕	诞〔誕〕	诼〔諑〕	谓〔謂〕
讶〔訝〕	诉〔訴〕	浒〔滸〕	诹〔諏〕	谖〔諼〕

谕〔諭〕
谥〔謚〕
谤〔謗〕
谦〔謙〕
谧〔謐〕
谟〔謨〕
谠〔讜〕
谡〔謖〕
谢〔謝〕
谣〔謠〕
储〔儲〕
谪〔謫〕
谫〔譾〕
谨〔謹〕
谬〔謬〕
谩〔謾〕
谱〔譜〕
谮〔譖〕
谭〔譚〕
谰〔讕〕
谲〔譎〕
谯〔譙〕
蔼〔藹〕
槠〔櫧〕

谴〔譴〕
谵〔譫〕
谳〔讞〕
辩〔辯〕
谯〔譙〕
雠〔讎〕①
谶〔讖〕
霭〔靄〕

饣

饥〔饑〕
饦〔飥〕
饧〔餳〕
饨〔飩〕
饭〔飯〕
饮〔飲〕
饫〔飫〕
饩〔餼〕
饪〔飪〕
饬〔飭〕
饲〔飼〕
饯〔餞〕
饰〔飾〕
饱〔飽〕
饴〔飴〕

饳〔飿〕
饸〔餄〕
饷〔餉〕
饺〔餃〕
饻〔餏〕
饼〔餅〕
饵〔餌〕
饶〔饒〕
蚀〔蝕〕
饹〔餎〕
铬〔餑〕
馁〔餒〕
饿〔餓〕
馆〔館〕
馄〔餛〕
馃〔餜〕
馅〔餡〕
馇〔餷〕
馈〔饋〕
馊〔餿〕
馐〔饈〕
馍〔饃〕
馎〔餺〕

𠃓

汤〔湯〕
扬〔揚〕
场〔場〕
旸〔暘〕
饧〔餳〕
炀〔煬〕
杨〔楊〕
肠〔腸〕
疡〔瘍〕
砀〔碭〕
畅〔暢〕
钖〔鍚〕
殇〔殤〕
荡〔蕩〕
烫〔燙〕
觞〔觴〕

纟

丝〔絲〕
纠〔糾〕
纩〔纊〕
纡〔紆〕
纣〔紂〕
红〔紅〕
纪〔紀〕
纫〔紉〕
纥〔紇〕
约〔約〕
纨〔紈〕
级〔級〕
纺〔紡〕
纹〔紋〕
纬〔緯〕
纭〔紜〕
纯〔純〕
纰〔紕〕
纽〔紐〕
纳〔納〕
纲〔綱〕
纱〔紗〕
纤〔纖〕

---

① 雠：用于校雠、雠定、仇雠等。表示仇恨、仇敌义时用仇。

纷〔紛〕　　经〔經〕　　综〔綜〕　　缚〔繛〕　　缡〔縭〕
纶〔綸〕　　苟〔薴〕　　绽〔綻〕　　缅〔緬〕　　潍〔濰〕
纸〔紙〕　　莛〔莚〕　　绾〔綰〕　　缘〔緣〕　　缩〔縮〕
纵〔縱〕　　绞〔絞〕　　绻〔綣〕　　缉〔緝〕　　缥〔縹〕
纾〔紓〕　　统〔統〕　　绩〔績〕　　缇〔緹〕　　缪〔繆〕
纼〔紉〕　　绒〔絨〕　　绫〔綾〕　　缈〔緲〕　　缦〔縵〕
哟〔喲〕　　绕〔繞〕　　绪〔緒〕　　缗〔緡〕　　缨〔纓〕
绊〔絆〕　　绔〔絝〕　　续〔續〕　　缊〔縕〕　　缫〔繅〕
线〔綫〕　　结〔結〕　　绮〔綺〕　　缌〔緦〕　　缧〔縲〕
绀〔紺〕　　绗〔絎〕　　缀〔綴〕　　缆〔纜〕　　蕴〔蘊〕
绁〔紲〕　　给〔給〕　　绿〔綠〕　　缓〔緩〕　　缮〔繕〕
绂〔紱〕　　绘〔繪〕　　绰〔綽〕　　缄〔緘〕　　缯〔繒〕
绋〔紼〕　　绝〔絕〕　　绲〔緄〕　　缑〔緱〕　　缬〔纈〕
绎〔繹〕　　绛〔絳〕　　绳〔繩〕　　缒〔縋〕　　缭〔繚〕
经〔經〕　　络〔絡〕　　绯〔緋〕　　缎〔緞〕　　橼〔櫞〕
绍〔紹〕　　绚〔絢〕　　绶〔綬〕　　缰〔繮〕　　缰〔韁〕
组〔組〕　　绑〔綁〕　　绸〔綢〕　　缤〔繽〕　　缳〔繯〕
细〔細〕　　绒〔絏〕　　绷〔繃〕　　缥〔縞〕　　缲〔繰〕
绅〔紳〕　　绠〔綆〕　　绺〔綹〕　　缣〔縑〕　　缱〔繾〕
织〔織〕　　绨〔綈〕　　维〔維〕　　缢〔縊〕　　缴〔繳〕
绌〔絀〕　　绡〔綃〕　　绵〔綿〕　　缚〔縛〕　　辫〔辮〕
终〔終〕　　绢〔絹〕　　缁〔緇〕　　缙〔縉〕　　缵〔纘〕
绉〔縐〕　　绣〔繡〕　　缔〔締〕　　缛〔縟〕
绍〔紿〕　　绥〔綏〕　　编〔編〕　　缜〔縝〕　　**収**
给〔紿〕　　绦〔縧〕　　缕〔縷〕　　缟〔縞〕　　坚〔堅〕
哟〔喲〕　　笃〔篤〕　　缃〔緗〕　　缝〔縫〕　　贤〔賢〕
　　　　　　　　　　　　　　　　　　　　　　　肾〔腎〕

377

竖〔豎〕 　 悭〔慳〕 　 紧〔緊〕 　 铿〔鏗〕 　 鲣〔鰹〕

⺌

劳〔勞〕 　 茕〔煢〕 　 荧〔熒〕 　 荣〔榮〕 　 荥〔滎〕 　 荤〔葷〕 　 涝〔澇〕 　 崂〔嶗〕 　 莹〔瑩〕 　 捞〔撈〕 　 唠〔嘮〕 　 莺〔鶯〕 　 萤〔螢〕 　 营〔營〕 　 萦〔縈〕 　 痨〔癆〕 　 嵘〔嶸〕 　 锛〔錛〕 　 耧〔耬〕

蛲〔蟯〕

见

览〔覽〕 　 揽〔攬〕 　 缆〔纜〕 　 榄〔欖〕 　 鉴〔鑒〕

只

识〔識〕 　 帜〔幟〕 　 织〔織〕 　 炽〔熾〕 　 职〔職〕

钅

钆〔釓〕 　 钇〔釔〕 　 钉〔釘〕 　 钋〔釙〕 　 钉〔釘〕 　 针〔針〕 　 钊〔釗〕 　 钗〔釵〕 　 钎〔釺〕 　 钓〔釣〕 　 钏〔釧〕 　 钍〔釷〕

钐〔釤〕 　 钒〔釩〕 　 钖〔錫〕 　 钕〔釹〕 　 钔〔鍆〕 　 钫〔鈁〕 　 钪〔鈧〕 　 钯〔鈀〕 　 钭〔鈄〕 　 钙〔鈣〕 　 钝〔鈍〕 　 钛〔鈦〕 　 钘〔鈃〕 　 钮〔鈕〕 　 钞〔鈔〕 　 钢〔鋼〕 　 钠〔鈉〕 　 钡〔鋇〕 　 钤〔鈐〕 　 钧〔鈞〕 　 钩〔鉤〕 　 钦〔欽〕 　 钨〔鎢〕

铋〔鉍〕 　 钰〔鈺〕 　 钱〔錢〕 　 钲〔鉦〕 　 钳〔鉗〕 　 钴〔鈷〕 　 钺〔鉞〕 　 钵〔缽〕 　 钹〔鈸〕 　 钼〔鉬〕 　 钾〔鉀〕 　 铀〔鈾〕 　 钿〔鈿〕 　 铎〔鐸〕 　 钗〔鏺〕 　 铃〔鈴〕 　 铅〔鉛〕 　 铂〔鉑〕 　 铄〔鑠〕 　 铆〔鉚〕 　 铍〔鈹〕 　 铊〔鉈〕 　 钽〔鉭〕 　 铌〔鈮〕 　 钜〔鉅〕

铈〔鈰〕 　 铉〔鉉〕 　 铒〔鉺〕 　 铑〔銠〕 　 铕〔銪〕 　 铞〔銱〕 　 铟〔銦〕 　 铷〔銣〕 　 铯〔銫〕 　 铥〔銩〕 　 铪〔鉿〕 　 铫〔銚〕 　 铵〔銨〕 　 衔〔銜〕 　 铲〔鏟〕 　 铰〔鉸〕 　 铳〔銃〕 　 铱〔銥〕 　 铓〔鋩〕 　 铗〔鋏〕 　 铐〔銬〕 　 铡〔鍘〕 　 铙〔鐃〕 　 银〔銀〕 　 铛〔鐺〕 　 铜〔銅〕

378

铝〔鋁〕	锁〔鎖〕	锰〔錳〕	锤〔鍾〕	镦〔鐓〕
铡〔鍘〕	锄〔鋤〕	锢〔錮〕	镂〔鏤〕	镨〔鐠〕
铠〔鎧〕	锅〔鍋〕	锟〔錕〕	锼〔鎪〕	镨〔鐯〕
铨〔銓〕	锉〔銼〕	锡〔錫〕	镓〔鎵〕	锏〔鐧〕
铢〔銖〕	锈〔銹〕	锣〔鑼〕	铴〔鐋〕	镥〔鑥〕
铣〔銑〕	锋〔鋒〕	锤〔錘〕	镔〔鑌〕	镤〔鏷〕
铤〔鋌〕	锆〔鋯〕	锥〔錐〕	镒〔鎰〕	镢〔鐝〕
铭〔銘〕	锵〔鏘〕	锦〔錦〕	镉〔鎘〕	镣〔鐐〕
铬〔鉻〕	锔〔鋦〕	锨〔鍁〕	镑〔鎊〕	镫〔鐙〕
铮〔錚〕	铜〔銅〕	锱〔錙〕	镐〔鎬〕	镪〔鏹〕
铧〔鏵〕	钢〔鋼〕	键〔鍵〕	镉〔鎘〕	镰〔鐮〕
铩〔鎩〕	铽〔鋱〕	镀〔鍍〕	镊〔鑷〕	镱〔鐿〕
揿〔撳〕	铼〔錸〕	镃〔鎡〕	镇〔鎮〕	镭〔鐳〕
锌〔鋅〕	锇〔鋨〕	镁〔鎂〕	镍〔鎳〕	镮〔鐶〕
锐〔銳〕	锂〔鋰〕	镂〔鏤〕	镎〔鎿〕	镯〔鐲〕
锑〔銻〕	锘〔鍩〕	锲〔鍥〕	镏〔鎦〕	镲〔鑔〕
锒〔鋃〕	锞〔錁〕	锹〔鍬〕	镜〔鏡〕	镳〔鑣〕
铺〔鋪〕	锭〔錠〕	锷〔鍔〕	镝〔鏑〕	镴〔鑞〕
铸〔鑄〕	锗〔鍺〕	锶〔鍶〕	镛〔鏞〕	镶〔鑲〕
嵌〔嵌〕	锝〔鍀〕	锴〔鍇〕	镞〔鏃〕	镬〔鑊〕
锓〔鋟〕	锫〔錇〕	锾〔鍰〕	镖〔鏢〕	
锃〔鋥〕	错〔錯〕	镆〔鏌〕	镗〔鏜〕	
链〔鏈〕	锚〔錨〕	锸〔鍤〕	镙〔鏍〕	
铿〔鏗〕	锛〔錛〕	镅〔鎇〕	镘〔鏝〕	
铜〔銅〕	锯〔鋸〕	锻〔鍛〕	镗〔鐋〕	

业

岀〔齣〕
学〔學〕
觉〔覺〕
搅〔攪〕

誉〔譽〕	莳〔蒔〕	轻〔輕〕	娈〔孌〕	涡〔渦〕
鲎〔鱟〕	释〔釋〕	氢〔氫〕	恋〔戀〕	埚〔堝〕
黉〔黌〕	箨〔籜〕	胫〔脛〕	栾〔欒〕	㖞〔喎〕
孝	**圣**	痉〔痙〕	挛〔攣〕	莴〔萵〕
译〔譯〕	劲〔勁〕	羟〔羥〕	鸾〔鸞〕	娲〔媧〕
泽〔澤〕	刭〔剄〕	颈〔頸〕	湾〔灣〕	祸〔禍〕
怿〔懌〕	陉〔陘〕	巯〔巰〕	蛮〔蠻〕	脶〔膃〕
择〔擇〕	泾〔涇〕	**亦**	脔〔臠〕	窝〔窩〕
峄〔嶧〕	茎〔莖〕	变〔變〕	滦〔灤〕	锅〔鍋〕
绎〔繹〕	径〔徑〕	弯〔彎〕	銮〔鑾〕	蜗〔蝸〕
驿〔驛〕	经〔經〕	孪〔孿〕	**呙**	
铎〔鐸〕	烃〔烴〕	峦〔巒〕	剐〔剮〕	

3. BIBLIOGRAPHY

(1) **Bào**, Kèyí, "Zěnyàng Chá Cídiǎn" [*How to Use a Dictionary*], Shànghǎi Jiàoyù Chūbǎnshè, 1981. 鲍克怡 《怎样查词典》，上海教育出版社，1981.

(2) **Chén**, Aiwén, **Chén**, Zhūhè, "Hànzì Biānmǎ de Lǐlùn yǔ Shíjiàn" [*Theory and Practice of Chinese Character Coding*] Xuélín Chūbǎnshè, 1986. 陈爱文，陈朱鹤 《汉字编码的理论与实践》，学林出版社，1986.

(3) **Chén**, Bǐngtiáo, "Císhū Gàiyào" [*Introducing Dictionaries*], Fújiàn Rénmín Chūbǎnshè, 1985. 陈炳迢《辞书概要》，福建人民出版社，1985.

(4) **Dīng**, Xīlín, děng, "Hànzì de Zhěnglǐ hé Jiǎnhuà" [*The Systemization and Simplification of Chinese Characters*] Zhōnghuá Shūjú, 1955. 丁西林等 《汉字的整理和简化》，中华书局，1955.

(5) **Fàn**, Yùzhōu, "Jiǎgǔwén" [*Oracle Bone Inscriptions*] Rénmín Chūbǎnshè, 1986. 范毓周 《甲骨文》，人民出版社，1986.

(6) **Fú**, Huáiqīng, "Xiàndài Hànyǔ Cíhuì" [*Modern Chinese Vocabulary*], Běijīng Dàxué Chūbǎnshè, 1985. 符淮青 《现代汉语词汇》，北京大学出版社，1985.

(7) **Fù**, Yǒnghé, "Zìxíng Biànxī hé Shízì" [*Discriminating*

and Recognizing the Shapes of Characters], Yǔwén Chūbǎnshè, 1985. 傅永和 《字形辨析和识字》，语文出版社，1986.

(8) **Gāo**, Jíngchéng, "Zhōngguó de Hànzì" [*Chinese Characters*], Rénmín Chūbǎnshè, 1986. 高景成《中国的汉字》，人民出版社，1986.

(9) **Hóng**, Chéngyù, "Gǔ Hànyǔ Cíyì Fēnxī" [*An Analysis of Ancient Chinese Word Meanings*], Tiānjīn Rénmín Chūbǎnshè, 1985. 洪成玉《古汉语词义分析》，天津人民出版社，1985.

(10) ISTRIN, V.A., Dù, Sōngshòu yì, "Wénzì de Fāzhǎn" [*The Development of Writing*], Wénzì Gǎigé Chūbǎnshè, 1966. V.A. ISTRIN, 杜松寿译，《文字的发展》，文字改革出版社，1966.

(11) **Liú**, Yèqiū, "Zhōngguó Zìdiǎn Shǐlüè" [*An Outline History of Chinese Dictionaries*], Zhōnghuá Shūjú, 1983. 刘叶秋《中国字典史略》，中华书局，1983.

(12) **Ní**, Hǎishǔ, "Xiàndài Hànzì Xíngshēngzì Zìhuì" [*A Glossary of Modern Chinese Picto-phonetic Characters*], Yǔwén Chūbǎnshè 1982. 倪海曙《现代汉字形声字字汇》，语文出版社，1982.

(13) **Sūn**, Jūnxī, "Hànzì Jīběn Zhīshi" [*Basic Knowledge about Chinese Characters*], Héběi Rénmín Chūbǎnshè, 1981. 孙钧锡《汉字基本知识》，河北人民出版社，1981.

(14) **Wáng**, Gāng, "Shūfǎ Zìdiǎn" [*A Dictionary of Calligraphy*], Chóngqìng Chūbǎnshè, 1982. 王纲《书法字典》，重庆出版社，1982

(15) **Wèi**, Tiānchí, "Shūfǎ Jīchǔ Zhīshi" [*Basic Knowledge of Chinese Calligraphy*], Shànghǎi Rénmín Chūbǎnshè, 1975. 尉天池《书法基础知识》，上海人民出版社，1975.

(16) **Wú**, Jīcái, "Mànhuà Hànzì" [*Essay on Chinese Characters*], Yúnnán Rénmín Chūbǎnshè, 1984. 吴积才《漫话汉字》，云南人民出版社，1984.

(17) **Wǔ**, Zhànkūn, **Wáng** Qín, "Xiàndài Hànyǔ Cíhuì Gàiyào" [*An Outline of Modern Chinese Vocabulary*], Nèi Měnggǔ Rénmín Chūbǎnshè, 1983. 武占坤，王勤《现代汉语词汇概要》，内蒙古人民出版社，1983.

(18) **Xiàng**, Sīxīn, "Biézì Biànxī" [*Discriminating Erroneously Used Characters*], Shànghǎi Jiàoyù Chūbǎnshè, 1985. 向思鑫《别字辨析》上海教育出版社，1985.

(19) **Xú**, Shìróng, "Pǔtōnghuà Yǔyīn Zhīshi" [*Knowing Putonghua Phonetics*], Wénzì Gǎigé Chūbǎnshè 1982. 徐世荣《普通话语音知识》，文字改革出版社，1982.

(20) **Yè**, Zíxióng, **Chén** Chén, "Wénzì" [*Writing*], Shànghǎi Jiàoyù Chūbǎnshè, 1983. 叶子雄，陈晨《文字》，上海教育出版社，1983.

(21) **Zhào**, Jiāxǐ, "Shàonián Xué Shūfǎ" [*Calligraphy for Youngsters*], Zhōngguó Shàonián Értóng Chūbǎnshè. 1986. 赵家熹《少年学书法》，中国少年儿童出版社，1986.

(22) **Zhèng**, Línxī, "Jīngjiǎn Hànzì Zìshù de Lǐlùn hé Shíjiàn" [*Theory and Piactice of Reducing the Number of Chinese Characters*], Zhōngguó Shèhuì Kēxué Chūbǎnshè, 1984. 郑林曦《精简汉字字数的理论和实践》，中国社会科学出版社，1984.

(23) Zhōngguó Dàbǎikē Quánshū "Yǔyán Wénzì Juàn" [*Chinese Encyclopedia: Language Volume*], Zhōngguó Dàbǎikē Quángshū Chūbǎnshè, 1988. 中国大百科全书《语言文字卷》，中国大百科全书出版社，1988.

[24] **Zhōu**, Yǒuguāng, "Hànzì Shēngpáng Dúyīn Biànchá"

[*A Guide to Pronouncing the Phonetic Components of Chinese Characters*], Jílín Rénmín Chūbǎnshè, 1980. 周有光 《汉字声旁读音便查》，吉林人民出版社，1980.

(25) **Zhū**, Tiānjùn, **Chén** Hóngtiān, "Wénkē Gōngjùshū Jiǎnjiè" [*A Basic Introduction to Literary Reference Works*], Jílín Wén-shǐ Chūbǎnshè, 1985. 朱天俊，陈宏天 《文科工具书简介》，吉林文史出版社，1985.

(26) **Zhū**, Xīng, "Hànyǔ Cíyì Jiǎnxī" [*A Simple Analysis of Chinese Word Meanings*], Húběi Jiàoyù Chūbǎnshè, 1985. 朱星《汉语词义简析》，湖北教育出版社，1985.

(27) **Zuǒ**, Anmín, "Hànzì Lìhuà" [*Some Examples of Chinese Characters*], Zhōngguó Qīngnián Chūbǎnshè, 1984. 左安民《汉字例话》，中国青年出版社，1984.

4. GLOSSARY

àn (bǐ) 按（笔） pressing (the brush) (calligraphy), 279

bāowéi jiégòu 包围结构 enclosed structure, 303

Běijīng Fāngyán Cídiǎn 《北京方言词典》 *Beijing Dialect Dictionary*, 316

běnyì 本义 original meaning, 179

biàntǐ 变体 changed form, 56

biétǐ 别体 alternate form, 56

biézì 别字 inappropriate character, 121;206

bǐhuà 笔画 stroke, 96

bǐshù cházìfǎ 笔数查字法 character referencing by number of strokes, 240

bǐshùn 笔顺 stroke order, 98; 291

bǐxíng cházìfǎ 笔形查字法 character referencing by stroke form, 242

bǐwèi 笔位 brush position, 277

bǐyù (yì) 比喻（义） metaphorical meaning, 184

bíyùnmǔ 鼻韵母 nasal final (vowel), 147

bùjiàn 部件 component part, 93

bùjú 布局 composition (calligraphy), 305

bùshǒu 部首 radical, 237;250;257

责任编辑　郁　苓　周奎杰
封面设计　朱　丹

现　代　汉　字

尹斌庸　John S. Rohsenow　（罗圣豪）

✲

华语教学出版社出版
（中国北京百万庄路24号）
邮政编码100037
北京外文印刷厂印刷
中国国际图书贸易总公司发行
（中国北京车公庄西路35号）
北京邮政信箱第399号　邮政编码100044
1994年（大32开）第一版
（英）
ISBN 7—80052—167—2/H·167（外）
02605
9—E—2507 P